RELIGION
AND
Reality

anne white, PhD
University of Calgary

Kendall Hunt
publishing company

Cover images © Shutterstock, Inc.

Kendall Hunt
publishing company

www.kendallhunt.com
Send all inquiries to:
4050 Westmark Drive
Dubuque, IA 52004-1840

ISBN 978-1-4652-2691-4

Printed in Canada
10 9 8 7 6 5 4 3 2

CONTENTS

CHAPTER 7

CHAPTER 8

CHAPTER 9

CHAPTER 10

CHAPTER 1

The Creation of Religion and Meaning: Human Ingenuity

INTRODUCTION

There have been many books written endeavouring to explain religion and the religious dynamic. The reason for this is that, despite a tumultuous and varied history, religion[1] is an intriguing part of our species' emotional and cultural identity. Indeed, through a methodological analysis of humankind's history, which we in the discipline of Religious Studies term *Religionswissenschaften*, there exists much evidence within all cultures to corroborate the claim that one of our speciel signatures as Homo sapiens is that we create religion. Addressing this reality or fact, our species is often dubbed *homo religiosus* or religious "man" due to our predilection for creating realms of religious meaning and expression through *myth, ritual, symbols, sacred art*, and often, where there is a culture of written word, sacred writings known as *scripture*. Whether we like it or not, the fact is that religion is part of the very essence of being "human" and it is one of the major ways humankind creates reality and identification. In spite of the secularization and materialism encountered within most cultures in our modern world, religion still endures. Even though the New Atheists[2] would vigorously dismiss the necessity for religion, the reality is that we, as a species, have always created religion to speak to our deepest needs and fears in order to cope with life and death, and have used it to aid us in our quest for *transcendence.*

In addition to these identifying signatures of religious expression, many of our human traits can be identified and classified using specific terminology. To illustrate this point consider the following terms and their explanations[3]: *Homo economicus:* economic man; *Homo faber:* man the maker; *Homo loquens:* talking man; *Homo ludens:* man who creates play; *Homo patiens:* suffering man; *Homo poetica:* man the meaning maker; *Homo reciprocans:* man living in reciprocity with others; *Homo religiosus:* man the religious; *Homo sociologicus:* social man, creating societies; *Homo socius:* man as a social being; *Homo symbolicus:* man who creates symbols; *Homo viator:* pilgrim man.

Walking sticks used on pilgrimage

WHAT MAKES US HUMAN: OBSERVING THE OBVIOUS

Developing out of the last term identified, that of *Homo viator,* any serious critical study of the religious dynamic as it creates an identifiable society or records thought and expression, will observe that many people seek "reasonable" answers to life and gravitate to guidelines on how to live and die in spiritually meaningful ways. In the creation of these comprehensible realities, humankind constructs a particular religious worldview, or *cosmology,* based on the specific religion's codes of conduct, interpretations of *spirituality,*[4] and the quest for *transcendence.*

Another observable fact is that many of us still need a link to something greater than ourselves; there is a need to experience spirituality, to rise above and overcome our own problematic conduct and nature, to create goodness through religious spheres of expression, and throughout all these endeavours, seek consolation and hope. This does not mean, as is argued by detractors, that it is a weakness or psychic drug, as claimed by Marx[5] or even a crutch, illusion, or opiate as Sigmund Freud opined.[6]

From a Religious Studies' perspective, it can be posited that the need for spiritual meaning, expressed in and through a religion, can be viewed as a genuine awareness of what it is to be human and vulnerable, small and lonely, loving and strong, finite and powerful. Religions, and the practical applications of their positive[7] teachings, through codes of conduct and order, can be appreciated in the ways that adherents incorporate religious reality into life through their genuine desires to transcend and improve their "inner" natures and enhance the quality of their physical experience.

These desires are based on affirmations of the good and constructive through which many humans hope to experience reaching out towards something or Someone in the supernatural realm that can help them overcome life's challenges and perhaps reorder society. In doing this we construct for ourselves the concept of space or place and *axis mundi*, whereby the religious space which we inhabit in mind and physicality, becomes the centre for our roles as important participants within a great realm of meaning.

THE COMPLEXITY OF HUMAN COGNITION

Arising out of these observations, a psychological, evolutionary, and philosophical question is often raised as to, "What makes us human?" Why do we need to construct intricate realms or webs of meaning and how do we sort and categorize them? There are many theories about why we order or explain things in the way that we do but there is no one clear and concise solution. The fact is that there are many explanations regarding what defines us as a species. One of the most viable theories, however, posits that it is through our cognitive capacities that we clearly distinguish ourselves from other primates. Cognitively speaking, what makes us as a species different from our closest relatives within the great ape genus is to be found in the way we create complex thought.[8] What the field of cognitive psychology will tell us is that the brain sorts raw information into finished assembling perceptions which then develop into a sophisticated process of cognition. This sorting and assembling mechanism provides us with useful patterns of discernment and levels of action. To achieve this multifaceted comprehension of the realities around us, our consciousness works on two levels and is thus divided into two stages: core (primary) consciousness and the higher (secondary) consciousness out of which flows problem solving and abstract thought. From the information we gather and retain through learning, remembering, and using knowledge, we form ideas and perceptions with which to navigate and construct our realities.

To illustrate this function, consider the following explanation given by Andrew B. Newberg, M.D., Associate Professor in the Department of Radiology and Psychiatry at the hospital of the University of Pennsylvania. Newberg also holds an adjunct appointment in the Department of Religious Studies at the University of Pennsylvania. He writes,

> The human brain does have a great propensity for trying to understand all aspects
> of the world that it perceives. One of the major functions of the brain is to name
> and define various concepts so that it may manipulate them in thought and
> utilize them for planning future behaviours. In addition to the abstract naming
> functions of the brain, the brain also attempts to order and categorize various
> concepts. The brain also attempts to define concepts via their opposites. Thus,
> as the brain attempts to define "spirituality" it does so in part by comparing this
> term to other related terms and also by setting it apart from discordant terms
> such as "atheism."[9]

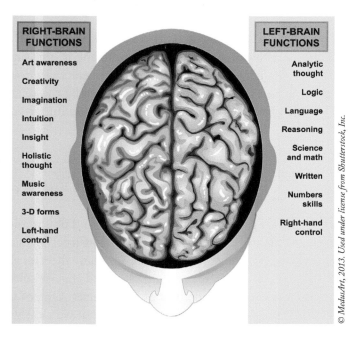

RIGHT-BRAIN FUNCTIONS	LEFT-BRAIN FUNCTIONS
Art awareness	Analytic thought
Creativity	Logic
Imagination	Language
Intuition	Reasoning
Insight	Science and math
Holistic thought	Written
Music awareness	Numbers skills
3-D forms	Right-hand control
Left-hand control	

In addition to this, another defining feature of our intellectual complexity is that we are aware of values and principles. We also engage in a quest for spiritual meaning and often for a fulfilling relationship with the ultimate, which for those who hold to a supreme being, is routinely described as God.[10] But what does this quest for meaning exactly mean? Who, or what, are we as a species and why do we seek some greater meaning outside of ourselves?

From a purely biological perspective, considering the data from a range of scientific disciplines, it would appear that our species is the product of evolutionary life processes that began over 3.5 billion years ago. The field of genetic science also tells us that each human being possesses approximately 30,000 genes, with their relating 3 billion base letters.[11] Scientists can also extrapolate back approximately 6 million years, to when humans and chimpanzees shared a common ancestor. Science will also tell us that as part of this evolutionary process we still share a 99.4 percent common genetic relationship with chimpanzees, thus making them our closest genetic relative.[12] The staggering biological reality is that, based on current scientific data, the sum total of our unique human identity is to be found in 0.6 percent of our genetic coding. In the context of our differing 0.6 percent genetic composition, we are an anomaly and an enigma.

ORDERING REALITY—DEFINING SPATIAL BOUNDARIES

Realistically speaking, all life forms on earth observe territorial boundaries or spaces and most species are aware of vulnerability, limits, and the dangers of exceeding spatial boundaries. To stray outside of group protection or familiar territory can lead to exposure, suffering and destruction. Although humankind is also aware of, and often practices these survival mechanisms, we exercise mental complexities that set us apart from other species, courtesy of our unique genetic coding. One of these distinctive speciel traits is that of creating logic and meaning from our multitasking thought processes.

Part of our human signature is that of *Homo poetica*, or man the meaning maker. Whether we hold to a faith or philosophy of any kind, we will seek some sort of meaning in life and crave significance through our actions. In the way humankind creates meaning, some of the most interesting academic studies on this inherent trait have been deduced by studying the production of space or place. The theory of place or space and meaning is a scholarly approach to defining humankind's ability to group significant events, rituals, or concepts into cultural memory and social codes, thus creating a consciousness of both social and ritual space in which we position or place ourselves. Place/space theory studies how our species has designed and defined the territory of mind and habitation; it speaks to how we have created significance of "dwelling" within the physical, emotional, and spiritual.

To demonstrate these concepts, and by way of illustration, the insights provided by the French sociologist, Marxist intellectual, and philosopher, Henri Lefebvre (1901–1991) will now be considered.

Neolithic standing stones

In "The Production of Space," published in 1991,[13] Lefebvre identified the creation of space, and defined four basic categories: physical, mental, spiritual, and the cognitive. Lefebvre also addressed what he classified as *cultural spheres*,[14] *social space*,[15] and *consecrated* space,[16] and argued that these all came together in a "multitude of intersections."[17] Later, in "The Production of Space," he also noted that this production was,

> "Not merely a space of ideas, an ideal space, but a social and mental space. An *emergence. A decrypting* of the space, that went before. Thought and philosophy came to the surface, rose from the depths, but life was decrypted as a result, and society as a whole, along with space."[18]

Lefebvre's general argument here is that humankind created a plethora of meaning derived from creating and defining the space which we inhabit. This can be a set of experiences such as social or cultural interaction whereby place/space is indicated by a specific role such as class, labour, duty, gender, reproductive designations, birth, age, and death. It can also be through a religious designation, such to devotees within a specific religion, with rights afforded to them which are not deemed accessible to others due to the obvious fact that those outside the tradition are considered nonparticipants. People "inhabit" these spaces without fully understanding why, or even being conscious of the subtleties or intricacies of the multitude of intersections which have shaped their experience of space and reality. These intricacies as "relations of exclusion and inclusion,"[19] form the reality in which a person is situated. Lefebvre stated,

> It is beyond dispute that relations of inclusion and exclusion, and of implication and explication, obtain in practical space as in spatial practice. "Human beings" do not stand before, or amidst, social space; they do not relate to the space of society as they might to a picture, a show, or a mirror. They know that they have a space and that they are in this space. They not merely enjoy a vision, a contemplation, a spectacle—for they act and situate themselves in space as active participants. They are accordingly situated in a series of enveloping levels each of which implies the others, and the sequence of which accounts for social practice.[20]

Continuing with this line of thought, the Religious Studies scholar, Thomas A. Tweed, also addresses the production of spatial significance and identification of place within it in his work, "Crossing and Dwelling: A Theory of Religion."[21] Tweed constructs a theory of religion, and emphasizes the cultural influences of religions over time and geographical space wherein he identifies two realities, (1) that of "dwelling and crossing," as movements across physical space, and (2) time.[22] For Tweed, *dwelling* is the process of homemaking wherein "religions orient individuals and groups in time and space, transform the natural environment, and allow devotees to inhabit worlds they construct."[23] Following on from this, the term *crossing* means that religions generate: "terrestrial crossings" (travel and communication); "corporal crossings" (traversing time and space—boundaries); and "cosmic crossings" (teleographies/representations of the ultimate horizon).[24] "Religions," he states, "are always in place and moving across,"[25] and this movement he believes is always subtly changing because devotees are consistently creating new realms of meaning in sacred space and physical time.

Cultural anthropologist Clifford Geertz also develops this theme with the identification of these realities of construction. Geertz addresses the intricacies of social and religious construction in his work, "The Interpretation of Cultures," written in 1973, argues that "man is an animal suspended in webs of significance he himself has spun…" and "[designated] culture to be those webs…"[26] Geertz stresses that there is a "conceptual envelope" woven throughout a culture and that within it there is a cultural dimension to understanding religion as culture and religion interact together to construct human realities and meaning. He states,

> … sacred symbols function to synthesize a people's ethos—the tone, character, and quality of their life, its moral and aesthetic style and mood—and their world view—the picture they have of the way things in sheer actuality are, their most comprehensive ideas of order. In religious belief and practice a group's ethos is rendered intellectually reasonable by being shown to represent a way of life ideally adapted to the actual state of affairs the world view describes, while the world view is rendered emotionally convincing by being presented as an image of an actual state of affairs peculiarly well-arranged to accommodate such a way of life.[27]

He also believes that human cultural activities are quite unusual and distinctive and that we accomplish nothing if we try to explain our creativity through scientific reductionism, as science alone could not explain *Homo faber, Homo religious, Homo poetica,* or *Homo viator* merely in terms of the natural biological order.

He observes that, as a species,

> We are, in sum, incomplete or unfinished animals who complete or finish ourselves through culture—and not through culture in general but through highly particular forms of it…. Man's great capacity for learning, his plasticity, has often been remarked, but what is even more critical is his extreme dependence upon a certain sort of learning: the attainment of concepts, the apprehension and application of specific systems of symbolic meaning. Beavers build dams, birds build nests, bees locate food, baboons organize social groups, and mice mate on the basis of forms of learning that rest predominantly on the instruction encoded in their genes…. But men build dams and shelters, locate food, organize their social groups, or find sexual partners under the guidance of instructions encoded in flow charts and blueprints, hunting lore, moral systems and aesthetic judgments: conceptual structures molding formless talents.[28]

The significance of the arguments presented by Lefebvre, Tweed, and Geertz is that these scholars approach the reality of meaning, culture, and consciousness from different disciplines but identify the same human traits. Each scholar places humankind at the centre in creating physical and spiritual significance through various realms of meaning. The identification of Homo sapiens' comprehension and resulting creation of "reality" again demonstrates our species' cognitive abilities to define and assign complex significance to life, reality, and meaning through identifying codes of conduct whether physical or spiritual.

These concepts, however, often present as overwhelmingly complex as they incorporate levels of meaning and cultural nuances. From a Religious Studies' perspective, one might ask as to what is the most practical approach to comprehending the development and function of religious structures in creating reality from primitive times into our modern twenty-first-century milieu. How can the enquirer systematically study and gain concrete understanding of religious systems that humankind has created through realms of being and existence in order to address the challenges of life? In answer to this, it is necessary to adopt specific methodologies through which one can chart the maze of our history, development, religious construction, and the building of knowledge.

BACKGROUND METHODOLOGICAL APPROACHES

The scientific study of religion, or *Religionswissenschaften*,[29] has allowed those who study religions and the realities they construct, to gain perspectives on just how sweeping this human signature is. What makes the discipline of Religious Studies so interesting is that we use the data found within religions in their great diversity and at the same time, compare this material with other various academic disciplinary perspectives. To prove this point, and by way of illustration, consider some of the other disciplines that we use in our approaches: Philosophy, Classical Studies, Anthropology, History, Psychology, Archaeology, Sociology, Women's Studies, Political Science, Economics, and the Philosophy of Law. Using this broad base of knowledge, we are able to construct a comprehensive evaluation of religion and reality that spans, to some degree, the breadth and complexity of *Homo religiosus*—man who creates religion—and *Homo sociologicus*—man who creates societies.

Another approach to further assist in our understanding and appreciation of the complexity through which humankind builds realms of reality is to view religions through their developmental processes over thousands of years. Sociologist Robert N. Bellah has done extensive work on the developmental aspects of human societies and has observed that religions, as part of the patterns established by *Homo religiosus* and *Homo sociologicus,* present as recognizable evolutionary stages in our construction of reality.[30] Indeed, as far back as 1976, in his work, "Beyond Belief: Essays on Religion in a Post-Traditional World,"[31] Bellah had developed an extensive model of these stages, categorizing them as: Primitive Religion, Archaic Religion, Historic Religion, Early Modern Religion, and lastly, Modern Religion.[32] As Bellah's material is extremely thorough and often complex, a paraphrased overview of his thematic classifications will be used to explain these stages as follows:

PRIMITIVE RELIGION
PRIOR TO FIRST MILLENNIUM B.C.E. (BEFORE COMMON ERA)

Worldview: cosmological *monism*

Exemplar: Australian Aborigines, African Dinka (Sudanese) People[33]

1. Religious persons could, through their religion rituals, transcend and/or dominate their circumstances.
2. From the meanings created through their religions, they were able to create symbolism and metaphor.
3. They created ritual as a means of expression and conduct to convey these insights or meanings.

THREE MAJOR FEATURES OF PRIMITIVE RELIGION:

i. Mythical world closely related to the actual world—no clear separation between the sacred and the profane. No separate religious organization or rituals that separated the sacred from the world of the living.

ii. Mythical sources were fluid in organization. There were stories of gods, monsters, spirits, and heroes who became gods [known as ancestral or cultural transcendence]. New heroes, gods, and events were simply added to the specific culture's mythos. The core of the myth was not enlarged by these additions and stayed the same; no increase in interpretive sophistication of the core myths. Players were simply added on and anything that challenged the myth's integrity was just added on [like an addendum]. It was unwieldy; did not adapt to its particular society; was difficult to change to reflect the needs of the evolving society.

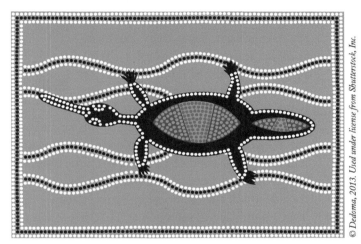

© Dedoma, 2013. Used under license from Shutterstock, Inc.

Australian Aboriginal mythology

iii. Characterized not by worship or sacrifice to a remote, mythical, transcendent entity or deity. In the ritual, participants became identified with the myths and identified with the specific entity through participation and acting out. Through their "acting out" they became the mythical being, took on its persona.

ARCHAIC RELIGION

Worldview: cosmological monism[34]

Exemplar: Greek mythologies and city-states

These are often classified by other scholars within the primitive religion category. They often include ancient Middle East, India, China, Africa, and Polynesia.

Ancient Egyptian depiction of worship

1. Archaic religions incorporate ritual and myth in a far more integrated system. There is still only one world, one reality with various deities that dominate the cosmology. Each deity possesses complex and multifaceted roles, meanings, and purposes. Religious action is reflected in cult (ritual observance, belief).
2. The distinction between humans as subject and gods as objects is more defined than in primitive religion. As the distinction grows, the possibility for the individual to shape his/her own religious purpose increases, but at the same time, so does the uncertainty of the divine response.
3. New degree of freedom, as well as an increased burden of anxiety. This is due to increased complexity of the relationship between man and the ultimate conditions of his existence.
4. The individual and society is still understood as united in a natural-divine cosmos, and traditional social structures and practices thought to be grounded in a divinely established cosmic order. Social conformity reinforced by religious sanction.

HISTORICAL RELIGION

Worldview: cosmological dualism, emergence of a transcendent universal higher reality beyond the natural world[35]

Exemplars: the great world religions of Confucianism, Taoism, Hinduism, Buddhism, Zoroastrianism, Judaism, Christianity, Greek philosophy, Islam. Note: increased differentiation among these world religions.

The development of thought during this period laid the foundation for all other religious ideas that followed. This period is unequalled for the development of thought and ideas of transcendence. Within this time frame there was a tremendous shift in attitude toward the world by the historic religions.

1. Whereas in primitive religion there was practically no distance between human beings and the community and the world around them in this period, people began to understand them-

selves solely as part of the community, of nature.

2. A transcendent is perceived beyond this world as these religions are dualistic in that there are two realities: this worldly and other worldly.

3. The superior transcendent world—essentially spiritual and must be sought through interior reflection. The transcendent sought is not so much in harmony with society and the world, as in primitive religion, or to placate gods, as in archaic religion. Transcendence is to be sought as a means to salvation.

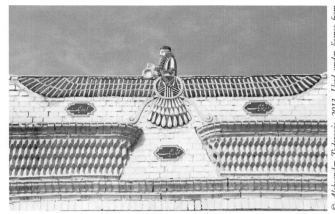

Zarathustra as founder of Zoroastrianism

4. The historical religions are concerned with salvation as they promise humankind the ability to comprehend the fundamental structure of reality. They promise that through salvation, humans can become active in their own transcendence. Along with growing awareness, however, comes the greater risk of failure.

5. The new dualism is expressed in the difference between this world and the life after death. The other religions focused on this life and some life after death, but historic religions focused on life in the other realm through participation in salvation in this world.

EARLY MODERN

Worldview: collapse of hierarchical structures, but retention of cosmological dualism except that mediation was removed, set aside, and salvation could be directly available to any seeker

Exemplars: most successfully institutionalized in the Protestant Reformation. (Note that something somewhat similar is associated with Vatican II. It is also increasingly being invoked as a desirable corrective to traditional/fundamentalist Islam.)

1. Development of a religious leadership class in the historic religions. This class develops separately from the political leadership class.

2. Although a major function of religion has been, and continues in historical religion to be, the legitimation and reinforcement of the existing social order, the rise of the separate religious elite now offers the possibility of conflict with the political leadership and of social change.

MODERN/CONTEMPORARY

A passage of speculation and uncertainty; part of a post-modern stage[36]

Worldview: collapse of dualism, especially through the ascendancy of the scientific perspective, a resulting "infinitely multiplex, infinite possibilities" worldview

Exemplars: Ethical Culturalism, Unitarian-Universalism, Humanism

1. Increasing analysis of the nature of symbolism itself.
2. The self is seen as endlessly revisable.
3. There is an increased self-responsibility and humanistic concern for humankind, together with social action.
4. Patterns of membership are flexible, no longer controlled by a specific; the group is endlessly revisable.
5. Humankind is to take responsibility for its own fate. Concept of *anthropodicy* whereby humans are the conduits for actions, which are either negative or positive.

CONCLUSION

Addressing the theories previously discussed, it is obvious that religion, like society, is a product of human construction. Both society as in the secular/profane or in the religious community, influence each other as human beings are the conduits in both contexts. In addressing and stressing the positives within religious systems in the way we build codes of conduct that govern our habitation of the secular world, an unfortunate reality still remains and is noted by supporter and critic alike in that religions can be unstable and volatile. Opponents of religion are always eager to emphasize that religions cause wars and suffering, but in reality, this is a rather superficial and simplistic answer to the major problems we find within ourselves as we build and interpret religions. Despite a very broad generalization towards the negative in religion, the reality is that it is not a system of religion per se that causes wars; religions are abstract thought mechanisms that are internalized by the devotee. As and of themselves, these beliefs do not have arms and legs; they merely represent ideas and do not "get up" walking and talking, wielding implements of torture and creating mayhem. Religions represent demonstrations of sophisticated and complex cognitive processes whereby we, as individuals and communities, create validation for peaceful or destructive codes of conduct in our search for meaningful existence.

Our religions throughout record have consistently addressed our intellectual consciousness by speaking to our deep spiritual and emotional problems concerning survival, fear, grief, loss, and hopelessness, as well as our need for love, comfort, transcendence, and peace. Religions have evolved over millennia to provide solutions and answers to issues for the individual and the community, all pertaining to this world and the next. The truth is that humans use the existing religious structures to find excuses for aggression and hate, as well as love and compassion. Sadly, as archaeological and historical records attest, aggression is one of the major identifying character signatures of our species. From a logical perspective, therefore, religions do not construct weapons, but human beings do. It is actually our problem-solving abilities that construct weapons and implements of torture—*Homo faber* (man the toolmaker) will use whatever means necessary to excuse or even promote our baser emotions, based on destruction and aggression.

Taking into account the reality of living life as an everyday experience, the study of our human history, as manifested in society at large and in the smaller circle of family and individual relationships, would easily indicate an identifiable drastic flaw in our psychological construction. Homo sapiens manifest inherent problems with regard to actions and will, often exhibiting alarmingly capricious and volatile traits. We are manipulative and often opt for the most expedient choices with little consideration for the suffering or consequences others experience as a result of our actions. As a case in point, one has only to study the unwise choices and practices we are utilizing with regard to the environment. Environmental devastation, pollution, and the mismanagement of resources merely for financial gain or political power, is and will, cause untold expressions of suffering around the planet. Most of us know at some level that what we are doing is inherently destructive, but we continue in our actions. We seem to manifest an illogical and short-sighted view of reality and our biological place in the biosphere. At the same time however, and even when faced with a clear indictment of our actions, most people will argue that we are basically good and that our actions cause little harm. This is an old dilemma, recognized by theologians and philosophers alike, and over time this human flaw has been addressed and/or defended through the concept of *anthropodicy*.[37] The term basically means the attempt to justify or validate human goodness in the face of the evils that we commit. The basis of this concept is that, whether it is a good action or a bad action, we act as a conduit for it. In many contexts, evil and suffering, goodness and healing, find their outlets and entry into the human and the natural environment through human agency. Wherever we go as active participants, we are somewhere in the centre of events that usher in some sort of chain reaction, be that negative or positive. The fact is that in many things pertaining to relationships and conduct, there is always a ground zero site from which problems or events spill over into many aspects of life. As such, we manifest as participants or epicentres, often acting as a centre of the world, and a catalyst for events, thereby becoming an *axis mundi* and thus creating through place or space, a world of reality in which people live and interact. This epicentre of the problem, or centre of events, is what religions and societies have manifested in general through an often bloody and checkered past. The history of the human race, in the building of our societies and organizations, reflects many of the political and philosophical realities surrounding and influencing us throughout our troubled history as a species. It is sadly, and most unfairly, however, in the context of the development of religion and spirituality, that only negative observations seem to make the headlines. To be balanced from an academic perspective, it can be strongly argued that the creation of religious realities over time and place has contributed much to understanding what it is to be human. This can be appreciated through the demonstration of altruistic love, compassion, nurturing, respect, and amazing artistic creativity which can be set alongside our other less positive character traits. The following chapters of this book will address some of these religious insights.

GLOSSARY

Anthropodicy: Attempts to justify the fundamental goodness of human nature in the face of the evils produced by humans. Arising out of this, humans cannot shift the blame for the cause of many evils and much suffering, away from themselves and on to God or some other supernatural source. As human beings, we must accept that our conduct has an immediate impact on others and upon all other sources and kinds of life forms.

Axis mundi: Cosmic axis, world axis, world pillar, and centre of the world. A symbol representing the centre of the world where the heaven (sky) connects with the earth. Different cultures represent the axis mundi by varied symbols such as a natural object (mountain, tree, vine, stalk, column of smoke or of fire). It can also be symbolized as a product of human manufacture (staff, tower, ladder, staircase, maypole, cross, church steeple, rope, totem pole, pillar, or a spire). Its proximity to heaven may carry implications that are chiefly religious (pagoda, temple mount, church) or secular (obelisk, minaret, lighthouse, rocket, or even a skyscraper). It can also represent the feminine (umbilicus providing nourishment) or masculine (phallus providing insemination in reproduction). Alternatively, is can be neither (navel).

Cognition: The physiological process of perception. The brain sorts raw information into finished assembling perceptions. These develop at various levels of cognition, thus providing useful patterns of discernment and levels of action. This perception, or consciousness, is divided into two stages: core (primary) consciousness and the higher (secondary) consciousness. Refers to all of the mental activities that are involved in learning, remembering, and using knowledge.

Cosmology: Religious worldview. Every religion, as part of its distinctive "signature," will contain a specific cosmology.

Homo economicus: The economic human. Man as a rational and singularly self-interested participant, possessing and utilizing judgments towards selfish, subjectively defined ends.

Homo faber: Man the smith, man the maker or toolmaker, fabricator man. Refers to a human being who controls his environment through personal abilities and tools, to be a maker of things.

Homo loquens: Talking man. Man as the only animal capable of complex communication through articulated language.

Homo ludens: Man the player. One who creates, initiates, and participates in play. Able to play alone or with others.

***Homo patiens*:** Suffering man. Human capability for suffering and enduring.

***Homo poetica*:** Man the meaning maker. Separates man from other animals in that he searches for meaning and significance.

***Homo reciprocans*:** Man living in reciprocity with others. Humans as cooperative actors who are motivated by improving their environment.

***Homo religiosus*:** Man the religious. Humans as religious beings who create religious meaning and codes of conduct.

***Home sociologicus*:** Social man. Prone to construct social groupings and societies.

***Homo socius*:** Man as a social being. Inherent within humans as long as they have not lived entirely in isolation.

***Homo symbolicus*:** Man who creates symbol. Communicates spiritual meaning in and through a material object which represents or stands for something abstract and sacred.

***Homo viator*:** Pilgrim man. Man as on his way towards finding God. The quest for transcendence inherent within the species.

Monism: The theory that reality consists of an unchanging whole in which change is mere illusion as there exists no separation between matter and mind; the person consists of only a single substance; there is no crucial difference between mental and physical events or properties.

Myth: Ancient, traditional story describing a central event of origin within a specific religion. Mythic event, ostensibly of an historical development or foundational belief. It serves to encapsulate the worldview of a people, or explain a practice, belief, or natural phenomenon.

Religion: The service and worship of God or the supernatural; commitment or devotion to religious faith or observance; a personal set or institutionalized system of religious attitudes, beliefs, and practices.

***Religionswissenschaften*:** The scientific study of religion. Incorporates many of the disciplines found within the social sciences, humanities, anthropology, history, philosophy, psychology, archaeology. Through all these disciplines the structure or presence of a "religious instinct" can be identified.

Ritual: Repetitive, solemn ceremony or action, performed by one or more persons. Held to a strict formula whereby a key event or central teaching of the religious tradition is remembered, observed, or celebrated in order to worship, placate, or to seek favour and/or forgiveness.

Sacred art: Paintings, carvings, sculptures also hymns, songs, and music, dedicated or set apart for the service or worship of a deity. Works, or expressions of sacred art, are symbols of faith. They

represent realities that cannot be seen and function to convey an interpretation of the "hidden" glories or meanings to a wider audience. Through their nuances, they function to make intelligible that which might be unintelligible due to a lack of general understanding.

Scripture: A sacred text specific to one religion. Contains the ancient belief patterns and teachings of the tradition. They are invested with an aura of authority, sacrality, and special power. The texts are believed to have been passed down from antiquity and are believed to have been revealed by some transcendent source. All major religious traditions possess sacred texts.

Speciel: Pertaining to Homo sapiens. General traits identified in all human groupings.

Spiritual: Relating to, consisting of, or having the nature of spirit; not tangible or material.

Spiritual enlightenment: Development of spiritual insight or knowledge; an ongoing process whereby the individual seeker "grows" in perception, understanding, insight as to what is important. This will encompass concepts of reality and truth.

Spirituality: An inner path enabling a person to discover the essence of one's being; or the "deepest values and meanings by which people live."

Symbols: Symbols are representational, using a sign that is agreed upon by members of a religious community, which represent a major theme within the religion. Utilizing this sign, devotees are able to access and make present the inner teachings of the tradition.

Transcendence: A reaching out to that which is indescribable, yet often tangibly sensed. Relating to the absolute, transcending all limitation; transcending experience; beyond human knowledge or consciousness; supernatural or mystical. To pass or lie beyond the range or limit of human understanding; to rise above, to surmount; to surpass; to exceed. Often equated with the process of enlightenment.

Typologies: Four basic classifications through which the world religions can be typed through their origins and core beliefs: Abrahamic, Indian, South East Asian, and Tribal.

ENDNOTES

1. The term *Religion* can be identified as: (i) uniquely concerned with God, deities, supernatural beings, and transcendent forces; (ii) distinguished by its special function in life (an institution or organization) rather than by a divine entity; (iii) how people come to terms with ultimate issues in life. See: Kenneth I. Pargament, "The Psychology of Religion and Coping," (New York: The Guilford Press, 1997), p 25.

2. The term "New Atheism" was coined by Gary Wolf in a 2006 article for the British magazine *Wired*. Wolf created the term in reference to three writers who had written very popular books advocating atheism and presenting a scathing criticism of religious belief and cultural respect for religion. These men were Sam Harris, "The End of Faith" (2004); Richard Dawkins, "The God Delusion" (2006); and Daniel Dennett, "Breaking the Spell" (2006). Later, in 2007, author and journalist Christopher Hitchens added his work "God Is Not Great" to the library of the New Atheists. See, Alister McGrath, "Why God Won't Go Away: Is the New Atheism Running on Empty?" (Nashville: Thomas Nelson, 2010).
    Also refer to Michel Onfray's international bestseller "In Defence of Atheism: The Case Against Christianity, Judaism and Islam," (Toronto: Penguin Canada, 2005).

3. Note: several of these terms are repetitious as they have previous been introduced.

4. In a broad sense, "spirituality" can pertain to all belief systems, whether or not they have a faith based on God, gods, spirits, or "emptiness" as in Buddhism.

5. Marx argued that, "Religion is the sigh of the oppressed creature, the heart of a heartless world, and the soul of soulless conditions. It is the opium of the people. The abolition of religion as the illusory happiness of the people is the demand for their real happiness." See, "Critique of Hegel's Philosophy of Right," 1843, http://www.marxists.org/archive/marx/works/1843/critique-hpr/index.htm (2 of 2) [23/08/2000 18:48:42]. Retrieved June 2, 2012.

6. Freud wrote that, "These, which are given us as teachings, are not precipitates of experience or end-results of thinking: they are illusions, fulfillments of the oldest, strongest and most urgent wishes of mankind." See, "The Future of an Illusion," (New York: Classic House Books, 2009), pp. 38 and 62.

7. Any religious system will have the elements of both negative and positive attributes. Stress upon the negative and destructive, creates a false sense of entitlement by and through which the devotee has licence to abuse others in order to gain the advantage for their specific religion. This destructive trait can also be identified in all other non-religious interactions in which *Homo socius* is a participant.

8. Robin Dunbar, *Why Are Humans Not Just Great Apes?*, "What Makes Us Human?," (Oxford, England: Oneworld Publications, 2007), ed. Charles Pasternak, pp 37-48. Dunbar discusses the critical difference between humans and other animals as interpreted through the "theory of mind" which is the capacity to imagine another individual's mind states. Dunbar states, "In terms of philosophy of mind, this is what is usually referred to as first order intentionality," and refers to a general concept "covering those mind states that involve beliefs is a critical difference between humans and animals," p 40.

9. Andrew B. Newberg, "Principles of Neurotheology," (Surrey, U.K.: Ashgate Publishing Limited, 2010), p 25.

10. Robin Dunbar, *Why Are Humans Not Just Great Apes?* p 73.

11. Base letters: The human genome has three billion base pairs, or DNA "letters" (A, T, C, and G). See, GNN's Genome Glossary, http://www.genomenewsnetwork.org/resources/glossary/s the critical difference between humans and other animals.

12. Rt. Revd. Richard Harries, *Half Ape, Half Angel*, "What Makes Us Human?" (Oxford, U.K.: Oneworld Publications, 2007) p 71.

13. Henri Lefebvre, "The Production of Space," (Malden, MA: Blackwell Publishing, 2012), trans. Donald Nicholson-Smith, pp 1-7.

14. Ibid., p 24.

15. Ibid., 27.

16. Ibid., p 34.

17. Ibid., p 33.

18. Ibid., p 260.

19. Ibid., p 294.

20. Ibid.

21. Thomas Tweed, "Crossing and Dwelling: A Theory of Religion," (Cambridge, MA: Harvard University Press, 2006).

22. Ibid., p 182.

23. Ibid., p 123.

24. Ibid., p 82.

25. Ibid., p 182.

26. Clifford Geertz, "The Interpretation of Cultures," (New York: Basic Books, 1973), p 5.

27. Ibid., p 90.

28. Ibid., pp 49-50.

29. Leonard and Paul Mojez, "The Study of Religion in an Age of Global Dialogue," (Philadelphia: Temple University Press, 2000), p 55.

30. Robert N. Bellah, "Religion in Human Evolution: From the Paleolithic to the Axial Age," (Cambridge, MA: The Belknap Press of Harvard University Press, 2011).

31. Robert Bellah, "Beyond Belief: Essays on Religion in a Post-Traditional World," (New York: Harper & Row, Publishers, 1976).

32. Ibid., pp 20-44.

33. http://web.pdx.edu/~tothm/religion/Religious%20Evolution.pdf, retrieved June 8, 2012.

34. Ibid.

35. Ibid.

36. Ibid.

37. Leonard Swidler, "The Study of Religion in an Age of Global Dialogue."

CHAPTER 2

The Creation of Social Codes of Conduct

In the field of Religious Studies, through applying the scientific study of humankind's behaviour, there are certain *archetypes*, or patterns of *modalities* that are easily identifiable. For the purpose of this chapter, the archetype of social codes of conduct will be examined in order to explore how and why we create parameters or boundaries by which we govern ourselves and the societies we inhabit. In addition to these archetypes, we will also review the development of certain early types of religio-social codes to trace continuity of a specific trait that our species used and continues to use in order to organize beliefs, conduct, and identity. Stemming from these early systems, it is easy to identify our own patterns of modern cognitive construction which promote group and individual identity. It should be noted that the amount of archaeological evidence regarding codes is enormous[1] and to discuss each one, whether religious or social, is far outside of the scope of these few pages. For the purpose of this chapter, therefore, only a few of the codes will be discussed in order to demonstrate our early, inherent but enduring cognitive abilities in building meaning and culture. The fact is that we have always drawn upon codes and "cultures" within our histories to establish psychic, psychological, and social navigational tools when interacting with those around us and the environment in which we live. Indeed, as microbiologist, environmentalist, and humanist, Rene Dubos (1901–1982)[2] observed in his 1968 work, *So Human an Animal*,[3]

> Except under unusual circumstances, man tends
> to accept the traditions of his group as embodying
> the truth. Even when he rebels against them, the
> attitudes he takes and the new ways he tries always
> incorporates many of the ancient traditions and thus
> keep him dependent on his social and cultural past.[4]

Dubos recognized that we work on the assumptions of culture in order to construct our social realities. In turn, it is our social realities that construct our own cultures, but what exactly is culture? The term itself is recognized and utilized within many fields of study such as political science, communication studies, advertizing and other forms of media enterprises, art, literature, government strategies, military studies, anthropology, sociology, social work, psychology, psychiatry, history, law, education, public relations, environmental studies, and, of course, theology, religions, and religious studies. Not surprisingly, with so many different approaches, there have developed various interpretative nuances reflecting a specific field of study and target goal or audience. Cultural historians, such as the late academic Raymond Henry Williams (1921–1988), acknowledge this, and wrote:

> Culture is one of the two or three most complicated words in the English language... partly because of its intricate historical development, in several European languages, but mainly because it has now come to be used for important concepts in several distinct intellectual disciplines, and in several distinct and incompatible systems of thought.[5]

Addressing this problem of incompatibility, one of the most direct ways of interpreting culture, and thereby the societies which construct this nebulous phenomenon of social codes of conduct, is to aim for an interpretative mean or basic definition. From the field of anthropology comes a key explanation that is broad enough to bridge the majority of specialized interpretations, and was defined by an eminent anthropologist named Clyde Kluckhohn (1905–1960), as that consisting of

> ...patterned ways of thinking, feeling and reacting; it is acquired and transmitted mainly by...human groups, including their embodiments in artifacts; the essential core of culture consists of traditional ideas and especially their attached values.[6]

In this basic analysis, three core phases or dynamic developments can be identified: culture as meaning, culture beyond meaning as practice, and culture in terms of "mediation."[7] The idea of "mediation" as the interpreter, purveyor, and distiller of cultural meaning and codes of conduct, is a key concept within any analysis of cultural identity and the shaping of personal reality.[8] This concept was clearly recognized by the great philosopher Plato, in his work *Laws*, written in 360 B.C.E., when through the discourse between an Athenian visitor to Crete and his two interlocutors (Megillus, a Spartan, and Kleinias, a Cretan), described the foundation of a just or good city.[9] Creating the *Laws'* twelve-book discussion, Plato has his characters address the concepts of the very foundation of a just or good city identified in its constitution, laws, offices, and other social institutions.[10] Through the mouth of the Athenian visitor, who is the main speaker, Plato described the age-old recognition of social encoding, or codes of conduct, through the inculcation of ethics and virtues in order to create a functioning, socially cohesive culture.

> Ath. You will wonder when I tell you: Long ago they appear to have recognized the very principle of which we are now speaking - that their young citizens must be habituated to forms and strains of virtue. These they fixed, and exhibited the patterns of them in their temples; and no painter or artist is allowed to innovate upon them, or to leave the traditional forms and invent new ones. To this day,

no alteration is allowed either in these arts, or in music at all. And you will find that their works of art are painted or moulded in the same forms which they had ten thousand years ago; - this is literally true and no exaggeration - their ancient paintings and sculptures are not a whit better or worse than the work of to-day, but are made with just the same skill.[11]

Plato's argument functions on the premise of perceived and accepted existence of norms and mores, but where do these values originate? *Culturalists*[12] will accept that "people build their worlds and their worlds build them,"[13] and that this world of self-construction is created through the cultural activity of mediation and interpretation. This means that, in the building of our cognitive and spatial worlds, we construct the communities in which we function. We use the codes of conduct that have evolved, sometime over millennia, during our interaction as individuals within a larger group which in turn builds the concept of belonging based on commonly held beliefs. In addition to this, communities also function as forms of societal control through the evolution of institutions, markets, individual and collective rituals, cult (*cultus*, Latin),[14] and government as the respective participants function within each grouping.[15]

Communities or societies, therefore, identify and understand themselves through the perception of their created realities. They do this by perpetuating, through their own significant stories, the justification and reaffirmation of their particular ways of life and institutions.[16] Many of these mechanisms of perpetuation are firmly based on religious beliefs and religious institutions because the religious cosmology defines rules as boundaries of being and conduct. These communal, institutional rules become psychological navigational points through which identity is created for the individual and the group, thus providing a cultural and communal setting. Social anthropologist Maurice Bloch describes this cultural process of validation by observing that there are two kinds of cultural processes that take place: (1) the ways in which a society talks about, understands, justifies, and perpetuates its own stories reaffirms its own particular ways of life and institutions; and (2) the ways in which individuals cope with their immediate experience, engage with others around them, and perceive and understand their social and natural environments.[17] In this context, the idea of a religious cosmology, relative to a specific social grouping, is acknowledged to play an influential role in the shaping of spiritual and physical reality; in other words, the "culture" of religion, with its inherent codes of conduct and specific identity, is a major form of mediation.[18] It is also, from an archaeological, textual, and anthropological perspective, one of the most easily identifiable, ancient, enduring forms of cultural and social profiling.[19]

PREHISTORIC RELIGION AND IDENTIFIABLE PATTERNS OF COSMOLOGY

Some of the earliest evidence of a social and religious code of conduct that provides the modern Religious Studies analyst with substantial scientific evidence comes from archaeological data. This material indicates a deeply significant background of prehistoric religious cultures spanning a time frame from the Middle Paleolithic (150,000 B.C.E.) to Late Paleolithic period which in itself spans a time frame of over ninety thousand years,[20] right through to the Neolithic, bordering on the Bronze Age, circa 30,000 B.C.E.[21]

The Middle Paleolithic provides substantial information regarding codes of conduct in and through burial sites and rituals, containing evidence of the oldest existent human burials yet to be found. This evidence relates to the Homo Neanderthalis' burials dating from around 60,000 B.C.E. and identifies our early ancestors' presence in Europe and areas located throughout southwestern and central Asia.[22]

From Smithsonian Magazine, June 2003 by Stan Fellows. Copyright © 2003 by Stan Fellows. Reprinted by permission.

Reconstruction of Neanderthal burial ritual

What is fascinating to note, courtesy of the Smithsonian Institution's findings, is that the Neanderthals' corpses were buried in shallow pits, their legs slightly flexed, or in a crouched position [fetal position], with their heads pointed towards the east. In addition to this in many instances "the graves contained animal bones, tools, or stones."[23] What is also a majority opinion among experts in the related fields, including Religious Studies, is that the Neanderthals intentionally and ritualistically buried their dead, as evidenced by the related behaviours in positioning their heads pointing towards the rising sun, in fetal position. There is also evidence that the corpses were sprinkled with red ocre, and that tools were situated within the grave, together with flowers placed as grave offerings.[24] The Smithsonian Institute also records that these, our early ancestors, created a

> … diverse set of sophisticated tools, controlled fire, lived in shelters, made and wore clothing, were skilled hunters of large animals and also ate plant foods, and occasionally made symbolic or ornamental objects. There is evidence that Neanderthals deliberately buried their dead and occasionally even marked their graves with offerings, such as flowers. No other primates, and no earlier human species, had ever practiced this sophisticated and symbolic behavior.[25]

This behaviour indicates a code of conduct in burying the body, coupled with ritualized, symbolic ritual in the placement of the body—sometimes covered in a bearskin,[26] adornment of ocre and flowers, and the practical "gifts" or tools stored with it. There is also evidence, based on cut marks on the bones, that our Neanderthal ancestors participated in some form of ritualized cannibalism, which would indicate a belief system held by the participants.[27]

In the same vein of codes, rituals, and symbols, the Late Paleolithic (35,000–10,000 B.C.E.) provides us with the first fossil evidence left by the first anatomically modern humans, known as Cro-Magnon.[28] The first discovery of our closely associated ancestors was made in southwestern France, and then subsequent finds were unearthed ranging from Britain, across Europe, North Africa, and into Southwest Asia. These Late Paleolithic ancestors made bows and arrows, spears; sewed fur clothes with needles and threads; fished with nets, fishing lines, and fishing hooks. In addition to this, they were accomplished artists who created the great cave paintings symbolic of the hunt, carved figures from soft stone, bone, ivory, or baked clay. Many of these artistic depictions in various mediums are ritualized symbols reflecting a pervading interest in animal fertility, human sexuality, female fecundity and, as it would appear, ideas about a Mother Goddess of fertility.[29] All of these artifacts again indicate the religious significance of life conduct on an individual and communal level, and indicate, as generated through their art forms, codes of conduct through hunt, ritual, and propagation of life.

© Erich Lessing/Art Resource, NY

The Neolithic period, dating from 8000 to 3500 B.C.E., saw the development of metallurgy circa 6500 B.C.E. with copper smelting, and then, around 3500 B.C.E., the development of early bronze metallurgy.[30] This is identified as a time when there was a major shift from nomadic life to settled farming communities and to the domestication of various animals for food, labour, and sacrifice. There was also a major change in community dynamics during this transition from hunting and gathering to the stable production of crops with the cultivation of grains and fruits. Human and animal communities, along with the domestication and cultivation of land, deeply affected social structures as settled life led to a broad division of labour and power within the emerging farming, artisan, and religio-political elite.[31] In addition to this, the increased use of blood sacrifice in ritual animal slaughter is also much in evidence, together with the offering up of humans for ritual cannibalization, and these all appear to indicate religio-social codes, cults, and community identity.[32]

What is also fascinating during the Neolithic is the development of the first religious architectural monuments in the form of the great standing stones or megaliths, and the complex burrows and mounds known as *tumuli*; it is also evidenced in the raised, rocky areas known as *tors* as sacred centres.[33] These great architectural monuments functioned as burial sites and open air sacred spaces for religious worship. Due to the sheer magnitude of construction, planning, and demand for manpower that would have been required to create each individual sacred space or axis mundi, it is evident that there had to have been concerted community efforts to construct these centres for worship and burial complexes due to the thousands of people needed to work on the projects. This, in turn, displays a social structure based on codes of conduct, identity, human participation, and consensus of religious belief in which individual and group participation was required.[34]

The Neolithic age also provides information through a varied system of proto-writing and pictographical techniques by which they described chronologies, histories, notices, communications, customs, totems, titles, and names. Each of these methods of communication, either on cave wall, on tortoise shell, or rock formation, clearly indicates defined religio-social codes of belief and leave no doubt as to clearly developed systems of cosmology and identity. The earliest evidence of written language develops out of the late Neolithic period, within established urban societies.[35] What becomes apparent from the evidence we now have is that, as our cultural histories evolved with the development of ancient urban societies, these mysterious codes of conduct, societal norms, and societal control become easier to identify due to their own records. We also know that the writing systems that were consequently developed in the Bronze Age evolved out of these earlier forms of visual communication or proto-writing.

DEVELOPMENTAL CODES IN THE ANCIENT HISTORICAL PERIODS

It is, however, with the advent of the Bronze Age (loosely identified around 3500–3000 B.C.E. to 1200 B.C.E.), that our history becomes easier to identify through specific script and text. Our various geographical communities developed written systems of communication and the ancient historical period pertains to the times when history began to be recorded through the written word. Thus begins the age of metal and writing and fortunately, due to our ancestors' need to record their world for practical, religious, and artistic purposes, these records become metaphorical windows through which we can view cultural perspectives.

The ancient scribes organized and documented various transactions, such as commercial activities, records of produce, and storage of grains and other goods. The priests recorded religious laws, the protocols of divination, the casting of spells, sometimes even the making of love potions, and also defined rituals for steering the deceased into the other world. In addition to all this, there was a specific genre of literature which dealt with life and cosmology through mythic stories.[36] From this diverse archaeological record we have a rich source of information, a time capsule from which to draw, regarding use of social and religious codes of conduct and human participation.

It was during the early Bronze Age, in Mesopotamia,[37] that the earliest, fully integrated writing system and written literature emerged in Sumer, which was a country located in southern Mesopotamia in present-day southern Iraq. Archaeological evidence dates the beginnings of Sumer to the fifth millennium B.C.E, and by the early Bronze Age, circa 3000, there was a flourishing civilization from which developed what we now classify as classical Sumerian script. The distinctive script that the Sumerians developed was a wedge-shaped writing system known as *cuneiform* and from this writing system emerged many codes and mythic stories which later manifest in culturally changed interpretations, within some of the great biblical stories of the Hebrew Bible or Old Testament.

Sumer gradually expanded to extend power over the surrounding area and culminated in the founding of the Akkadian dynasty circa 2340 by Sargon I. The language and cuneiform script evolved

Cuneiform script

and later developed into the Akkadian writing system and language. It is from the Sumerian and Akkadian texts that much of our earliest social codes and myths develop. After 2000 B.C.E., the Sumerian civilization gradually declined and was absorbed by Babylonia and Assyria.

One of the earliest and most important pieces of Sumerian text, dating from around 2700 B.C.E., was discovered during an archaeological dig undertaken at an ancient Sumerian city named Shuruppak or Shurappag ("The Healing Place") on the banks of the River Euphrates. The city of Shuruppak was considered to be one of the five *antediluvian*[38] cities of Sumerian tradition, and was dedicated to Ninlil (also named Sud), the goddess of grain and air.[39]

Among the clay tablets found and classified as *Wisdom Literature*,[40] was a text entitled, *The Instructions of Shuruppak*, the legendary founder of the city, who in Sumerian myths, predated the Deluge or Flood. The *Instructions*[41] were addressed to Shuruppak's son, and eventual Flood hero Ziusudra (in the Akkadian, known as Utnapishtin). The work is also viewed by many scholars as a very significant, if not the most important, piece of Sumerian *wisdom literature* ever discovered.[42]

Within the *Instructions of Shuruppak*[43] lie many recognizable concepts familiar to those acquainted with Hebrew Bible or biblical literature, resembling precepts taken from the Decalogue or the Ten

Commandments, the Levitical laws within the Book of Leviticus, and the Book of Proverbs (wisdom literature).[44] The *Instructions* present clearly defined codes of conduct—practical, philosophical, and religious—and demonstrate the early codification of societal standards and existing wisdom passed down from one generation to another. The Shuruppak instructions can also be said to be the Sumerian forerunner to the Ten Commandments and some Proverbs of the Bible: Line 50: Do not curse with powerful means (third commandment); line 28: Do not kill (sixth commandment); lines 28–31: Do not steal or commit robbery (eighth commandment); line 36: Do not spit out lies (ninth commandment); and lines 33–34: Do not laugh with or sit alone in a chamber with a girl that is married (seventh commandment).[45]

A few other examples of Shuruppak's wisdom read as follows:

> 28–31 You should not steal anything; you should not ...... yourself. You should not break into a house; you should not wish for the money chest (?). A thief is a lion, but after he has been caught, he will be a slave. My son, you should not commit robbery; you should not cut yourself with an axe.
>
> 65–66 The eyes of the slanderer always move around as shiftily as a spindle. You should never remain in his presence; his intentions (?) should not be allowed to have an effect (?) on you.
>
> 101–102 Property is something to be expanded (?); but nothing can equal my little ones.
>
> 103–104 The artistic mouth recites words; the harsh mouth brings litigation documents.
>
> 202–203 A loving heart maintains a family; a hateful heart destroys a family.
>
> 255–256 You should ... not question the words of your mother and your personal god.

The next code to be identified comes from 2050 B.C.E., and is called *Urukagina's Code*.[46] This code was named after another legendary king named Urukagina, ruler of the Mesopotamian city-state of Lagash, who reigned circa 2380–2360 B.C.E., after deposing the previous unjust king named Lugalanda. Urukagina's Code is considered to be the first recorded example of government reform and within the text it is stated that the king believed himself to have been divinely appointed to effect these sweeping legal, economic, and social reforms.[47] He sought to protect the poor from their more powerful neighbours, protect the widows and orphans, and to abolish the exorbitant taxes levied by his predecessor, Lugalanda. King Urukagina also limited the overall power of the priesthood as well as codifying laws against usury, unfair business, theft, and murder. His laws are thought to be the first legal code recorded in history, and although no known example exists, they have been referenced in other ancient Mesopotamian codes.[48]

Still within the Bronze Age, another code, the *Code of Hammurabi*, emerged between 1772 and 1780 B.C.E. This code not only had a significant influence on the contemporary cultures of the time, but also because of its literary longevity influenced some of the concepts identified within the Mosaic Code, which was constructed around 1300 B.C.E.[49]

Hammurabi's code is presented as the laws of a Babylonian king who claimed that his laws were given under the divine authority of the sun-god Shamash. The story and rulings are depicted on a black diorite (a type of granite) obelisk or stele, written in old Babylonian cuneiform script, and shows the bestowal of these laws and authority. The stele has a large carving at the top of the laws, depicting Hammurabi standing before Shamash who, as the sun god, is seated upon a throne. Shamash holds in his hand the scepter and ring and is seen conferring the authority of rulership upon his servant Hammurabi, who stands facing the deity, with his right hand raised in prayer as he prays for guidance and wisdom. From the inscription information supplied, it was engraved for the temple of Shamash at Sippar, and that another copy stood in the temple of Marduk in the city of Babylon.[50] The discovery of various fragments makes it probable that more copies had been set up in different cities, thus indicating an organized disbursal of law and legal system.

The expression "an eye for an eye" has come to symbolize the principle behind Hammurabi's code. Certainly, within our modern context, many of the laws would seem barbaric, but in the context of the time, the code was the first clearly encoded standard of cultural laws within a system of empire. The code contains 282 legal clauses and, for example, regulated a vast array of obligations relating to professions and rights including commerce, slavery, marriage, theft, and debts.[51]

Analysis of these laws demonstrates a social and moral code which is reinforced by commonly held religious beliefs in the divine right of a king, a plethora of gods, a diversified cosmology, and a clearly defined hierarchy of order. It also identifies a culture, strictly set within a religious and social context, and presents an outline of a stringent code of conduct through societal control.

Code of Hammurabi

Further ideas dating from the Bronze Age concerning codes, beliefs, and structures are easily located within Egyptian sources. The *Egyptian Book of the Dead*, originating in the New Kingdom, and written in hieroglyphs around 1550 B.C.E., formed part of an accepted grouping of ancient funerary texts and art, including the *Pyramid Texts* and *Coffin Texts*. This religious literature functioned as a collection of ritual spells and guidance for the dead, and was painted upon objects. As such they form the "oldest collection of religious spells preserved from ancient Egypt."[52] Some of the spells were drawn from works dating from the Old Kingdom of the third millennium B.C.E. Other spells were composed later in Egyptian history, up to and including the Third Intermediate Period, from the eleventh to seventh centuries B.C.E. The *Book of the Dead* was placed in the coffin or burial chamber of the deceased and contained instructions and codes of conduct to be used in order to ensure safe passage and preservation of the deceased's soul and body.

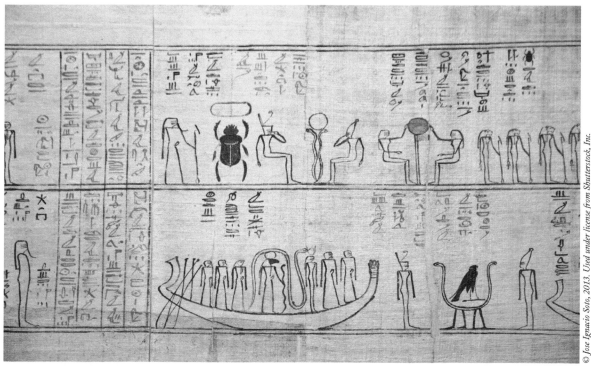

Funerary text

EGYPTIAN FUNERY TEXT

Another insightful text emerges from around 1300 B.C.E., and is now contained within the sacred scriptures of the Hebrew Bible or Tanakh.[53] This code is known as the Mosaic Law Code, or the Pentateuch, and can be divided into three parts: (1) the moral code, known as the Decalogue or Ten Commandments; (2) the ceremonial code, which concerned sacred space, the Levitical priesthood, the holy days and sabbaths, offerings, sacrifices, and feasts; and (3) the social code, which organized diet, hygiene, quarantine, tithes, laws of evidence, crime, land conservation, slavery and freedom, the poor (including widows and orphans), the military, and the economy.

THE DECALOGUE

The Decalogue, generally known as the 10 Commandments, is part of the Pentateuch, and is one of the most ancient enduring socio-religious ethical codes of conduct for many faith communities. As such is still socially relevant for many religious and to varying degrees, also secular societies in the application of moral and social codes. To this day, due to the core ethics that were applied through early Christianity, then absorbed into late Antiquity, and later into to the development of the European countries, remnants of these concepts still remain. So far reaching is this ancient code that adherents to Judaism, Christianity, and Islam can easily trace the origins of many of their beliefs and practices to the Mosaic Code that is believed to have been instituted by the Israelite reformer Moses, the Lawgiver, in 1300 B.C.E. Further, what is interesting to note is that traces of Hammurabi's code can be found within the ancient Pentateuchal laws, with the ancient, but adapted concept of an "eye for an eye" in punitive law.

There were, however, also other civilizations from India and China that evolved their own systems of social and legal coding within the Bronze and Iron ages.[54] Due to the complexity of their cultures and diversity of texts it is often difficult to select a particular code through which to illustrate a central enduring theme within their systems. The following examples reflect only a brief overview of central beliefs but demonstrate their enduring influence on systems today.

In the context of the codes of conduct within the Hindu systems,[55] it is necessary to consult the Vedas, which represent some of the oldest texts within the Bronze Age in order to construct a cultural navigational aid. The Vedas consist of four "books" and all presuppose an established sacrificial system, with hymns, myths, and the role of the priest.[56] The first Veda is known as the *Rig Veda,* and is the oldest text with material dating from around 2000 B.C.E., which reached its final form around 1200 B.C.E.[57] The second, third, and fourth Vedas—the *Sama Veda, Yajur Veda,* and *Atharva Veda*, respectively—were all compiled after the *Rig Veda*. Together, this early body of work is referred to as the *Samhitas*[58] and they are considered to be texts of divine origin, referred to as *Shruti*.[59] The second body of material falls under the heading of *Smriti*, or "that which is remembered," and forms a codified unit of Hindu customary law which is not considered to be of divine origin. This secondary body of work, however, although much later in origin, provides a particularly interesting code of social conduct, and one which still has lasting influence in the majority of Hindu belief systems. The code describes the caste system and the relative duties or *dharma* for members within each social grouping. The explanation for the four castes comes from *The Institutes of Vishnu,*[60] and defines the sacred duties the Brahmins (priestly and religious officials), the Kshatriyas (rulers and warriors), the Vaishyas (traders, merchants, farmers, craftsmen), and the Shudras (servants of the upper three castes). The *Institutes* states that the "first three of these are called twice-born.[61] They must perform with mantras

Performance of ritual before a Brahmin priest

[sacred words or syllables chanted to create cosmic spiritual power].[62] These ideas of social hierarchy remain an integrated part of Indian social codes to this day.

The final code to be considered is that found within the diverse Chinese matrix of relationships. The code itself is called *The Five Relationships* and although emphasized by Master K'ung (Confucius 551–479 B.C.E.),[63] found its roots in the more ancient system of Chinese relationships dating from the Middle Kingdom[64] of family, community and extended village life, and the concept of filiality.[65] Observance of, and compliance to, the concept of the *Five Relationships* (father and son; ruler and minister; husband and wife; elder brother and younger brother; older friend and younger friend) were based on a formulation of superordination and subordination.[66] These concepts were also based on the idea that it was "perfectly appropriate that individual desires be sacrificed for the larger good." In

Father and son

ancient China the family relationship was based upon a patrilinear descent, with ranking usually age based. Thus "one was always in a system of dynamic relationships in which one was superior to some members of the family and subordinate to others."[67] Family property and assets were held in a corporate ownership and as long as the family stayed together, their property remained intact within the unit. This meant that the importance of the family unit held dominance over the desires of the individual.[68] Many of these ideas can still be identified within traditional Chinese families and cultural life and, in Mainland China, through the acceptance of a controlled political and social philosophy for the good of the collective community.

WHAT ALL RELIGIOUS CODES CONTAIN

From the codes reviewed in the preceding pages, certain cognitive modes of expression emerge, and can be identified as the theoretical, the practical, and the social,[69] or TPS. From a structural functionalist perspective,[70] these organizational systems function as modes of expression and experiential reality[71]:

> The *theoretical* is described as the verbal aspect, as that which is told and described, as in a core religious system of beliefs. It explains the cosmology of the group through its myths and doctrines, and provides teachings on how the universe is organized and provides a map of the invisible world. In other words, it functions to provide the authority behind fundamental truths and guidance for life through the respective religious path, and seeks to explain why things are the way they are in the reality of the individual and the community.

> The *practical* level or mode pertains to the visible as contained within ritual, worship, and ethics. It stresses the performance or acting out in our experience of the sacred within life and community. It stresses participation and adherence to codes of religious conduct through our physical selves as we live within the context of everyday life.

> The *social* incorporates the practical within a communal experience. It is demonstrated by a community that adheres to beliefs and enforces codes of conduct through everyday life. It establishes leadership and authority through designated lawgivers, kings, or priests and through an integrated system of beliefs and/or laws which influence the larger society. The social level of expression functions as a purveyor of these beliefs through their respective community structures. In other words, how the religion is set up to preserve and implement its teachings and practices through the codification of social rules and interaction, vested with the aura of divine sanction or ancient rule.

CONCLUSION

What we have seen evidenced within the construction of codes is that they contain belief systems which are embodied within the practical application of rules exerted to effect social control or social order. They are thus archetypal as exhibited through the TPS. To varying degrees these religious and moral laws have been an enduring influence in the lives of our ancestors and are still exerting their influence today through the dynamic of religious belief and traditional teachings. It is clear, therefore, that the genius of our ability to construct these modes of expression constitute a fundamental element in the way we absorb religion into our realities, both past and present.

GLOSSARY

Ancient Near East: Mesopotamia (modern Iraq, southeastern Turkey, northeastern Syria); ancient Egypt; ancient Iran (Elam, Media, Parthia, Persia); Anatolia/Asia Minor (modern Turkey); the Levant (modern Syria, Lebanon, Israel, Palestine, Jordan); Malta; the Arabian Peninsula.

Antediluvian: Before the Deluge. Time between the creation of the earth and the Great Flood as recorded within ancient Sumerian, Akkadian, and biblical texts.

Archetype: A universally understood symbol, term, or pattern. A model or original used as an archetype. A person or thing considered worthy of imitation. A plan; one that is worthy of imitation; a model. One that is typical or representative; an example. An ideal that serves as a pattern; a copy, as of a book, diagram, or model to be followed in making things: a dress pattern. A representative sample of behaviour, a prototype upon which others are copied, patterned, or emulated.

Bronze Age: Loosely identified around 3500–3000 B.C.E. to 1200 B.C.E.

Code of Hammurabi: Law code that emerged between 1772 and 1780 B.C.E.

Cult: A system or variety of religious worship. Identifies a pattern of ritual behaviour in connection with specific objects, within a framework of spatial and temporal coordinates. Ritual behaviour would include (but not necessarily be limited to) prayer, sacrifice, votive offerings, competitions, processions, and construction of monuments. Some degree of recurrence in place and repetition over time of ritual action is necessary for cult to be enacted, to be practiced.

Cuneiform: One of the earliest forms of written script. Distinctive wedge-shaped characters used in Mesopotamia, Persia, and Ugarit.

Decalogue: The Ten Commandments.

Egyptian Book of the Dead: Funerary text.

Filiality: Compliance to the Five Relationships. Based on the concepts of superordination and subordination.

Five Relationships: Chinese system of relationships: father and son; ruler and minster; husband and wife; elder brother and younger brother; older friend to younger friend.

Hieroglyphics: Early Egyptian writing system. Pictographic script in which conventional, recognizable pictures are used.

Hindu caste system: Social classification of Brahmin (priestly caste); Kshatriyas (rulers and warriors); the Vaishyas (traders, merchants, farmers, craftsmen); and the Shudras (servants of the upper three castes).

Institutes of Vishnu: A codified unit of Hindu customary law (codified popular law and customs) written anywhere between 300 and 1000 C.E. [common era]. Modern scholarship fixes it around 700 C.E., originating out of Kashmir. It also contains the first reference to Sati—widow immolation (voluntary burning) when a wife, in an act of devotion to her dead husband, would burn herself alive on her husband's funerary pyre.

Iron Age: Period in the Middle East and Europe, circa 1200 B.C.E., and in China circa 600 B.C.E.

Middle Paleolithic: Period dating from 200,000 to 28,000 B.C.E.

Modalities: The ceremonial forms, protocols, or conditions that surround formal agreements or negotiations.

Modality: A tendency to conform to a general pattern or belong to a particular group or category.

Neolithic: Period dating from 8000 to 3500 B.C.E.

Pentateuch: Hebrew scriptural text. Law code. Known also as the *Five Books of Moses*. Generally identified as containing three parts to the codal system: moral, ceremonial, and social.

Samhitas: Four books, or collections; commonly referred to as the Vedas.

Shruti: Referring to early Hindu texts considered to be of divine origin. Defined as "that which is handed down; of divine truth and origin."

Shuruppak: Legendary founder of the city, who in Sumerian myths, predated the Deluge or Flood.

Smriti: Referring to Hindu texts considered to be of human origin. Defined as "that which is remembered." Transmitted by tradition.

Structural functionalism: Identification of the distinct structures or institutions that shape a society; each structure has a specific function or role to play in determining the behavior of the society.

Urukagina's Code: Named after legendary King Urukagina, ruler of the Mesopotamian city-state of Lagash, who reigned circa 2380 to 2360 B.C.E.).

Vedas: Earliest body of Hindu scriptures. Four books within this collection.

Wisdom literature: Genre of literature common in the Ancient Near East. A way of looking at life based on experience.

ENDNOTES

1. The Schoyen online manuscript collection provides an impressive overview of literature representative of our diverse cultures over thousands of years. See http://www.schoyencollection.com/collections.htmle

2. René Dubos, credited for the maxim "Think globally, act locally," performed groundbreaking research which led to the discovery of major antibiotics.

3. Dubos was awarded the Pulitzer Prize for Nonfiction in 1969, for *So Human an Animal*.

4. René Dubos, "So Human An Animal: How We are Shaped by Surroundings and Events," (New York, Charles Scribner's Sons, 1968), p 61.

5. Angela Zito quotes Raymond Williams from his work, "Keywords: A Vocabulary of Culture and Society," in her work, *Culture*, "Keywords in Religion, Media and Culture," (New York: Routledge, 2008), ed. David Morgan, p 69.

6. Clyde Kluckhohn, as quoted by Julia Jahansoozi, et al, in *Mago Mago: Nigeria, Petroleum and a History of Mismanaged Community Relations*, "Culture and Public Relations: Links and Implications," (New York: Routledge, 2012), eds. Krishnamurthy Sriramesh and Dejan Vercic, p 106.

7. Angela Zito, *Culture*, p 70.

8. Ibid., p 81.

9. Christopher Bobonich, ed., "Plato's Laws: A Critical Guide," (Cambridge: Cambridge University Press, 2010), p 1.

10. Ibid.

11. *Laws* by Plato, written 360 B.C.E., Book II, translated by Benjamin Jowett, The Internet Classics Archives, http://classics.mit.edu/Plato/laws.html, retrieved June 30, 2012.

12. Those who study cultures and the dynamics, both human and environmental, that cause societies to develop and evolve.

13. David A. Morgan, ed., "Key Words in Religion, Media and Culture," p xiv.

14. *Cultus* in Latin or "cult" describes a system of religious institution and worship surrounding a specific religion.

15. David A. Morgan, ed., "Key Words," p 17.

16. Richard K. Fenn, *Key Thinkers in the Sociology of Religion*, (Trowbridge: The Cromwell Press Group, 2009), pp 207-208. Fenn discusses the work of social anthropologist, Maurice Bloch (b. 1939).

17. Richard K. Fenn, *Key Thinkers in the Sociology of Religion*, pp 207-208.

18. Anita Zito, *Culture*, pp 80-81.

19. Roger Schmidt et al., "Patterns of Religion," (Belmont: Wadsworth Publishing Company, 1999), p 52.

20. Ibid., p 61.

21. Ibid., p 57.

22. Smithsonian database at: http://humanorigins.si.edu/evidence/human-fossils/species/homo-neanderthalensis. Retrieved July 10, 2012.

23. Ibid., p 58.

24. Roger Schmidt et al., "Patterns of Religion," p 58.

25. Smithsonian database at: http://humanorigins.si.edu/evidence/human-fossils/species/homo-neanderthalensis. Retrieved July 10, 2012.

26. http://www.smithsonianmag.com/science-nature/neanderthals.html. Retrieved July 16, 2012.

27. http://www.livescience.com/1187-neanderthals-cannibals-study-confirms.html. Retrieved July 10, 2012.

28. Cro-Magnon was named after a rock shelter in southwestern France, where the first remains were found in 1868. See, Roger Schmidt et al., "Patterns of Religion," p 58.

29. The Venus of Hohle Fels, circa 35,000 B.C.E. Carving discovered in the Hohle Fels cave in Germany. Also, the Venus of Willendorf, carved circa 25,000 B.C.E. The Venus of Willendorf is believed to have been a childbearing talisman.

30. Roger Schmidt et al., "Patterns of Religion," pp 62-63.

31. Ibid., p 60.

32. Ibid., p 67.

33. As is the case of site of the Glastonbury Tor in Somerset, England, which is the site of Neolithic and later Celtic, Roman, and Saxon occupancy. As it rose from a plain which was flooded at high tide, the site was bestowed with significant spiritual and logistical importance.

34. Evolving out of this tradition, the great standing stones of Stonehenge were erected in the Bronze Age. There was also a prehistoric wooden centre named "Woodhenge" which was developed around 23,000 B.C.E. At Woodhenge there is definite archaeological evidence of human sacrifice, with one fully excavated skeleton of a three-year-old child whose skull had been cleaved open in what appeared to be an almost predetermined way, and placed within the centre of the wooden complex. See, Woodhenge: http://www.this-is-amesbury.co.uk/woodhenge.html. Retrieved July 6, 2012.

35. During the excavations in the 1980s of 30 tombs in Juxian, the paleographer Tang Lan, identified certain very early Chinese characters inscribed on pottery wine vessels. These artifacts are identified as belonging to the late period of the Neolithic Dawenkou Culture (4500-2500 B.C.E.). Arche-

ologists and paleographers have since recognized 14 of the more than 20 drawings as pictographs and deciphered them as seven characters, including "fan" (ordinary), "nan" (south), and "xiang" (enjoy). http://english.people.com.cn/english/200004/21/eng20000421_39442.html. Retrieved July 6, 2012.

36. Initially, written language was believed to be the gift of the gods and only given to and used by priests of the specific cult.

37. Mesopotamia was located between the Tigris and Euphrates rivers, the area now identified as modern-day Iraq.

38. Term referring to before the Flood or Deluge. Time between the creation of the earth and the great deluge.

39. The city was discovered in 1900 and, over intermittent periods of excavation lasting into the 1970s, many clay cuneiform tablets, some baked by a catastrophic fire, and other "unfired" pottery shards were unearthed.

40. Type of literature common in the Ancient Near East: Mesopotamia (modern Iraq, southeastern Turkey, northeastern Syria); ancient Egypt; ancient Iran (Elam, Media, Parthia, Persia); Anatolia/Asia Minor (modern Turkey); the Levant (modern Syria, Lebanon, Israel, Palestine, Jordan); Malta; the Arabian Peninsula.

   This genre of literature is characterized by sayings of wisdom intended to teach about divinity and virtue. The key principle of wisdom literature is that while techniques of traditional storytelling are used, books and existing codes of conduct also presume to offer insight and wisdom about nature and reality.

41. This text appears to have been a popular one and forms a central teaching within Sumerian and Akkadian literary canons.

42. Paul-Alain Beaulieu, *Wisdom Literature in Mesopotamia and Israel*, 2007, p 4, ed. Richard J. Clifford.

43. The Instructions of Shurppak, from W.G. Lambert Babylonian Wisdom Literature. (Eisenbrauns, Winona Lake, Indiana, 1996). See also on-line English translation of the text: http://www.gatewaystobabylon.com/myths/texts/life/instruction-shruppak.html

44. From the Schoyen Collection on-line.
   MS 3396 Instructions of Shurppak, Proverb Collection.
   MS in Sumerian on clay, Sumer, ca. 2600 BC, 1 tablet, 8,7x8,7x2,5 cm, 2 columns + 2 blank columns, 8+8 compartments in cuneiform script, reverse blank. Context: For the Old Babylonian recension of the text, see MSS 2817 (lines 1-22), 3352 (lines 1-38), 2788 (lines 1-45), 2291 (lines 88-94), 2040 (lines 207-216), 3400 (lines 342-

345), MS 3176/1, text 3, and 3366.
   Context: For the Old Babylonian recension of the text, see MSS 2788 (lines 1-45), 2291 (lines 88-94) and 2040 (lines 207-216).
   Commentary: The present Early Dynastic tablet is one of a few that represent the earliest literature in the world. Only three groups of texts are known from the dawn of literature: The Shuruppak instructions, The Kesh temple hymn, and various incantations (see MS 4549). The instructions are addressed by the ante-diluvian ruler Shuruppak, to his son Ziusudra, who was the Sumerian Noah, cf. MS 3026, the Sumerian Flood Story, and MS 2950, Atra-Hasis, the Old Babylonian Flood Story. http://www.schoyencollection.com/historySumerian.html.

45. http://www.schoyencollection.com/historySumerian.html.

46. See: http://www.duhaime.org/LawMuseum/LawArticle-44/Duhaimes-Timetable-of-World-Legal-Hist

47. http://cuip.uchicago.edu/~bobfinn/2003/sample-timeline3.htmlory.aspx#2350bc.

48. The Science Forum: http://www.thescienceforum.com/history/24301-first-tax-reformer.html. Retrieved July 10, 2012.

49. http://cuip.uchicago.edu/~bobfinn/2003/sample-timeline3.html

50. Both gods were sun-gods.

51. http://cuip.uchicago.edu/~bobfinn/2003/sample-timeline3.html

52. Erik Hornung, David Lorton, *The Ancient Egyptian Books of the Afterlife* (Ithaca: Cornell University Press: 1999), pp 1, 14.

53. Tanakh: T = Torah or Law; N = Nav'im or Prophets; K = Ketuv'im or Writings.

54. Middle East and Europe, circa 1200 B.C.E., China 600 B.C.E.

55. Hinduism represents a diversity of religious beliefs which developed over thousands of years. It is often less confusing to approach the religious systems in the context of polytheism, which represents millions of different concepts of gods and goddesses. In fact, there are at least 330 million belief systems within Hinduism. It is also better to think of Hinduism representing the religious traditions of India as the "religions of the Hindi speaking people."

56. Robert E. Van Voorst, *Anthology of World Scriptures* (Canada: Thomson Learning Inc., 2003), 4th ed., p 30.

57. Ibid., p 31.

58. Theodore M. Ludwig, *The Sacred Paths: Understanding the Religions of the World* (New Jersey: Prentice Hall, 2001), p 70.

59. That which is handed down.

60. The Institutes of Vishnu, Sacred Books of the East, (Oxford, the Clarendon Press, 1880), Vol. 7., trans. Julius Jolly. NOTE: This text has been dated anywhere from 300 B.C.E. to 1000 C.E. [common era].

61. The rite of initiation only allowed the three upper castes. They are allowed to participate in Hindu rites that are exclusive to their groups and listen to the Vedas. Traditionally, no Shudras were allowed to participate in any of these ritual observances.

62. Robert E. Van Voorst, *Anthology of World Scriptures,* pp 40-41.

63. Hsu Dau-Lin, *The Myth of the "Five Human Relations of Confucius,"* Monumenta Serica Institute, http://www.jstor.org/stable/40725916.

64. The Middle Kingdom dates back to at least 1000 B.C.E.

65. Bradley K. Hawkins, *Introduction to Asian Religions,* (New York: Pearson, 2004), pp 179-180. Filial piety means the relation or attitude of a child to a parent.

66. Hsu Dau-Lin, *The Myth of the "Five Human Relations of Confucius."*

67. Ibid., p 180.

68. Ibid. p 181.

69. Joachim Wach, *Sociology of Religion,* (Chicago: University of Chicago Press, 1944) pp 17-34.

70. Identification of social structures.

71. Theodore M. Ludwig, *The Sacred Paths of the West,* (New Jersey: Pearson, 2006), pp 8-9.

CHAPTER 3

Developments in Laws and Construction of Typology Laws

The way our species builds connection through society, history, and culture is easily identified by means of patterns of construction. This construction methodology is evident in the enduring modes of social order, based on religious cosmologies that have developed. Examples of just a small selection of laws will illustrate how we have assigned values which in turn have influenced the evolution of various cultures, together with civil and religious states. Some of these include classical Hindu law[1]; Greek law (the law of Athens during fifth to fourth centuries B.C.E.)[2]; Roman law (The Twelve Tables, 450 B.C.E.[3]); Christian canon law[4]; Celtic law (seventh and eighth centuries C.E.)[5]; traditional Chinese law, T'ang (617–926), Ming (1369–1644), and Ch'ing (1644–1911)[6]; The Anglo-Saxon Dooms (560–975 C.E.)[7]; English law (Magna Carta, 1215 C.E.)[8]; Germanic law (circa seventh century C.E.)[9]; Russian law (Law of Yaroslav, eleventh century C.E.)[10]; Talmudic or Jewish law (Halakhah)[11]; and Islamic law (Shariah).[12] Existing even today within our current legal codes are traces of these culturally respective foundational law and perspectives established by ancient rules of adjudication. Our cultures have merely built upon, extracted, enhanced, amended, and reinterpreted according to their social evolutionary needs and perceptions.

Of note also in this context of law is the insight that religions offer to the researcher. Religious codes have, as we have seen, been part of our social structures from early in recorded history. Enduring and extending into our modern cultural and global experience is the reality that in many parts of the world, religious laws still form the basis of a nation's governance. These ancient rules sometimes present in rather startling law codes which we still see as prevalent in our twenty-first-century world. A country, state, or religious community that is governed by religious law is called a *theocracy* or *theocratic state*.[13] Within these theocratic systems of religious laws it is sometimes difficult to find continuity or even consistency due to differences within a specific governing religious sect's own understanding and bias. This can mean that a specific religious law code can have a variance of interpretations regarding severity and implementation of the actual law. In addition to this, the ingrained belief that these laws were "handed down" by God, prophet, divinely enlightened leader, or revered ancestor, may cause loyalty, and blind devotion. This in turn engenders reluctance to, or may even initiate the violent rejection of changes that are often required to legitimately reflect the specific needs of the always evolving society around them.

THE DOUGLAS MODEL

To illustrate this religious reality and the tension encountered regarding change in a religious structure, one must accept that differing factions—some based on reform and others based on maintaining the status quo—will sometimes interpret the same codes of conduct from differing perspectives. This often causes sectarian splintering or even the establishment of a new religious system. These developments therefore contribute to the evolution of social, cultural, and religious systems, thereby reflecting historical development, change or even upheaval.

In order to understand this dynamic of change some descriptions given by cultural anthropologist Mary Douglas will now be examined to illustrate how these changes occur. In two works, "Cultural Bias"[14] and "Natural Symbols: Explorations in Cosmology,"[15] Douglas used a grid-group-constructional analysis to explain the tension encountered within a group of people sharing the same cosmology as they react to the pressures of competing demands both religious and social. She defined the dynamic as a three fold encounter experienced by a group sharing a common grid or belief system. The three fold experience was classified as *culture, cosmology,*[16] and *individualism* or *individual need.*[17] Douglas also analyzed the classification of a shared belief or faith as the *grid,* referred to as A. She then described the *group* in two ways: the ego controlled by D exerted pressure on the more compliant group C whose ego was controlled by D; and at the bottom of the group layout there was a system of private classification or individualism known as B. The most simple way to understand this structural function analysis is through a very useful diagram used by Robert McCutchan in his work, "The Social and the Celestial: Mary Douglas and Transcendental Meditation."[18]

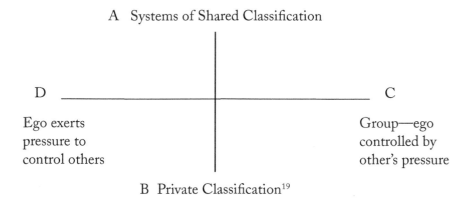

A Systems of Shared Classification

D ————————————————————— C

Ego exerts
pressure to
control others

Group—ego
controlled by
other's pressure

B Private Classification[19]

Expanding upon the Douglas model, and arising out of her classification system, the tension which runs through this interrelated dynamic, in the context of how religions change or develop, is simple. Initially, A (the *grid* or shared belief system) defines a religion or cosmology and there are three groups within this system. In the community's construction of the grid, group D emerges as the dominant hierarchy through consolidated leadership or the control exerted by an alpha leader. This group exerts pressure through edicts and comprehensive control mechanisms, and maintains this influence by using the existing cultural construct, governed by central law codes often perceived to be divinely received. Group C, being the masses or ordinary devotees, then responds to pressure brought upon it by the dominant group D, through compliance and obedience to the codes of belief and conduct. The growing, often despotic, hierarchal control of D places extreme pressure on C, which subtly finds a relief valve through individual interpretations of their religious system and this is identified as B group. There is a wild card factor to this private system of belief because it contains the seed elements used for religious and social reform, often voiced by a leader or specific group which bands together to effect change through the articulation of these contending beliefs. This dynamic causes either lasting changes espousing the system or a religious revolution culminating in the formation of another religion or a sect within the existing cosmology. This is simply how religions purge themselves of cumbersome, often outdated, religious and social traditions.

AN ANALOGY

On a more general level, the following analogy of a cart wheel will now be presented to explain how individuals within societies effect change within their religious systems and cause cultural change. It demonstrates how people are influenced by their surrounding infrastructures and, in turn, how they also influence the cosmological societies in which they live.

© Budipig, 2013. Used under license from Shutterstock, Inc.

If one studies the cart wheel it is apparent that there are three parts to its construction: (1) the hub at the centre, (2) the spokes that connect to the hub, and (3) the rim which holds the other two parts in position.

The functional purpose of the wheel, when in motion, is to affix to a cart via an axle and transport a larger, perhaps more unwieldy item in size and weight from one place to another. To use an analogical interpretation, it is the wheel through its structural design that keeps things in motion, providing function and purpose.

The design can be used to illustrate the social role of law and religion throughout history by interpreting the hub as the central belief system found within each society—usually representing the core religious cosmology. The spokes become the cultural customs that have evolved through the course of that society's evolution and are established within the particular religious system. Finally, it is the rim which holds in balance the other two parts of the structure. The rim represents the community; one that is ever in motion and consequently changing as it responds to its environmental, historical, and political surroundings in the material world. These factors have all combined to shape the respective religious identifications throughout history and have produced the variance in religious beliefs, customs and cultures that surround us.

As the cart wheel moves it will routinely encounter uneven terrain and will eventually suffer wear and tear. This leads to the fracturing or weakening of the spokes which are themselves essential to the integrity of the wheel. When a spoke becomes weak it must be replaced in order for the wheel to be righted, balanced, and aligned. Spokes are representations of cultural systems, practices, or outdated traditions, which the community has the discretion to remove and replace with new, stronger, interpretive, and culturally relevant systems. These replacement "spokes" are still anchored within the hub or cosmology, and do not affect its strength as the hub is the indispensible "signature" of core spiritual beliefs. It is the rim that replaces the customs but retains its connection to the spiritual core identification of the group. When a religion is no longer culturally "relevant" it atrophies and becomes obsolete for many within its systems, thereby causing people within its cosmology to look for more meaningful alternatives. This is where hierarchal opposition can manifest through violent repression and the rejection of change by implementing religious sanctions, threats, ostracism of the individual, and isolation of the group from outside "corruption." Sadly, as far as the historical data attest, there is not one religion that has been exempt from this evolutionary convulsion, as each religion, existing in a social and cultural infrastructure, has manifested the reluctance to change for the good of its devotees. Realistically, the freedom of spirituality, for the individual or small group seeking change, is never an easy task and is often fraught with risks and challenging consequences.

CATEGORIES

On the positive side, however, this is the way that religions evolve gradually or spasm into manifestations of differing systems of belief. In the discipline of Religious Studies these systems are categorized and explained by Roger Schmidt in his work, "Studying Religion," in *Patterns of Religion*,[20] as *theistic, nontheistic, ethnic,* and *universal* religions. These traditions will be identified as follows:

> *Theistic* cosmologies incorporate religions such as Zoroastrianism, Judaism, Christianity, Islam, Hinduism, Sikhism, some forms of Shintoism, and many of the tribal traditions existing today. These traditions believe in a divine person or persons, God or many gods. They can be *monotheistic* or *polytheistic* but systematically believe that there exists a personal interaction between the human and the divine.

> *Nontheistic* beliefs are specifically identified within Buddhism, Confucianism, Jainism, secular or humanistic Judaism, and a branch of Hinduism known as philosophical Advaita Ve-

danta. This concept can also be "extended to include quasi-religious movements such as communism and humanism which affirm nontheistic and explicity atheistic worldviews." These belief systems perceive the sacred as an impersonal form, a power, process, liberating truth, or way of being.

Ethnic or *tribal* traditions link people together with their association through ancestry, kinship, and culture. These traditions represent thousands of tribal groups, and localized ethnicnational religious, such as early Israelite religion (1300–586 B.C.E.) now known as Judaism, Shinto, Taoism, Druze, and Jainism.

Universal religions are conversionist by nature and seek converts by proselytization, whereby they recruit others of different faith systems in various parts of the world. The mainstream groups within these religions actively seek to convert others, thus creating a global family which spans ethnic boundaries. They do this by uniting people of various national and ethnic groups into a broad cosmology specific to the universal religion in question. The specific religion will present an exemplary founder such as Buddha, Jesus Christ, Mohammad, Nanak, Joseph Smith, or Bahá'u'lláh as the guide to self-transcendence and/or salvation. The religions represented by these founders are, respectively, Buddhism, Christianity, Islam, Sikhism, Latter Day Saints, and Bahai.[21]

THE TYPOLOGIES

There is, however, much more complexity and diversity within the religions and their characteristic structures and, as a consequence, a more comprehensive and detailed system of analysis has been developed over the past 150 years.[22] This system of classification is referred to as *Typological Signature*. This analytical methodology places religions within a type of core belief patterns found in religious structures and is called *Typological Identification*. Through this system it is possible to group the major world religions into four basic *typologies* or *trees,* notably the Abrahamic, Indian, South East Asian, and Tribal/Indigenous. Each tree will now be explained.

THE ABRAHAMIC TREE: THEIST, UNIVERSAL (JUDAISM, CHRISTIANITY, AND ISLAM)

These faith traditions are historical religions as their origins lie within a specific time frame. They consider themselves to be of biblical origin as they claim one common religious "ancestor" named Abram, later known as Abraham, who passed on his revelation. This revelation was then handed down through oral transmission and later recorded through the medium of the written word known as scripture. It is believed that Abraham lived circa 2000 B.C.E., in the vicinity of the modern Persian Gulf area.

Abraham's concept of God was as "Supreme Being" and creator of all, and it was this perspective that provided the foundation for monotheism in the Semitic cultures. Such a belief meant that there was one who was Creator and moral overseer of life and history. Further, although God was altogether radically separate and different from humans—Creator and the creation—there existed a personal interaction between them. As a consequence to this, the deepest significance in human life was to be gained through love, worship and obedience to this God.

Each of the Abrahamics believe themselves to be recipients of God's unique revelation and that these revelations were recorded within their specific holy scriptures (Tanakh, Christian Bible, Qur'an, respectively). These truths were delivered through divinely appointed messengers who were themselves the founders of each of the religions and that the revelations within the scriptures reveal the personality and nature of God. The messengers who brought these revelations are highly revered, namely Abraham and Moses for Judaism, and Prophet Mohammed for Islam. In the context of Christianity, most branches of the tradition do not merely revere Jesus Christ as Son of God and Saviour, but centre their worship of Him as being the incarnation of God's sheer essence and nature, thus considering Him to be God.

The Abrahamics also believe in heaven and hell, the individual judgment of the dead, and the resurrection of the body at the end of time. It is imperative, therefore, that the individual should obey God in this life and seek the genuine good of others. In addition to all this is the fact that within each of these traditions there are some who believe in reincarnation, although this doctrine is not found within any of their respective scriptures. Biblically, it is: one soul, one life, one chance.

NOTE: Zoroastrian contains monotheistic beliefs but believes their founding prophet was one named Zarathstrusta. They do not believe in reincarnation.

INDIAN TREE: THEIST, NONTHEIST, ETHNIC, AND TRIBAL (HINDUISM, BUDDHISM, JAINISM, AND SIKHISM)

These religions trace their ancient origins within India, over millennia, and reflect a multitude of cultures, ancestral traditions, and tribal belief systems all linked to their respective ethnic origins and associated with their local regions. As such, the Indian tree itself reflects of diversity of cultures, local systems, tribal gods, varying gods (estimated within Hinduism alone to be 330 million in representation), one God (Sikhism), and no gods (Jainism and Buddhism).

© Ostill, 2013. Used under license from Shutterstock, Inc.

Although each of the religions have varying characteristics unique to their specific cosmologies, it is reasonable to state that they express fields of influence wholly independent from biblical ideas, and contain elemental and similar core belief sets specific to the subcontinent of India. As such, they possess their own unique construction of religious values pertaining to perceptions of reality, concepts of impermanence, transmigration of the consciousness, reincarnation, punishment, and the law of karma.

Central to all their beliefs systems, however, is that the world is understood as an interplay of relative, limited, illusory human perception on the one hand and cosmic reality in the process of the consciousness's enlightenment on the other. In the evolution of a human being's enlightenment there is an interplay between his/her real identity and the ignorance of everyday life which shrouds awareness and consequently leads to yet another rebirth into either the human realm or other realms of existence which are usually not conducive to enlightenment. This is referred to as the wheel of Samsara which is the unending process of birth, death, reincarnation, birth, death, etc. It is believed that only in human form can the consciousness attain liberation or *Moksha* and be released from karma for a period of cosmic time.

NOTE: The Bahai tradition originating on the Indian subcontinent is theist in so far as it emphasizes only one God, but this god is not directly accessible. In regards to life after death, they do not believe in a final judgment or in the resurrection of the dead. They believe in a series of experiences that unfold after the cessation of one's physical life. Heaven is described as being near to God and hell is the opposite where one is separated from God's presence. This cosmology incorporates many other religious belief systems, including Islamic interpretations, into its own tenets and seeks to spread its teachings through proselytization. As such it is regarded as universalist.

SOUTH EAST ASIAN TREE: NONTHEIST, TRIBAL, SHAMANISTIC (TAOISM, CONFUCIANISM, SHINTO)

The primary image of religiousness native to China, Korea, and Japan is harmony within the given order of the world. It stresses filial piety, which is a central virtue expressing the primary duties of respect, obedience, and care for one's parents and elderly family members. This concept also broadens into respect for hierarchy within government and the creation of an orderly existence through which every person observes his/her duty within the given order of society. The primary spiritual value is thus to behave in appropriately fitting relationships with the world and the Tao. The Tao is defined as the "way, path, or energy force, which manifests within nature, responsibility, and order."

The origins of the religion now known as Taoism are tribal, ancestral, and shamanistic, representing a conglomeration of belief in spirits (both benign and malignant), spirit possession by ancestors, powerful animal forces, and gods to be found within the Tao. As the religions came to be consolidated and written about by the charismatic sage Lao Tzu, the legendary founder of the newly emerging religion, Taoism developed the ancient traditions that interpreted a core Chinese concept of harmony and balance within the Tao in terms of nature metaphors. Further, it incorporated ancient beliefs in ancestor worship, and also created the concept of the Tao as Mother. All things came from and returned to the Tao and so the individual sought to maintain an harmonious relationship with all things according to the flow of the Tao as the life force or energy within all natural systems. When an individual died they merely returned to the Tao to be reincarnated, or processed into another form, or to exist on some sort of ancestral plane, thus accommodating the enduring Chinese belief in ancestor worship. Taoism to this day incorporates a variety of different, even conflicting beliefs into an harmonious view of the "Way and its Power" or the Tao.

Confucianism, as constructed by Master K'ung or Konzi (Confucius), emphasized social relationship, virtues, and proper conduct. Right relationship was of the highest value and the idea of salvation through any kind of deity worship, or liberation that could be achieved through rejection of material wealth, was rejected. The eternal Tao (way, balance, harmony) of things was to be known through seasoned wisdom and the cultivation of the character. Confucianism stressed only proper behaviour through filial piety and social balance, but later also formally accepted and incorporated the enduring idea of ancestor worship within its cosmology. These concepts are still signature identification markers within Confucianism today.

Shinto (The Way of the Gods/Spirits), as the original Japanese religious cosmology, contains at its core a tribal, indigenous religious tradition. In addition to this, it also exhibits the

common markers found within Taoism and Confucianism, but includes the concept of the kami as gods or revered spirits, to be worshipped. There are three tiers to kami identification: the celestial kami, nature kami, and ancestral kami. Right relationship as in filial piety, together with ancestor veneration, and the worship of all other kami, lies at its centre.

TRIBAL TREE: THEIST, NONTHEIST, SHAMANISTIC (AFRICAN, FIRST NATIONS, AUSTRALIAN ABORIGINAL CULTURES/RELIGIONS)

Each religion generally functions independently of other surrounding tribal religions. This is because in general, each has its own self-contained religious logic which is often indigenous to its own local community and actual physical location. This means that each religion is often tied to the confines of its own tribal lands and possesses a path or cosmology commensurate with its own cultural goals and visions. Further, each religious system is not easily transferred over to another culture or indigenous group. This religious reality, placed within a demographic, makes it very difficult to thoroughly identify specific, uniting patterns. Realistically, taking into consideration that there are over 232 million tribal adherents within a multitude of localized, indigenous religions, comprising 4 percent of the global population, it proves to be a daunting task to identify numerous consistent themes.[23]

Prevalent beliefs, however, can be loosely identified within tribal cosmologies by their general adherence to ancestor worship—both out of fear and devotion; the practice of shamanism; the veneration of the shaman or shamaness; the belief in spirit possession; ghosts; good and evil spirits; spells; animism; and respect for nature.[24]

CONCLUSION

In conclusion, there are many realities in our existence as a species. In the context of how we have generated and constructed religions and laws, it is a breathtaking scenario. The drive of *Homo religiosus* to seek meaning, order, and protection has created a many-faceted realm of reality in which we live even in our modern world. This instinctive requirement does not die, but merely morphs into new directions of meaning and in the quest for lives which manifest some sort of worth to ourselves and to others. The religious typologies evolved over thousands of years to meet the specific requirements of ever changing societal needs. In addition to this, our species has been identified as one that is always in motion, always seeking answers, whether consciously or unconsciously, as to the meaning of life and the quest for safety, whether spiritual or physical.[25] The fact is, we seek because it is within our biological composition; and the material, as discussed, describes part of our journey. At the very centre of the journey is the search for transcendence and comfort. In the next chapter we will discuss the phenomenon of transcendence.

GLOSSARY

Animism: The belief that natural objects, natural phenomena, and the universe itself possesses soul; that natural objects (i.e., animals, plants, mountains, rocks and rivers) have souls that may exist apart from their material bodies and that they manifest spiritual powers.

Canon law: Regarded as the oldest continuously functioning internal legal system in Western Europe. It formed the foundation for many of the European countries' own law codes as they developed out of the Holy Roman Empire commencing in the ninth century C.E., and predates the evolution of modern European civil law traditions. It was established by the dominant Church of the time, which was the Catholic Church. The Catholic Church established these laws or canons using the Roman prototype of infrastructure and civil law. The use of Roman law, the "canons" or rules claimed to have been adopted by the Apostles at the Council of Jerusalem circa 45 C.E., together with New Testament norms. Canon law also incorporates elements of Hebrew or Old Testament law, Visigothic, Saxon, and Celtic legal traditions. Many of these concepts are still subtly encoded within Canadian law (Canadian Criminal Code).

Classical Hindu law: In Hinduism, dharma refers to a wider range of human activities than law in the usual sense and includes ritual purifications, personal hygiene regimens, and modes of dress, in addition to court procedures, contract law, inheritance, and other more familiar "legal" issues. In this respect, Hindu law reveals closer affinities to other religious legal systems, such as Islamic law and Jewish law. Dharma, as part of both religious and legal duties, in part of this system. It has been widely criticized.

Halakhah: "Jewish Law" or "the path that one walks." It is derived from three sources: the Torah (the first five books of the Bible), laws instituted by the rabbis, and from long-standing customs. It is believed that, at the heart of *halakhah* lies the unchangeable 613 mitzvot (commandments) that God gave the Jewish people through the Torah. It is upheld by devotees as an all-inclusive way of life that brings the believer nearer to God.

Magna Carta: Signed in 1215; enduring principles of liberty. Composed by a group of thirteenth-century barons to protect their rights and property against a tyrannical king. It is concerned with many practical matters and specific grievances relevant to the feudal system under which they lived. The interests of the common man were hardly apparent in the minds of the men who

brokered the agreement. But there are two principles expressed in Magna Carta that resonate to this day and form the basis of human rights: "No freeman shall be taken, imprisoned, disseised, outlawed, banished, or in any way destroyed, nor will We proceed against or prosecute him, except by the lawful judgment of his peers and by the law of the land…To no one will We sell, to no one will We deny or delay, right or justice."

Monotheism: Belief in one personal God through whom salvation is granted. Stresses personal relationship between the human being and God.

Polytheism: Belief and worship of many gods.

Shariah or **Sharia:** Islamic law; applies both to civil and criminal justice as well as regulating individual conduct in all things personal and moral. Systematized during the second and third centuries of the Muslim era (eighth to ninth centuries c.e.). It teaches total and unqualified submission to the will of Allah. Known as the Shariah (literally, "the path leading to the watering place"), the law constitutes a divinely ordained path of conduct. Shariah as a source of law is, by definition, both arbitrary and discretionary. It is interpreted through a system known as *fiqh* which is the human attempt to scientifically study and comprehend divine law. It therefore contains a degree of flexibility as it is believed that, while Allah's laws are immutable, human interpretations always contain an element of fallibility. In Islamic law, religious lawyers, practicing Shariah, are called *fakih* (plural *fukaha*).

Theocracy: Government of a state by immediate divine guidance through sacred laws, or by officials who are regarded as divinely guided.

Traditional Chinese law: Confucianism, as articulated between the fifth and third centuries b.c. by Confucius, Mencius, and Hsuntzu, emphasized "teaching and moral guidance" as the key instruments of governance. When teaching failed and law had to be applied, it was to be invoked in a manner that upheld the fundamental human relationships that shaped society: ruler and minister/subject; husband and wife; older and younger brother. Moreover, the law was to encompass the ruler's concern for the moral and physical welfare of his people by allowing mitigation of punishment for the aged, young, infirmed, impoverished, and repentant.

Typology: Systematic classification of religions that have characteristics or traits in common.

ENDNOTES

1. In Hinduism, dharma refers to a wider range of human activities than law in the usual sense and includes ritual purifications, personal hygiene regimens, and modes of dress, in addition to court procedures, contract law, inheritance, and other more familiarly "legal" issues. In this respect, Hindu law reveals closer affinities to other religious legal systems, such as Islamic law and Jewish law. See, *New World Encyclopedia*, http://www.newworldencyclopedia.org/entry/Hindu_Law.

2. The Law of Athens: http://www.britannica.com/EBchecked/topic/244633/Greek-law.

3. Ancient History Sourcebook: *The Twelve Tables*, 450 B.C.E., http://www.fordham.edu/halsall/ancient/12 tables.asp.

4. Canon law is regarded as the oldest continuously functioning internal legal system in Western Europe and formed the foundation for many of the European countries' own law codes as they developed out of the Holy Roman Empire commencing in the ninth century C.E. It predates the evolution of modern European civil law traditions.

5. Raimund Karl, *Celtic Law: A Short Summary*, http://draeconin.com/database/celtlaw.htm#THE%20 SOURCES%20FOR%20CELTIC%20LAW.

6. Geoffrey MacCormack, *The Spirit of Traditional Chinese Law*, (Athens, GA: University of Georgia Press, 1996). Reviewed by Jonathan Ocko, Professor of History, North Carolina State University and Adjunct Professor of Legal History at Duke University Law School. © McGill Law Journal 1997, (1997) 42 McGill *L.L* 733.

   Oko states, "Confucianism, as articulated between the fifth and third centuries B.C. by Confucius, Mencius and Hsun-tzu, emphasized 'teaching and moral guidance' as the key instruments of governance. When teaching failed and law had to be applied, it was to be invoked in a manner that upheld the fundamental human relationships that shaped society: ruler and minister/subject; husband and wife; older and younger brother. Moreover, the law was to encompass the ruler's concern for the moral and physical welfare of his people by allowing mitigation of punishment for the aged, young, infirmed, impoverished and repentant." See p. 734.

7. The Medieval Sourcebook: *The Anglo-Saxon Dooms*: http://www.fordham.edu/halsall/source/560-975dooms.asp. *These are the Dooms of Wihtræd, King of the Kentish-Men*. "....18. Let a priest clear himself by his own sooth, in his holy garment before the altar, thus saying: "Veritatem dico in Christo, non mentior." In like manner, let a deacon clear himself.

19. Let a clerk clear himself with four of his fellows, and he alone with his hand on the altar, let the others stand by, make the oath."

8. Magna Carta, 1215: Enduring Principles of Liberty: Written by a group of thirteenth-century barons to protect their rights and property against a tyrannical king. It is concerned with many practical matters and specific grievances relevant to the feudal system under which they lived. The interests of the common man were hardly apparent in the minds of the men who brokered the agreement. But there are two principles expressed in Magna Carta that resonate to this day: "No freeman shall be taken, imprisoned, disseised, outlawed, banished, or in any way destroyed, nor will We proceed against or prosecute him, except by the lawful judgment of his peers and by the law of the land... To no one will We sell, to no one will We deny or delay, right or justice." http://www.archives.gov/exhibits/featured_documents/magna_carta/

9. Medieval Sourcebook: The Law of the Salian Franks: www.fordham.edu/halsall/source/salic-law.html

10. Under Yaroslav the codification of legal customs and princely enactments commenced, and this work served as the basis for a law code called the Russkaya Pravda ("Russian Justice"). Encyclopedia Brittanica: http://www.britannica.com/EBchecked/topic/652106/Yaroslav-I

11. *Halakhah* means "Jewish Law" or "the path that one walks." It is derived from three sources: from the Torah (the first five books of the Bible), from laws instituted by the rabbis, and from long-standing customs. It is believed that, at the heart of *halakhah*, lies the unchangeable 613 mitzvot (commandments) that God gave the Jewish people through the Torah. It is upheld by devotees as an all inclusive way of life that brings the believer nearer to God. http://www.jewfaq.org/halakhah.htm

12. Shariah, also spelled Sharia. Islamic law, applies both to civil and criminal justice as well as regulating individual conduct in all things personal and moral. Systematized during the second and third centuries of the Muslim era (eighth and ninth centuries C.E.). It teaches total and unqualified submission to the will of Allah God. Known as the Shariah (literally, "the path leading to the watering place"). http://www.duhaime.org/LegalDictionary/S/ShariaLaw.aspx

13. From the Greek *theokratia*, from *the-* + *-kratia* −cracy. First known use: 1622.

14. Mary Douglas, *Cultural Bias,* (Royal Anthropological Institute of Great Britain and Ireland, 1978). Occasional paper.

15. Mary Douglas, *Natural Symbols: Explorations in Cosmology,* (Toronto: Random House Inc., 1970).

16. Douglas used the term *Cosmology* widely when addressing religious systems.

17. Mary Douglas, *Cultural Bias,* pp 1, 19, 41.

18. Robert McCutchan, The Social and the Celestial: Mary Douglas and Transcendental Meditation, *The Princeton Journal of the Arts and Sciences,* vol. 1(2), Fall 1977, p 130.

19. Ibid.

20. Roger Schmidt, "Studying Religion," *Patterns of Religion,* (Belmont, CA: Wadsworth Publishing Company, 1999), pp 18-21.

21. Roger Schmidt, "Studying Religion," *Patterns of Religion.*

22. Systematic classification of religions that have characteristics or traits in common.

23. Demographic data is to be found at: http://www.religioustolerance.org/worldrel.htm

24. The attribution of conscious life and spiritual powers to nature or natural objects. http://www.merriam-webster.com/medical/animism

25. Refer back to Chapter 1: *Homo poetica, Homo patiens,* etc.

CHAPTER 4

Transcendence and the Question of Meaning

OVERVIEW OF TERMS AND CONTEXTS

For the Religious Studies researcher the word *transcendence* presents a multitude of differing interpretations. In fact, even a brief overview of the phenomenon is overwhelmingly complex within the existing scholarly publications. The reason for this complexity is that explanations describing transcendence can be found within numerous realms of reality that our species has created. Descriptions defining or addressing the meaning of this elusive concept of transcendence are to be found within philosophy, psychology, music, the visual and performing arts, the written word in poetry and prose, neuroscience, psychiatry and even the history of war, and all this before one even addresses the complexity of the religious quest. The simple explanation for this variance is that human beings inhabit multitudinous realms of being and meaning through our cognitive processes; this is why, through all of the disciplines aforementioned, its reality can be identified.

To commence our discussion, therefore, it is first necessary to identify or perhaps define what the word *transcendence* means. According to the *Oxford English Dictionary* it means "the act of rising above, surmounting, excelling, and surpassing." It connotes the idea of elevation or extension beyond ordinary limits. In this context, it can also refer to "existence or experience beyond the normal or physical level and also to the possibility of spiritual transcendence or cultural transcendence through heroic and altruistic acts in the modern world."[1]

The word speaks to the human quest for something greater and outside of one's physical and mental limitations; it seeks to raise the sensitivities and consciousness of the individual through experiential interaction. In this context, it can be related to the beauty expressed in art, music, or literature, where the observer can enter into an emotional and intellectual connection with the reality expressed through the gifted communicator. Further, it can also describe the quality and nature of the divine or transcendent as perceived and explained through finite human comprehension and the limitations of language. This experience is what theologian Rudolf Otto defined as the *Wholly Other*.[2]

It can also describe some fully enlightened consciousness that has metaphysically transcended the physical plane of being into some realm of enlightened existence. Quite simply put, it can be understood as the ultimate voyage of the "heart" or awakened consciousness through a process of understanding and perception of greater reality. Transcendence addresses levels of consciousness or self-actualization, which transform or alter one's life, and in a broader context, can subtly or radically influence the quality of the society in which one lives.[3]

To illustrate this interrelated process of the journey of the self, consider the brilliant humanistic psychologist Abraham Maslow's (1908–1970) categorization of how our species cognitively comes to grip with life through living in and through experience, reflection, and emotional maturation.[4] Maslow, in company with fellow humanistic psychologists, believed that within each person lay the strong motivation or wish to realize their full potential; this Maslow termed "self-actualization." Maslow believed that every person possessed a strong desire, whether consciously and subconsciously, to realize his or her full potential, and that for many this was identifiable through various stages of personal growth and realization. This composite of the personal self, on its way to self-actualization, is depicted in the following chart:[5]

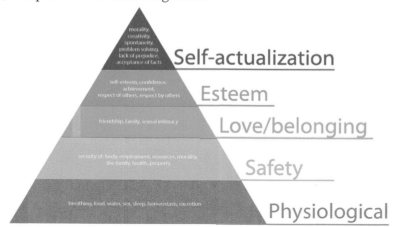

MASLOW'S HIERARCHY OF NEED

Maslow's theory did not go uncontested by his critics who observed that human experiences and needs tend to not follow an orderly upward path. Maslow identified a higher-order category of self-actualization, and a lower order of awareness and need (esteem, belonging, etc.). Further, he seemed to overlook the problem that psychological and physical needs, together with oppressive cultural indoctrination or social control, tended to hinder the luxury of full self-actualization for people living in precarious situations. However, what Maslow's theory did was to successfully present a classification of needs and provide guidelines for the exploration of those levels of needs and satisfactions during periods of stability and peace, and also acknowledge the potential for growth even during periods of danger created by war and famine. In other words, what were people's needs at various times and in various cultures and how did these affect or fit into the journey towards self-actualization? Strikingly, what arose out of Maslow's research on *Hierarchy of Need* remained a constant in that given these variables, the fact remained that people, when given the opportunity for safety and/or serious reflection, would yearn for "something greater," whatever that intangible was.

Maslow also asserted that self-actualized people seemed to live in a more "realized" cognitive reality within their various environments, thus making life more significant and meaningful. The more one was in a cognitive state of receptiveness, the more frequent would be the "peak" experiences of meaning within one's daily life; thus making for a more stimulating and gratifying life span.[6]

Maslow addressed some of the needs and character traits of the self-actualized person as follows:

> Truth, rather than dishonesty.
> Goodness, rather than evil.
> Beauty, not ugliness or vulgarity.
> Unity, wholeness, and transcendence of opposites, not arbitrariness or forced choices.
> Aliveness, not deadness or the mechanization of life.
> Uniqueness, not bland uniformity.
> Perfection and necessity, not sloppiness, inconsistency, or accident.
> Completion, rather than incompleteness.
> Justice and order, not injustice and lawlessness.
> Simplicity, not unnecessary complexity.
> Richness, not environmental impoverishment.
> Effortlessness, not strain.
> Playfulness, not grim, humorless, drudgery.
> Self-sufficiency, not dependency.
> Meaningfulness, rather than senselessness.[7]

The problem that arises, however, within these criteria, is that they do not fully address the breadth or complexity of the forms of self-realization or transcendence that are recorded within our historical, philosophical, and religious annuls. Transcendence is not merely a more rarified quest for self-improvement or the development of an all-rounded compassionate nature. There is something deeper, almost intangible in the energy or drive that fuels our quest for discovery of what might be described as the self, or soul, or consciousness. Nevertheless, suffice it to say, from a Religious Studies' perspective, Maslow's *Hierarchy of Need* provides a basic foundational understanding upon which to create an introduction to the mystery of human transcendence. The *Hierarchy of Need* can and does explain the steps towards self-actualization, and he does accept the presence of human *spirituality*, but, in the context of religion and reality, he cannot describe the actual, mysterious force which impels us along in our quest. The question persists, "What is this unquantifiable force or energy that drives us?" This is not some grievous flaw within Maslow's theory, however, as the whole phenomenon of human consciousness is an anomaly within itself. From a scientific perspective there is no empirical, quantifiable test that can be conducted to establish the existence of the "inner self."[8] In fact, scientists "do not even know what exactly it is that should be measured" and acknowledge that at present there is no scientific evidence even for the existence of consciousness.[9]

Yet, the existence of this inner self, the quest for transcendence, the quest for meaning and expression, is identifiable as an enduring human signature throughout history. The reality of transcendence is that it has been exhibited throughout nearly every demonstration of human creativity and yearning spanning history and even extends back into the prehistorical artifacts as record. In addition to this, the reason for the existence of transcendence is also very easy to isolate; it is simply that many people desire it. Transcendence in its various forms functions to address deep-felt needs and instincts of inadequacy, helplessness, emptiness, finitude, longing, and creativity; to give us hope, direction, comfort, and peace. As the great psychoanalyst Carl Jung (1875–1961) once wrote concerning the loss of transcendence or belief

> … in our time, there are millions of people who have lost faith in any kind of religion. Such people do not understand their religion any longer. While life runs smoothly without religion, the loss remains as good as unnoticed. But when suffering comes, it is another matter. That is when people begins to seek a way out and to reflect about the meaning of life and its bewildering and painful experiences.[10]

The reality behind the transcendence offered within various religious perspectives, whether these are theistic, nontheistic, or even secular belief systems, such as humanism with its ethical codes, is that it functions to allow us to navigate and find purpose when we encounter chaos. Self-transcendence, or self-actualization, is an integral part to our cognitive processes and is a part of that which makes us fully human.

DEFINING CATEGORIES

From the records that we have, facts emerge as to how we order chaos, fear, grief, disillusionment, despair, and hope. The reality is that our species yearns for meaning but often this longing is not even named or sought after until some emotional trigger is engaged. This emotional engagement can occur either as a steadily growing unease and longing for something outside of oneself, or through some radical "conversion" or awakening into reality. Through our copious records—be they represented in pictographs, paintings, carvings, sculptures, the written word as in poems, epic stories, great myths, the magnificent scripture texts, music, art, ceremony/ritual, law codes, or the historical records—there are identifiable categories into which we organize transcendence. What emerges into tangible reality is that there are three major identifiable categories of self-realization or transcendence. These three basic categories will now be explained in order to assist the researcher in understanding and appreciating the phenomenon which, although common to humankind, is as unique as the person embarking upon the journey.

First, as has been discussed previously in some measure, there is *self-transcendence,* or self-actualization. Self-transcendence is an awareness of connectedness to a larger universe—that is, to see everything, including the self, as part of a greater totality as contrasted to the non-self-transcendent person who manifests a distinctly self-centred myopic viewpoint.[11] It widens our perspectives on how we define self and the way we relate to the greater whole. In theory, it functions to increase our compassion and respect for self and others and spans both religious and nonreligious interpretations.

Secondly, there is *social transcendence.* This is a logical and easily identifiable motivation that is generated out of self-transcendence. It manifests in commitment to others, including selfless humanitarian pursuits as in the pursuit of science and medicine for good causes. It is also manifested in social activism and social reform movements through which the needs of the powerless, such as disenfranchised people, child exploitation, abuses of all kinds, unjust labour practices, animal rights, and law reform are brought to the fore as burning issues for awakening social consciousness. In addition to this, social transcendence also addresses environmental concerns, seeking to protect the environment in matters ranging from exploitation and destruction, through to pollution and climate change, public educational platforms and sometimes peaceful or even somewhat confrontational active protests.[12] There is a passion for social justice whereby a direct challenge is made to the prevailing oppressive and exploitive mechanisms of social control through active lobbying, local campaigning or networking and publicity. Once again, this social consciousness can be identified within humanistic secular philosophies and religious cosmologies.

Thirdly, there is spiritual transcendence. This does not necessarily evolve out of self-transcendence and social transcendence, although many who are involved in these movements can develop a specific form of religious outlook.[13] In the case of spiritual transcendence, however, there is something markedly different in its influence upon the individual. While it will often display many of the characteristics involved with identification, compassion and social justice found within the other two categories, it possesses the dynamic ability to open up a further realm of cognition or consciousness. It will

manifest in a radical change in attitude and behaviour, not merely psychological or intellectual but deeply revelatory in nature. It inspires the pilgrim to look deeply within the self while at the same time, granting to the individual the ability to reach out to a greater wisdom through spiritual, meditative enlightenment or to that which is considered to be God as one who can be experienced. Its mechanism appears to span both the temporal and the metaphysical, allowing the individual to grasp a broader view of reality and to heighten awareness of self and relationships towards others. One of the distinctive markers of spiritual transcendence will be to incorporate unconditional love; and manifest in long-term, enduring, positive changes which continue to develop throughout the life process. It will never, categorically never, manifest in sheer hatred and violence as that runs contrary to transcending our basic human self-centredness and aggression. It will maintain an enduring quest towards the ultimate, whatever that is believed to be. The irony of trying to explain this metaphysical state is that this is a tangible experience based on intangible longings, and evidenced throughout our respective cultural histories, by those who seek ultimate connection with the divine or enlightenment and release.

TOWARDS DEEPENING SIGNIFICANCE

Bearing the three classifications in mind, it can be appreciated that the human quest for meaning and often sublime yearning for something outside of human *creatureliness* is not merely another intellectual endeavour based on a need to always feel contentment or a comfortable psychological numbness. It is based in tangible material physicality but displays the intangible characteristics of some higher nature or consciousness. Indeed, its search, as attested through the studies of all religions in their various manifestations is, as classicist William A. Johnson observes, to be that "which is prompted by the individual's search for a deeper and more profound meaning of life and for a sanitizing and intensification of human experience."[14]

Thus the physical and the metaphysical interact with each other and flow outwards towards a greater understanding of what it is to be a spiritual human being living in relationship with life itself, not merely living in it. From the global historical evidence, therefore, we have a reality that presents itself in that there is an impulse on the part of many humans throughout time, cultures, and religious cosmologies, to aspire to something greater than the self. What is an observable fact is that for many within our species, there exists a quest or search within the self which drives the person "from the ordinary dimension of life"[15] in order to find a personal link associated with a greater meaning to life and existence beyond their current limited experience of being human. It is the perennial angst or consciousness of a void within, which causes many people to ask "What is the purpose to life?" or to seriously ponder, "Is this all there is?" It can also be noted that generally shock, or at least unease, will be experienced as the spiritual "sleeper" begins to awaken. The awareness brings the uncomfortable feeling of unfamiliarity, vulnerability, and loneliness, almost like being a stranger in a strange land. The acknowledged irony of life that many seekers of truth, or people who have experienced an awakening of consciousness, will encounter along their journey is well summarized by The Preacher, who as writer of the Book of Ecclesiastes[16] observed:

> When one is afraid of heights, and terrors are in the road; the almond tree blossoms, the grasshopper drags itself along and desire fails; because all must go to their eternal home, and the mourners will go about the streets; before the silver cord is snapped, and the golden bowl is broken, and the pitcher is broken at the fountain, and the wheel broken at the cistern, and the dust returns to the earth as it was, and the breath returns to God who gave it. Vanity of vanities, says the Teacher; all is vanity.[17]

As a general observation, consider the words of Socrates in Plato's *Apology*.[18] On trial before his Athenian accusers who see his teachings as challenges to the accepted norm of philosophical reasoning, Socrates demonstrates the quintessential dilemma often encountered by a seeker of truth. Answering his detractors who want him to physically relocate or simply disappear, and to refrain from urging his listeners to seek something greater than the norm, the aged philosopher points to the quest for realization and understanding. Socrates acknowledges that the quest for self-actualization or transcendence is often fraught with alienation and incurs rejection from those who wish to remain within the pale of mediocrity.

> Some one will say: Yes, Socrates, but cannot you hold your tongue,
> And then you may go into a foreign city, and no one will interfere with
> you? Now I have great difficulty in making you understand my answer
> to this. For if I tell you that to do as you say would be a disobedience
> to the God, and therefore that I cannot hold my tongue, you will not believe
> that I am serious; and if I say again that daily to discourse about virtue,
> and of those other things about which you hear me examining myself
> and others, is the greatest good of man, and that the unexamined life is
> not worth living, you are still less likely to believe me. Yet I say what is
> true, although a thing of which it is hard for me to persuade you.[19]

Here, Socrates makes the point that an unexamined life is not worth living but this statement falls on dulled intellects that do not wish to seek something greater outside of themselves. In other words, they are comfortable with their construction of truth and wish to silence him; they eventually do this by imposing upon him the penalty of death by his own hand. Notably, Socrates' quote is one that has endured throughout the ages as an inspiration to philosophers and reformers, and is held with great respect within scholarly enclaves.

These truths are also noted by the great philosopher and Hasidic[20] theologian Martin Buber (1878–1965) in his work, "I and Thou."[21] Buber observed that we prefer the simple and orderly path which offers understanding without challenge, but noted that nothing was ever neat and simple. Sadly, many people preferred a "simplicity" which was tantamount to stupidity because it did not question or address complexity. He wrote: *Mundus vault decipi* or *the world wants to be deceived.*[22] Truth in and of itself was challenging and often frightening because the traveler on the path to understanding had to look within oneself and observe the complexity of self and others. Buber argued that this could be done only by entering into relationship with, in this context, God. The path then became one of reciprocity whereby the seeker no longer looked at reality as an observer viewing the subject—the "I-It" experience—but as "I-Thou" or a relationship in reciprocity and love. Buber emphasized that people who chose the I-It opted for the standard, comfortable approach of being told what to think and do by some eloquent writer, pundit, or charismatic charlatan, who lulled them into stupefaction or separation from truth.[23] Instead, the seeker in the I-Thou dynamic embarked upon a voyage towards understanding in which life was lived through divine sustenance in the reality of the present and not just in objective experiences as filtered, secondhand through the conventional wisdom of a particular leader, so that "What is essential is lived in the present [not as] removed objects in the past."[24] Buber stated further that it is through this transformation of thought and awareness that one could then "act, help, heal, educate, raise [and] redeem.[25]

In this context, philosopher of religion and theologian John Hick (1922–2012) observed that the meaning to life was to become self-aware of our spiritual consciousness and the need to embark upon the journey of spiritual discovery. He wrote:

> The beginning of wisdom is to become aware of our own presuppositions as options that can be examined and questioned. Otherwise, we are wearing mental blinkers without even being conscious of them.[26]

These mental blinkers, as Hick defines our presuppositions, refer to a veil of ignorance that we all experience during our lives. We live, together with our religions, amidst cultural and materialistic veils, all existing within our human perceptions, and constructed out of the same emotional fabric of our shared cognitive, physical nature. This emotional fabric with which we create reality can blind and bind us, but it also contains the mechanism for seeking truth and reality in a world in which we can find meaning. Metaphorically speaking, this fabric presents to us a world within a world, in which we function and engage. We can be blissfully unaware of the existence of an inner world but when we do become conscious of this sphere of existence, it provides the possibilities to access a deeper reality. This deeper reality is defined by one or a variant combination of all forms, as that which our species has identified as transcendence or self-actualization. By its very nature, transcendence will cause us to change.

IDENTIFYING EMOTIONAL, INTELLECTUAL,
AND SPIRITUAL TRIGGER POINTS

Referring back to Socrates' general observation, "An unexamined life is not worth living," the question can be raised, "Why bother, when it is so much hard work and can cause so much unease?" The problem is, many human beings are driven to reflect upon the self through some irresistible and undeniable yearning. So, what does examination of the self consist of and why do we engage in this? What contributes to our identity and makes us who we are as persons, whether reflective, caring people, or self-centred and superficial? There are many social and psychological theories and explanations, each with valid points of scientific accuracy, but is it merely a nature/nurture influence that makes us who we are? How is our cognition engaged in the path of transcendence? What causes the spark within us to even begin to think about reality, not as we are told to accept physical truths, but in the way we look for deeper meaning within the intangible? Not belying higher learning in any way, one can be permitted to ask whether many of our respective disciplines really do lead us onto a path of inner peace and enlightenment? Do our many and varied disciplines give us peace or merely furnish props that we can build our lives and realities on, establish career goals and pursue financial gain? Is it possible for philosophy, theology, artistic training, the sciences, or financial expertise to lead us to a path of understanding or happiness or deep peace whereby we may face life's vicissitudes with a degree of serenity? What about learning such things as compassion, humility, and altruism, and simply seeking knowledge about selfhood and what we want out of life quite apart from physical and temporal gain or intellectual superiority? What happens to our emotional lives when we are faced with enormous tragedy, disappointment, failure or betrayal, or the crippling misery of realization when we candidly ask with a sinking dread "Is this all there really is?"? In fact, realistically, do our lives really mean anything at all? Are we not just evolutionary manifestations or mistakes, possessing reasoning powers that cause us so much sadness? Most people will claim or perhaps hope that their lives have meaning; but how do these lives have meaning? What constitutes meaning? Is it power, monetary gain, hedonism, hubris? The great leveling reality is that, despite all our philosophies or scientific materialism, we all die whether we have accomplished great things or lived in the mundane, so perhaps what we do between life and death is merely a diversion to keep us from thinking about the fact that we die!

Questions about the meaning of life, in all their variant hues, will change according to our station in life and experience within it. Our physical needs will change due to whether we live in a pampered environment or whether we are among the poverty stricken, living in slums and often eaking out an existence rummaging through garbage dumps. The depth of self-contemplation will vary according to whether we have suffered at our own hands or at the whim or intent of another. For example, we are born, and then as children we live at the mercy of adults, albeit fortunately for many, benign protectors; but not everyone has a pleasant childhood. Children are abused and often sold into slavery; young people are sold into vice and suffer horrendous degradation at the hands of the depraved. Are these abused lives as important as those who make productive contributions to society? Are those who are valued because of their physical prowess or beauty more important than those who are mentally handicapped or physically maimed? Do those living in poverty have any purpose or harbour the same significance as those who are privileged? By what criteria do we establish value? If one is physically suffering does it matter if he or she is affluent or poverty stricken; whose pain is the more valid? The questions raised regarding the significance of life become so complex and heart wrenching that it overwhelms reason.

Another alarming question posed is, how do people relate to each other or feel compassion for others when they have been indoctrinated to hate or fear for specific religious or secular purposes? How do we feel when we realize we are, like Herbert Marcuse the philosopher and political theorist, observed, trapped within a culture that subtly but aggressively "impinges itself on man's consciousness of himself"?[27] What happens when we become aware of the void within us, and much like Winston Smith in George Orwell's *1984*,[28] we feel a strange discontent with our own many and various models of the "Ministry of Truth,"

whereby *War is Peace, Freedom is Slavery, Ignorance is Strength*? To paraphrase Marcuse, the most effective state (or system) is one that manipulates consciousness and inculcates "false needs" into the consciousness of its members. This manipulation is effected by culture and environment and shapes a distorted view of the individual's perception of self and encourages a misconception of what "the authentic self" is.[29] The tragedy is that without an extensive debriefing of ourselves within whichever society we are located, we fail to see the stark realities that surround us. We do this because, just like Socrates' protagonists or those living within Buber's I-It mentality, we find comfort in the buffers that our respective cultures or societies have made for us. Sadly, even alarmingly, many cannot stand the examined life and this can be identified within both secular and religious communities in our modern societies today. We have at our fingertips access to so much knowledge and information, yet so many of us succumb to popular culture and convenient, though often very flawed political or religious logic, which supposedly flows from reliable information sources. One must not ask uncomfortable questions, one must not challenge, even if one's consciousness is screaming on the inside that things definitely are not right. For those who stand on this brink, reality can be a lonely and frightening experience, but it is exactly this crisis of awareness that many within the various religious and secular structures have faced, written about and discussed for centuries. Fortunately, much of this information is still accessible and can be incorporated into the seeking person's voyage to understanding self in complexity and truth. It is at the point where we become uncomfortable that, just like Socrates, we understand that an unexamined life is a wasted life and our journey towards true self-awareness and transcendence begins. In other words, we begin to grow wise. Simply explained, the emotional trigger points have initiated an understanding of genuine reality.

ACKNOWLEDGING RESPONSIBILITY: SIN, GUILT, DEATH, JUDGMENT, AND REDEMPTION

To add to the complexity of self-actualization within society is the issue of what happens when we encounter a heightened sensitivity to our actions and their consequences. How do we react to understanding that we have caused pain and grief to others? By what means do we deal with remorse and guilt or the fear of metaphysical consequences? Are the horrible feelings of remorse and guilt ever remitted and is there any hope for release or salvation? Can we ever make adequate restitution or heal that which we have hurt or damaged? What happens when we face the prospect of death, both for ourselves and for others of whom we are aware; perhaps we, ourselves, have also acted in cruel ways that would under ordinary human assessment require some sort of just punishment? What about those who have caused great suffering and death? Is there punishment for those who have led lives full of violence and have caused the mental and physical agony of others, leading even to their deaths? These questions present a mere fraction of the examples we find that have been posited by our various religious traditions, especially from the Axial age onwards.[30] These are just a few of the emotional triggers that our ancestors identified and that the religions have incorporated through the centuries into their cosmologies, together with various coping mechanisms to deal with the realities. As has been noted by Gavin Flood, human beings are concerned with being born, living, dying, and the encounter with the metaphysical universe. It is only religions that have addressed

> … these concerns in a systematic way and only religions have provided structures
> for communities to negotiate the difficult transitions into and out of life and have
> provided forms of mediation or processes in which we can deal with, and attempt
> to understand, what we might call 'mystery' or 'transcendence' or 'the invisible.'[31]

SOTERIOLOGY AND TRANSCENDENCE

Being trapped within an unpleasant reality that one has either made for oneself or had thrust upon one, is a distressing and emotionally imprisoning experience. Experiencing the sting of whichever emotional conflict we find ourselves trapped within, we as problem-solving animals seek intellectual and sometimes chemically enhanced means of escape. We find ourselves faced with coping and navigating our way through the maze of human existence. Through this emotional awareness we seek means of escape either superficially without looking within, or through adopting the path of spiritual self-realization—transcendence, which is a slow but therapeutic answer to our chaos.

For many, the deep-felt need to find answers and assistance in their plight has led to religions developing the concept of *soteriology,* or the study of salvation and deliverance as a part of their theoretical component. There is within the religions a series of teachings that provide hope and also peace, as one faces extremity. The hope encoded in the various cosmologies addresses the belief that life has meaning and at "the end of life, or a series of lives, or at the end of time, all will be made complete, whole and healed."[32] Nearly every religion also teaches in some way that in life we encounter a limit to our understanding of reality, that there is peace in sometimes accepting that which we cannot fathom, and that we can reach out to something greater than ourselves for navigational assistance.[33]

The concept of soteriology is most easily identified within Christian theology which teaches that salvation, forgiveness of sin, and spiritual regeneration come through God as manifested in Jesus Christ as Lord. As the application of soteriology or salvation/liberation was expanded within the study of religions comprising the various typologies, certain identifiable and characteristic soteriological themes became evident as they dealt with meaning, hope, codes of conduct, and ethical perspectives and sought to address fear and grief.[34] To illustrate this point certain teachings will be discussed as embodied in the four typologies.

THE ABRAHAMIC TREE

In Judaism, the concept of salvation is to adhere to the Torah, as part of the revealed will of God[35] and to apply the concept of *Teshuvah*[36] or heartfelt repentance. There are four steps in the process of repentance as the word means "to deliberately turn from one's negative and destructive actions." It is a very serious process as it requires (1) completely stopping the sinful practice; (2) experiencing regret and shame for one's action; (3) confession before God and, if there is a person wronged by one's action, confession, apology, and when required, restitution; and (4) resolving intently not to return to the sin. Thus, in Judaism, forgiveness is given by a merciful God and peace can be given to the individual, thus empowering him or her to draw closer to Him.

In some groups within Judaism there is no belief in an afterlife; in other traditions there a belief in life after death whereby the soul will enjoy some sort of consciousness with God. In other traditions, there is the belief in life after death as in reincarnation. Whatever the belief in the soul's survival, the emphasis in Judaism is on living within the covenantal laws given by God in this life and being in right relationship with the divine.

Whichever group one considers, however, the familiar human needs for comfort and sustenance, identity and solidarity, protection and hope, can be seen in the strong identification with the covenant people of Israel. There is support in group belief, shared ritual, and ceremony in a community that in theory takes the member through every stage or passage of the life cycle and at the end provides comfort that in death one is returned to the *Bosom of Abraham.*[37] Thus, transcendence is realized through an individual living as part of an ancient religious community, who is encouraged or nurtured to develop deep roots of self-awareness in and through God's laws and the traditions of the people.

In Christianity, the concept of soteriology is easily and simply explained. It is through Christ's atonement upon the cross, remission of sin, and the gift of new spiritual life and a fresh start that one can find peace, hope, and assurance in this life and the next. Assurance is also given through the physical resurrection of Christ as proof of His saving work in dying and overcoming death on behalf of and for the repentant person. The corollary to attaining these great gifts is heartfelt repentance on the part of the individual who must come to Christ, confess his or her sins, and repent of the actions. Once this act of repentance is committed, Christians are assured unequivocally of God's forgiveness and guilt is remitted. This soteriological perspective provides for Christians the amelioration of guilt for the consequences of their negative actions and offers peace to the soul but does not necessarily take away the sting of the memory of past deeds. A life spent with God means that there is a responsibility to act according to his guidance and sin should be taken very seriously—one is saved to serve God and one's neighbour. Thus, one's life must reflect compassion and humility in the service of others.

Transcendence is interpreted as an individual personal relationship with God in and through Christ whereby the Christian grows in "grace" or *sanctification*, developing a deep awareness of the life lived in the spirit of God.[38] This is, for Christians, the practical reality of transcendence.

In Islam, salvation takes on a very specific meaning. The name *Islam* means unequivocal *submission* to *Allah* and a *Muslim* is one who submits to Allah through obedience, love, and respect. Islam is also based on the idea that salvation can only occur when there is total belief in the oneness of Allah, *Tawheed*, and all the teachings of Islam, plus right practice or actions permitted, required, and observed by the devotee, which are categorized as orthodoxy and orthopraxy. Through Islamic theology, or *kalam*, and faith, *or iman*, in both Allah and the divine revelation known as the *Qur'an* as inerrant holy scripture, personally given to the Prophet Muhammad, one can hope for salvation or divine mercy at the resurrection on the Day of Doom. Thus Islam is governed by submission to the perfect will of Allah revealed in Qur'an, the judicial code, known as *Sharia*, or law, and observance of the *Five Pillars of Islam*. Right practice, or orthopraxy, is described by the *Five Pillars of Islam* as follows: (1) Shahada—the Islamic Creed, "There is no God but Allah and Muhammad is the messenger of God"; (2) Salat—prayer, which is generally sanctioned as being mandatorily observed five times per day; (3) Sawm—fasting during the ninth lunar month of Ramadan; (4) Zakat—the giving of charitable donations, or alms, generally set at 2.5 percent of one's gross income. There are also other occasions for personal almsgiving where even though the disclosed amount is kept confidential it can be a substantial donation. In the case of the Shi'ia Ismailis, it can range from 12.5 percent to as high as 20 percent of one's gross income; (5) the Hajj—the pilgrimage to the holy city of Mecca conducted during the twelfth month of the Islamic lunar year. It is stipulated in the Qur'an that every Muslim who is financially and physically able should make Hajj once in their lives. The Hajj is considered to be a time when Muslims devote themselves to Allah and reflect spiritually on their personal faith.

Soteriology or salvation in the Islamic context means that by submitting to Allah and observing his laws, one lives within the Islamic community, or *umma*. It also means that one can hope for leniency, help, and guidance as Allah is merciful.

The Indian Tree

In Hinduism, ideas pertaining to soteriology and/or enlightenment and liberation are complex and varied. The reason is that this cosmology provides for belief in an almost incomprehensible number of belief systems. For example, at the root of nearly all Hindu belief systems there is the concept of an ultimate source of all things, know as *Brahman* (god), who pervades and yet transcends human thought and the universe itself. Brahman can be conceptualized in two ways: Saguna Brahman and Nirguna Brahman. Saguna Brahman applies to the intellectual and emotional perception of the ultimate, as personified in the deities; Nirguna Brahman is the concept of god which teaches that Brahman is beyond human perception and can only be meditated upon as a source of enlightenment leading to liberation of the *atman* or soul. According to the influential advaitic philosophical tradition,[39] the level of one's spiritual maturity determines how one sees "god." The more developed one's comprehension, the more one interprets god without attributes, or Nirguna Braham. Saguna Brahman, god with attributes is, however, the most widespread perspective within popular Hinduism, which is known for its millions of gods and goddesses. Some of the main deities such as Shiva, Vishnu, Krsna, Kali, or Durga can be the object of singular or favourite devotional practices known as Bhakti in order to attain salvation through a degree of respectful relationship. At the root of all these systems of belief, however, is the concept of the atman, illusion, ignorance, attachment, and karma. According to one's ability to live within the dharma[40] and as an outcome of karma, caused both by physical and mental action, one will experience the cycle of birth, death, and rebirth into higher or lower states which can be animal or human, with humans being born into a four-tier caste system. Within the caste system the groups can be identified as priests, rulers, merchants, and servants. In most general interpretations of the castes, males within these upper three are known as the twice-born who are considered to undergo a spiritual rebirth through an initiation ritual and are inducted at that time into the ruling hierarchy. The twice-born can usually move up through successive reincarnations to reach enlightenment and release, but it is usually accepted that the priestly caste, or Brahmins, are not demoted in rebirth. The lower caste, or Shudras, are the labourers, menial cleaners, disposers of carcasses, and cremation ground attendants. It is generally believed that a Shudra cannot reincarnate into the upper three castes. In the case of females within all systems, their gender denotes negative karma, as a woman is not considered to be able to reach liberation; as a consequence to this, most women would aspire to being reborn into male form.

In order to achieve liberation one is required to study, meditate, and adhere to *dharma* or castely and gendered codes of conduct as taught within the Hindu scriptures or Vedas, including the ancient Dharmashastras.[41] The object is to finally realize through inner enlightenment that atman is Brahman and Brahman is atman and this requires a highly advanced understanding and years of meditation. One will in this way undergo a radical change in perception which will lead to correct mental and physical action. This in turn will lead for a period of time to liberation from the samsaric cycle.

In Buddhism, Siddhartha Gautama or Buddha,[42] sought to simplify the complex concepts within Hinduism. Through Siddharth's teachings on enlightenment, the philosophical tradition of Buddhism was developed. It was originally perceived as a philosophical tradition because it dispensed with the idea of gods and goddesses, and so was basically atheistic in its perception of reality.

Buddha incorporated many of the central Indian concepts regarding samsara, karma, illusion—*maya*, ignorance, and liberation, but he rejected the need for deities in order to achieve enlightenment and liberation. He also dismissed the idea of the atman and taught that there was no self or soul but that there were five aggregates or skandhas, also known as the five heaps which were defined as (1) form or matter; (2) physical or mental sensation; (3) perception; (4) mental attitudes, predilections and biases; and (5) mental consciousness or thought based on what we perceive as perception of the self. Together, these aggregates create the illusion of a self. Instead of this, what was at the core of our being was dharmakaya, or Buddha nature, which constituted the transcendental, blissful, eternal pure consciousness.

Through meditation, observance of the teachings of Buddha known as the dharma of the Buddha containing the concepts of the Middle Way, the no self, shunyata (emptiness), Nirvana, and centred on the Four Noble Truths and the Eight Fold Path, the Buddhist believes that transcendence comes through enlightenment.

The central idea within Buddhism is contained within the *Four Noble Truths* which consists of the teachings that (1) life means suffering; (2) the origin of suffering was attachment and craving manifested through our ideas of the self; (3) the cessation of suffering and thus, samsara, was possible through enlightenment; and (4) the path to cessation of suffering was to be found within the dharma of Buddha as explained in the Eight Fold Path of right view, right intention, right speech, right action, right livelihood, right effort, right mindfulness, and right concentration. If a Buddhist observes and practices the dharma he or she could attain nirvana or liberation and break the cycle of rebirth. Thus liberation or transcendence is accepted to be through enlightenment which opens the way to release in Nirvana. Through balance, or the Middle Way of avoiding extremes, the Four Noble Truths, the Eight Fold Path, and understanding the Five Aggregates, Buddhists can alter the perception of attachment and free themselves from incorrect thought and action which leads to suffering. Thus, the Buddhist path to transcendence is through Buddha nature and enlightenment.

In Jainism and Sikhism, as part of the Indian Tree, the central ideas regarding karma and samsara remain the same as those of Hinduism and Buddhism. For the Jaina tradition, there is no need for a deity as liberation eventually occurs through one's own efforts as one gradually overcomes negative karma and becomes a conqueror or jina. Consciousness is identified as the *jiva* or living substance which is subject to karma and samsara until the living substance achieves liberation.

In the Sikh tradition, the central belief in one God interprets karma and rebirth as part of God's cleansing judgment. A person is able to change his or her karma through sincere love, repentance, and devotion to God. This is achieved through following the *four fruits of life,* which are truth, contentment, contemplation, and the observance of Naam Simran which is the remembrance of God through mediation on, and repetition of, His name which is *Naam.* Accordingly, if one has developed a pure spirit, reincarnation is no longer necessary and the devotee is allowed to live eternally in the presence of God. Thus salvation or soteriology is always in the hands of God and based on personal devotion.

South East Asian Tree

In the cosmological systems of Shamanism, Confucianism, Daoism, various forms of Buddhism, and also Shinto transcendence is interpreted as harmony or balance and sin is not emphasized as a concept. On the other hand, inappropriate action causing shame, such as in not giving due respect to ancestors, family, spirits, and/or gods, is clearly emphasized and reinforced with strong consequences for noncompliance. Departure from the traditionally designated paths will result in dishonor and sometimes punishment from ancestors and definitely alienation from earthly family. To ensure an orderly and purposeful life, a strict observance of moral and social codes of conduct is believed to be the best way to avoid suffering and achieve harmony. It will also affect the life hereafter as a dishonorable ancestor is not given the same reverence or devotion as one who has been a great role model. In those traditions that believe that upon death one becomes an ancestor, great emphasis is laid upon being revered in the afterlife through sacrifices and prayers. It is therefore necessary to incorporate the necessary virtues in this life so that transcendence will be a natural outcome of one's life. In addition to this, according to some of the other religious systems there may be karmic consequences in the form of an inauspicious rebirth, which is fraught with suffering, so one must adhere to acceptable codes of conduct in order to achieve the best rebirth possible.

Another development in the South East Asian typology was the acceptance of Zen Buddhism and Pure Land Buddhism. Zen, with its meditative techniques and emphasis on enlightenment, and Pure Land with its soteriological emphasis on faith in the Amitabha Buddha (Chinese Buddhism) and Amida, the Buddha of Infinite Light (Japanese) as the way to salvation, gradually became popular forms of South East Asian Buddhism. Zen taught sudden enlightenment and thus offered the prospect of achievable transcendence or liberation within Nirvana, for the practitioner. On the other hand, Pure Land emphasized salvation and transcendence through the grace of Amitabha or Amida.

The Tribal Tree

In tribal systems, transcendence and release presents complex research patterns as each religion is unique unto itself. In some cases, rituals can be similar in certain contexts as in American Indian groups, pertaining to the sun dance, but other ceremonies concerning cleansing rituals, passages of life, and initiation rituals, will be so varied that there is little similarity by which to make comparison. It can, however, be noted, that there are certain broad core ideas that can be identified in most indigenous groups throughout the world.

The tribal systems have close links to territory or tribal land and their mythology regarding origins and customs will usually associate with the ancestors who founded their tribal group. Ancestors play a significant role in the lives of many groups ranging from Australian aboriginal, to African tribal, to North and South American Indian religious systems. As ancestors play such an integral role in the history of the tribe and also in the governance of the family and home, they are revered. Most tribal groupings will believe that their ancestors are very much a part of life on earth and are engaged in the activities of their descendants. Thus, transcendence means that one becomes a revered member of a group that lives in another realm and is essential in the lives of the living.

As the tribal system depends on the participation of the group, there are complex traditions regarding conduct and order within the membership. To create disharmony is to create the danger of destabilization which would in turn affect survival. In consequence, sin, judgment, fear of reprisal, and punishment within the group or by the ancestors are always sensitive issues within the individual systems. These destabilizing events are regarded as negative, destructive actions, which are considered to be sins.

There is also disharmony through causing harm to one's life support system, which is the environment and through any offensive action which would displease the Creator or spirit beings, or even gods and goddesses. As a consequence of this, great emphasis is put in traditional teachings on respect towards land, animals, ancestors, living elders, treatment of family, and conduct with one's own contemporaries. If any of these rules of order are breached, punishment will or may be apportioned.

Soteriological transcendence in the tribals will be viewed as something accessed through rituals, vision quests, sacred ceremonies such as the peyote ritual or the use of other hallucinogenic drugs in order to contact the ancestors or to achieve heightened awareness. Ceremonies of repentance, cleansing—both physical and spiritual—together with restoration, can also start the healing process needed when heartfelt remorse or grief are experienced by the individual or the group.

CONCLUSION

Siddhartha Gautama, Buddha, observed in his philosophical teachings that to live is to suffer; a consequence of sentient life or consciousness is that we will feel pain and often remorse during our lives due to attachment and incorrect perspectives. The Lord Jesus Christ, addressing his followers, observed that "In the world you will have hardship, tribulation, but be courageous, I have conquered the world."[43] Each religious tradition in some way addresses our human need to find answers, to find peace, and to have hope that our lives and the outcome of our deaths will be validated by the quality with which we have existed in the physical world. For those seekers of transcendence throughout our religious histories, these values have remained constant. It speaks to our cognitive problem-solving skills and to the creativity with which we have sought to express our longings and devotion, and to convey what we have learned through successive generations, on to others. At the heart of transcendence lies the need to connect with greater meaning within ourselves and with the greater reality of life. Religions, with their unique ability to access this central seam of common human nature have, over centuries, developed complex ways to speak to our intricate needs. At the very heart of human nature the quest continues; it is manifested in our creative ability to make connection with the intangible through our physical and emotional natures. Through transcendence we address the ultimate questions of "Why?" and "How?"

GLOSSARY

Allah: The Arabic name for the one, true God.

Bosom of Abraham: Ancient tribal concept of being return to one's ancestor, Abraham, where one is protected; also belief that it is the place where a righteous Jew enjoys a blissful state.

Four Fruits of Life: Sikh concept of truth, contentment, contemplation, and the observance of Naam Simran.

Hasidim: Hebrew for "the Pious." Refers to those who lead pious lives. This religious sect within Judaism emphasizes devotion to God which manifests in scrupulous ritual purity and scrupulous observance of the law. It was originally developed by Israel Ben Eliezer (Baal Shem Tov) in the eighteenth century, and stressed a strongly mystical leaning. Baal Shem Tov taught that all human beings were created equal before God and that purity of heart was superior to study. He emphasized a loving devotion to God, expressed through joy and warmth in prayer, which in turn led to a joyous obedience to God's laws. During the Second World War the movement suffered major persecution and destruction but reemerged and continues to exert a considerable influence on Judaism.

Hierarchy of Needs: Theory of self-actualization and psychological growth. Invented by Maslow who identified a higher-order category of self-actualization and a lower order of awareness and need (esteem, belonging, etc.).

Labyrinth: An intricate structure of interconnecting passages through which it is difficult to find one's way; a maze.

Sanctification: The gradual process through which one's consciousness is transformed by God's influence, from base self-centred human nature into a spiritually sensitive and changed person.

Self-transcendence: An awareness of connectedness to a larger universe. To see everything, including the self as part of a greater totality as contrasted to the non-self-transcendent person who manifests a distinctly self-centred viewpoint.

Social transcendence: Evolving out of self-transcendence. Can manifest in a passion for the environment, social justice, selfless humanitarian pursuits as in the pursuit of science and/or medicine, social activism, and social reform.

Soteriology: The study of salvation and deliverance. Originally applied to Christian theological concepts of the atonement, salvation, reformation of the individual. Included ideas regarding spiritual regeneration or new birth in and through Christ. Hope in Christ and a joyous life after death through His resurrection. Now broadened to apply to concepts within most religions

that will involve teachings regarding liberation and fulfillment through transcending self.

Spiritual: Relating or concerned with the soul or spirit; relating to religious matters.

Spirituality: Attachment to all that concerns the life or the soul; quality of being spiritual.

Spiritual transcendence: Manifestation of a radical change in attitude and behaviour. Unconditional love, long-term positive changes within the self which incorporate self-transcendence and social transcendence.

Teshuvah: Repentance or return to God. There are four steps in the process: (1) leaving the sin; (2) regret and shame for one's actions; (3) confession before God; and (4) acceptance for the future (resolving to not return to the sin again and consciously making every effort to avoid the sin again). In the case where one has sinned against God personally, Teshuvah is done in contrition directly to God. In the case where our sins are committed against another person, one must first ask the forgiveness of that person and make restitution to them if one has taken or destroyed something belonging to them, before God will accept the Teshuvah.

Transcendence: To "rise" towards, or aspire to closeness with the supreme being; surmounting, excelling, and surpassing. It connotes the idea of elevation or extension beyond ordinary limits. In this context, it can also refer to "existence or experience beyond the normal or physical level: the possibility of spiritual transcendence in the modern world."

Wholly Other: That which is beyond the sphere of the familiar and the intelligible. It falls outside the limits of human-limited understanding and is contrasted with it, filling the mind with blank wonder and astonishment.

ENDNOTES

1. Oxford Dictionaries online.
2. This will be discussed at length in another chapter describing mysticism.
3. William A. Johnson, ed., The *Search for Transcendence: A Theological Analysis of Nontheological Attempts to Define Transcendence,* (New York: Harper Colophon Books, 1974), p 11.
4. Maslow's theory of the Hierarchy of Needs has come under criticism because it is argued that he presents an oversimplification of the developmental stages; where one begins and one ends is not always that easily identifiable. Sufficient to say, what Maslow puts at the pinnacle of cognitive realization is self-actualization. One's whole life is a voyage towards some understanding of reality. Self-actualization incorporates the awareness of spiritual or humanistic sensitivity.
5. https://www.google.ca/search?q=abraham+maslow.
6. Dr. C. George Boeree, *Abraham Maslow:* http://webspace.ship.edu/cgboer/maslow.html. Retrieved May 10, 2012. Boeree lists some of the criteria required by the self-realized.
7. Ibid. Boeree.
8. Mario Beauregard, Ph.D., Denyse O'Leary, *The Spiritual Brain: A Neuroscientist's Case for the Existence of the Soul,* (New York: HarperOne, 2007), p 109.
9. Ibid., p 109.
10. *Classics of Western Thought: The Modern World,* Edgar E. Knoebel, ed., (Fort Worth: Harcourt Brace Jovanovich College Publishers, 1988), vol. III, 4th ed., p 562. Carl Jung et al., "Approaching the Unconscious," *Man and His Symbols* (New York: Dell Publishing, 1964), Copyright 1964 Aldus Books, Ltd., London.
11. Ibid., p 49.
12. Ibid.
13. As in *green religions,* or *deep ecology,* whereby they imbue the environment with a particularly spiritual depth and character.
14. William A. Johnson, *The Search for Transcendence: A Theological Analysis of Nontheological Attempts to Define Transcendence,* (New York: Harper Colophon Books, 1874), p 1.
15. Ibid.
16. Generally believed to have been written mid to late third century B.C.E.
17. Ecclesiastes, Chapter 12:5-8. The New Oxford Annotated Bible, (Oxford: Oxford University Press, Inc., 1973), 3rd ed., p 957.
18. The Greek word *apologia* means "explanation."
19. *The Apology* is Plato's account of the trial and execution in 399 B.C.E. of the Greek philosopher Socrates (469–399 B.C.E.), who was a prominent philosopher in Athens. He was on trial for impiety and the corruption of youth, for which the penalty was death. The great philosopher was found guilty with a sentence of death at his own hand, by Hemlock poisoning. At the time of the sentence and death, Socrates was an old man, around the age of 70. Plato's *Apology,* translated by Benjamin Jowett, (New York: C. Scribner's Sons, [1871]), www.sacred-texts.com/cla/plato/apology.htm
20. Mystical Jewish movement founded in the eighteenth century. The term *"Hasidim"* means "those who lead a pious life." See, Dan Cohn-Sherbok, *A Concise Encyclopedia of Judaism* (Oxford: Oneworld, 1998), p 91.
21. Martin Buber, *I and Thou,* (New York: Touchstone, 1970).
22. Buber, p 9.
23. Ibid.
24. Buber, p 64.
25. Buber, p 66.
26. John Hick, *The Fifth Dimension: An Exploration of the Spiritual Realm,* (Oxford: Oneworld Publications, 2004), p 1.
27. Herbert Marcuse, *One-Dimensional Man: Studies in the Ideology of Advanced Industrial Society* (London: Routledge Classics, 2002). See, Charles Reich's discussion of Marcuse in, "Transcendence as Personal Liberation," *The Search for Transcendence,* p 15.
28. George Orwell, *1984* (New York: Signet Classics, 1950).
29. Charles Reich's discussion in "Transcendence as Personal Liberation," *The Search for Transcendence.* p 15.
30. Refer to Robert Bellah's developmental stages.
31. Gavin Flood, *The Importance of Religion,* (Chichester: Wiley-Blackwell, 2012), p 4.
32. Ibid., p 6.
33. Ibid.
34. Chester Gillis, *A Question of Final Belief: John Hick's Pluralistic Theory of Salvation,* (New York: St. Martin's Press, 1989), p 100.
35. Many Jews disapprove of writing the full name of God but will accept the Name being described as God.
36. http://www.ou.org/chagim/elul/foursteps.html. Teshuvah implies return to God's laws through repentance and resolve to leave sin behind and not engage in it again.

37. Ancient tribal concept of being returned to one's ancestor, Abraham where one is protected; also belief that it is the place where a righteous Jew enjoys a blissful state.

38. The gradual process through which one's consciousness is transformed by God's influence, from base nature to a spiritually sensitive and changed person.

39. Known as Advaita Vedanta, it refers to the study of the Vedas, or Hindu scriptures, and emphasized Nirguna Brahman, or god without attributes.

40. Natural universal laws whose observance provides humans with the capacity to live in appropriate moral ways and observe correct spiritual discipline. Considered to be the very foundation of life itself.

41. Ancient Indian religious and legal treatises that were written by various theological schools. They were collections of rules and prescriptions regulating the social and personal life of individuals, depending on class and caste; contained not only legal but also religious, moral and ethical directives and other standards of conduct.

42. Siddhartha Gautama was probably born in the sixth century B.C.E., in Napal.

43. John 16:32, *The New Jerusalem Bible*, (New York: Doubleday, 1985).

CHAPTER 5

Human Creativity: Reflections on Our Descriptions of Reality

EXPRESSIONS WITHIN RELIGIOUS OR SPIRITUAL CONTEXTS

In our systems of social, visual, artistic, and textual expression throughout millennia, there is little room for doubt that our species has created realms of meaning and constructed many ways of conveying that meaning to others. Through the use of our intellectual and artistic abilities, together with the creation of sociocultural, traditional, and religious realities, we have developed means of visual and audible communication to express that which is beyond the normal physical realm. Arising out of this construct we then translated and still do translate, that which is subjective and intuitive into a formed means of tangible interpretative expression. What is impressive about this is that by using varied means of interpretation we have developed culturally identifiable mechanisms which transmit or act as routes of interpretation between that which is considered *profane*[1] and that which is considered *sacred*.[2]

In the context of Religious Studies, adopting a simply sociological and/or scientific deterministic[3] perspective to understand the profound gravity and scope of human religious creativity does to some degree hamper research. This is due to the fact that human creativity is enormously complex, varied, quirky, and intuitively subjective. These traits will necessitate that the researcher recognizes certain ethereal qualities and interpretative approaches. Interpreting and appreciating these aspects of meaning and creativity, must be undertaken with an attitude of respect, and sometimes awe, wonder when seeking to understand the "otherness" of the grand scale of human consciousness. In religious expression, it is clear that this creative consciousness is linked to the desire for transcendence and so reflects something of our innermost subjective and spiritual nature.

The problem is, how does one cognitively comprehend this very complex function within religion? What is the process whereby our species conceptualizes and conveys through human perspectives and various artistic mediums that which is rationally not within scientific paradigms? How can we analyze religious consciousness and explain spiritual reality? Do we ground ourselves in so much empirically proven data that we lose sight of the inspiration that lies behind that which we study? On the other hand, to merely be swept away by emotion might be pleasant for a short period of time, but does it contribute to one's intellectual growth or understanding? Emotion speaks to us but we must also be able to cognitively understand the rationale behind the experience. In other words, one must be able to understand the process and the meaning and make decisions based on comprehension and not blind stupidity.

THE LOGISTICS OF ANALYSIS

The renowned historian of religion and philosopher, Mircea Eliade (1907–1986) observed that in all religions there was a clear cognitive process which occurred whereby the sacred was known to the observer through the means of physical conveyance. This was experienced in physical reality and time, and its significance commemorated through the division of the sacred and the profane. He also observed that we organized these experiences through dividing our religious realities into sacred and profane spaces, situating them within our experience of time; we did this through rituals, pilgrimages, myths, and traditions. He argued that we negotiated these realities and lived within their webs of significance because we had experienced the phenomenon of transcendent occurrences known as *hierophanies* which formed the basis of all religion. Thus our experiential reality of the spiritual realm was made comprehensible and navigable through our organization and compartmentalism of time, space, and specific events. Eliade believed that humankind became aware of the sacred because it manifested itself as something wholly different from the profane and that this experience, or "act of manifestation of the sacred" was an event of hierophany, whereby the sacred showed itself to the observer in and through easily identifiable ordinary objects.[4] These objects did not morph into other forms but were simply identified as the divine manifesting through a physical object such as a "stone or a tree," or in the case of Christianity, the supreme hierophany being the "incarnation of God in Jesus Christ."[5] These hierophanic encounters enabled us to fix and commemorate our religious reality through physical participation in the ritual observances. This process Eliade defined as the process or *Myth of the Eternal Return*, whereby the devotee literally relived and became part of the hierophanic encounter.[6]

Another perspective on this creative participation can be taken from author and researcher Matthew Alper's[7] work on the argument for a generalized spiritual awareness arising out of brain function. He wrote

> All humans have practiced a belief in the existence of a spiritual realm, a God or
> gods, a soul, and an afterlife. Strange that every culture should perceive reality
> with this same "spiritual" bent, that we should all hold similar beliefs and then
> express them through such similar rites and practices. Are we to believe this is

the result of some vast coincidence, or is it possible that   we are compelled to maintain such beliefs as well as to engage in such practices as the result of a very sophisticated series of reflexes or instincts?[8]

To further examine this creative dynamic or instinctive behavioural pattern and its encounter with the divine, consider another perspective, this time expressed by the great poet William Wordsworth (1770–1850). Wordsworth was Britain's Poet Laureate from 1843 until his death in 1850. Writing about a deeply moving, emotional, and intuitive experience during his visit to the banks of the Wye River in July 1798, he wrote

And I have felt
A presence that disturbs me with the joy
Of elevated thoughts; a sense sublime
Of something far more deeply interfused,
Whose dwelling is the light of setting suns,
And the round ocean and the living air,
And the blue sky, and in the mind of man:
A motion and a spirit, that impels
All thinking things, all objects of all thought,
And rolls through all things.[9]

INCORPORATING A CRITIQUE— PHENOMENOLOGY VERSUS REDUCTIONISM

The concepts as per these three given examples demonstrate the argument for *phenomenology* which is basically the study of appearances or identified types within the context of cognitive experience. The instinctive creativity by which we express this contact with that which is God, the divine, or spiritual essence, is contextualized within the concept of spiritual experience, situated in physical reality. It refers to an analytical form of enquiry which seeks to situate human activities within certain general forms or fixed patterns of subjective significance that can be discerned by the trained observer.

Phenomenology is a complex analytical process of enquiry which applies to the study of structures of experience, or consciousness. It studies how our consciousness experiences reality or events from a subjective or first-person perspective. The study of *phenomena* applies to the appearances of things as they appear in our experience of them and how these events provide meaning for us. The phenomenological approach also studies how and why we apportion conscious meaning and significance to things from both profane and cultic/ritual perspectives. These things, or objects of significance, are manifested and subjectively experienced in our lives and environments. This relationship of significance relates to concepts of time and events; to the self within that setting, and to objects and tools which we consider meaningful. It furnishes the context of background for the self or individual as it functions in the parameters of roles, both sacred and profane. It also manifests in actions, boundaries, social understanding, and interrelationships within a community that places self in the context of temporal and metaphysical awareness.[10] Phenomenology interprets this consciousness as something deeply subjective, emotive, "reasonable," practical, and functional; it pertains to the intellectual examination of spiritual survival skills and spiritual language.

From the perspective of Religious Studies' scholarly analysis, the researcher should, however, also consider other variables or arguments in order to arrive at a broader understanding of human intellectual, emotional, and spiritual creativity. Often the argument for *reductionism* is posed as a preferable intellectual alternative. It can be too overtly and also subtly antithetical to the phenomenological approach and is argued by its proponents to be a more scientific methodological approach. Reductionism does offer interesting fields of enquiry and perspectives in that it argues that religious experience or motivation can be reduced to, or explained by, fixing it within the context of historical, psychological, or sociological factors. It thus removes the confusion which often lies behind our perception of reality and places it squarely within the boundaries of empirical fact and logic.

The objective of reductionism is to explain religion through identification of a reason or cause for its construction, and locate the influences upon it that sparked its development; these causes are then explained by cognition, genetics, and sociopolitical structures. This means that its methodological approach will endeavour to explain the root, origin and development of religion and spirituality as that arising out of external causes. These causes will mainly be presented as factors such as primitive superstition based on lack of knowledge, or a fear of disease through impurity, or the spectre of death which is ever present to the human consciousness, together with the manipulation of the lower mass population within a dominant elitist hierarchal environment. Thus the origin of the phenomenon of religion is structurally perceived as a complex coping mechanism of psychological and social need for order that can be traced through evolutionary psychology and cultural development and rendering it logical through structural function.

Modern reductive interpretations can therefore be explained by dividing the system of analysis into two central analytical systems. First, there is *naturalist/eliminative*[11] reductionism centred within the realms of science. This incorporates theories of cognition, evolution, and the resulting interpretation of evolutionary psychology along with philosophical justification for each aspect of emotional and religious reality. Second, there is *cultural reductionism*,[12] and this pertains to the spheres of influence within politics, structure of hierarchy, and social control that create boundaries, law codes, identification of self, religious structures, and the interpretation of religious experience. As both forms of reductionist theory interpret religious belief from an external perspective, neither methodological approach will consider intuitively creative religious worlds of being and subjectivity. Reductionism will by the mandate of its discipline, reject the generation of religion from the perspective of emotional creativity.

Having pragmatically addressed the two major methodological interpretations—that of phenomenology and reductionism—the researcher is still ultimately left with the observable, quantifiable, cold hard fact that our species, through our creativity and need for meaning, constructs and expresses religious concepts. The reality is these expressions of the inner self are historically conveyed through art, ritual, symbol, myth, and scripture. The only point of dissention in these analytical approaches is the reason for the genesis and motivation of religion in the first place. The reality is that whatever the cause, the need to create and express religious sentiment is easily identifiable and indisputable.

THE REALITY OF THE INNER SELF

From the material body of evidence that surrounds us culturally and historically, we know that humankind's innovative religious reality has been transmitted through millennia and has expressed our inner longings and revelatory self through the respective religious structures. In addition to this, our ancestors and persons of religious persuasion today, have taken what was and is revealed, sensed, or comprehended, and placed it into the realm of the physical by means of communication through art which is displayed in the making of visual symbols, ritual worship, devotional music or chant, sacred spaces, myth, and scripture. In this way they have encoded it within the religious structures so that all religions within each of the typologies will still exhibit the same basic components.

This culturally observable fact can be explained by the subjective and very creative process of *revelation, interpretation, and communication* by and through which the recipient or originator of a special religious insight uses a special cognitive interpretive process to pass on their vision or message. Each of these processes can be explained as follows: (1) *Revelation*: through creative insight the recipient becomes aware of a deep spiritual reality or truth; (2) *Interpretation*: routinely, this insightful experience is so profound that it takes time to process and decipher the complex content of the subjective revelation. The interpretive process will always be in accordance with the recipient's cultural, thinking modalities, and time frame but will contain a certain profound insight that changes the spiritual environment of his/her perspective. It may also contain elements of other outside subtle influences such as a reinterpretation of specific universal symbols, myths, or even "foreign" writings and art forms. (3) *Communication*: after a period of time, during which the truth becomes explainable through the process of thought and logical organization, it will then be conveyed to a wider community or audience and discussion, acceptance, or persecution will ensue.

To dismiss this creative phenomenon or relegate it to merely a physiological process is to blithely overlook something deeply ingrained in our species. The process in itself, within a spiritual and psychological context, is a way of becoming, or growing into something greater than what presently appears. Take, for example, the process of becoming, as described by Dr. Erich Fromm the great psychologist, psychoanalyst, sociologist, and humanistic philosopher. Fromm related the story of a conversation which occurred between an Hassidic student and his esteemed teacher, a rabbi. The student observed his master/rabbi in a state of great sadness, and asked him,

> "Master, why are you sad? Are you sad that you have not reached the highest knowledge, that you have not the greatest virtues?" The master said, "No, I am not sad about that. I am sad not to have become myself totally."[13]

Fromm argued that people possess the latent optimum of what they could become but neglect that potential by seeking other sources of purpose whilst forgetting their inner drive for things that are greater.[14] In a work entitled *The* Anatomy *of Human Destructiveness,* written in 1973,[15] Fromm addressed the creative impulse within our species and stated that there was a "great deal of psychological evidence that striving for creativeness and originality [were] deeply rooted impulses" and "that the striving for creativity and originality [were] 'built in' the systems of the brain."[16]

Arising out of this, from a Religious Studies' perspective, and applying either a reductionist or phenomenological interpretation, certain intangible sensitivities or inspirations become evident in the creative process. Whether we are suspicious or dismissive of these and consider their display simply manifestations of abherent behaviour, or whether we respect them as valid expressions of deep sincerity and insight, the fact remains that they have repeatedly occurred throughout prehistory and recorded history.

Our creativity reflects in sensitive aspirations of expression such as aesthetics, *numinosity* or *numinous[17]* (the holy and nonrational aspect of human communication with the wholly other), compassion, emotion, profound empathy, sorrow, or joy. We seem driven to provide means of expression for each of these human components and endeavour to present tangible descriptions, thus we use the physical senses, through creative artistry, to form the tangible out of the intangible.

Unfortunately, this does not mean, however, that every expression will be uplifting or even benign in its manifestation. Our creativity also embodies, or manifests, in negative, cruel, destructive, violent impulses and calculated acts of depravity, that each one of us has the potential to display when exposed to the pertinent emotional triggers. This alarming human signature was aptly described by psychiatrist and psychoanalyst Carl Jung (1875–1961), as *the Shadow.*[18] Jung wrote

> Unfortunately there can be no doubt that man is, on the whole, less good than
> he imagines himself or wants to be. Everyone carries a shadow, and the less it is
> embodied in the individual's conscious life, the blacker and denser it is…. if it is
> repressed and isolated from consciousness, it never gets corrected.[19]

Simply stated, the shadow is an integral part of our psychological construction. When this drive is left uncontrolled it manifests in aggressive, self-seeking, manipulative, and narcissistic conduct. From the perspective of religionswissenschaften, the historical, philosophical, artistic, and religious evidence clearly attests to the fact that this self can be easily manipulated through various sociological, political, and religious ideologies that favour control, repression, coercion, hatred, and violence. This is also the reason why some of our creative genius has been channeled into creating cultures of abuse and degradation. Using an argument taken from anthropodicy, we choose to apply either corrosive or life-affirming choices to much that we do. Hence humans become the portal through which positive or negative influences are exhibited and any approach to, or analysis of, the ways in which we explain and create our religious realities must always accept the human potentials of beauty or revulsion.

IDENTIFYING THE MEANS OF CREATIVE TRANSMISSION

That our species possesses a special intelligence is beyond argument and this not based on arrogant speciesism which would consider us superior to all other creatures. It is simply to make the observation that, as a signature aspect of our species, we have routinely demonstrated and recorded particular ways of operating in and through our physical and spiritual realities. To illustrate this point, review again the terms of reference used to classify what we as a species accept as the norm within our creative experience: *Homo economicus*: economic man; *Homo faber*: man the maker; *Homo loquens*: talking man; *Homo ludens*: man who creates play; *Homo patiens*: suffering man; *Homo poetica*: man the meaning maker; *Homo reciprocans*: man living in reciprocity with others; *Homo religiosus*: man the religious; *Home sociologicus*: social man, creating societies; *Homo socius*: man as a social being; *Homo symbolicus*: man who creates symbols; *Homo viator:* pilgrim man. Each of these descriptive terms indicates ways in which we have existed and found means to express our problem-solving adaptation to various modes of survival and interaction. To carry this analysis further, it is evident that within each of these realms of human expression we can locate artistic expression through *archetypes* or archetypal classifications such as symbol, metaphor, ritual (including pilgrimage), myth, and scripture.

Archetypal forms or classifications have been and still are routinely expressed throughout cultures and can be identified as early as Palaeolithic or Stone Age art depicting dramatic rituals and early community structure and sacred spaces like the standing stones.

What can also be noted is that throughout history archetypes have been central to religious ideas and have formed integral components within our basic universal language of the mind. As a consequence of this, from the basic functions of religious composition, it can be observed that we hear the sacred with our hearts and express our concepts through given archetypal forms anchored within physical realms of communication. Hence all our religious traditions have core ideas such

© TnT Designs, 2013. Used under license from Shutterstock, Inc.

as mythic beginnings, sacred spaces, concepts and stories of the divine origins of their deities, individual communities founded by divine or exceptional and/or mythic ancestors. Included in these concepts there are designated cultic objects, words, gestures conveying sacred significance, and the establishment of specific rituals given by God, the Creator, gods, spirits, ancestors, or enlightened sacred leaders. In addition to all this, using the medium of ritual and the drama of participation, archetypal concepts will also relate to that which is set apart as holy and that which is considered profane, and they will apply rules of inclusion and exclusion through some form of initiation.

Arising out of these facts, a plethora of historical and anthropological evidence exists that traces the inclusion and adaptation of specific archetypal myths or stories containing these ideas, which have then been transmitted into many religions. This can be identified through the mediums of folklore and art, the use of song and dance, and dramatic presentations such as sacred stories and drama plays. During this whole creative process they will still retain identifiable archetypal structures or patterns that are found within all religious societies. This is the reason why religions within a specific religious typology will reflect some general motifs of common views but, at the same time, display their own distinct identities. In other words, religions evolve out of specific cultural matrices and routinely incorporate various forms of syncretistic adaptation while still developing their own very individual cosmological identities.

From a Religious Studies' perspective, these archetypal ideas have influenced the formation and character of the many and various religious communities throughout history. The archetypal mediums of expression are identified as symbol, ritual, myth, and specific text classified as scripture. These types of expression and communication remain integral elements within the respective religious cultures and they provide "easy" patterns by which one religious community can distinguish itself from another.

FUNCTIONS OF THE ARCHETYPAL MEDIUMS

SYMBOL—THE THREE BASIC CATEGORIES

The most basic interpretation of a symbol is that of a representational sign, which by conversion or stipulation, stands for or suggests something else by reason of relationship, association, convention, or accidental resemblance. Simply put, symbols stand for something else and in the context of religion, they function as visible signs representing a quality contained in some metaphysical concept or teaching but are represented in a physically tangible form. In this way, symbols play a fundamental role in that which is humanly imaginable as perceived or believed within each specific religion. For example, consider how water as a symbol of life and also of spiritual purity and/or purification is taught in religions such as Hinduism, Shinto, Judaism, Christianity, Islam, and specific native North American tribes or bands that participate in the sweat lodge ceremony.

The function of a symbol is to act as a sign describing the intangible, whilst placing the guide points for accessing this metaphysical reality within the context of physical experience. This can be seen in the way that symbols convey concepts through a particular religion's designation of that which is holy, and is communicated through particular words, gestures, and objects. In so doing, symbols shape human perceptions of the relative cosmology in which they exist, together with the identity of self, others, society, and the world in the context of a specific religious reality. For example, for the majority of Muslims, the Ka'ba in Mecca represents not only the visible reminder or symbol of Allah's historical revelatory presence, but also represents the symbol of faith and submission as taught within the Qur'an on the part of those observing the ritual of tawaf.[20] Pilgrims performing tawaf believe that the angels in heaven participate in the same devotional act around the throne of Allah, who himself is situated in the seventh heaven, directly above the Ka'ba.[21] Thus the Ka'ba is a symbol of the close proximity of Allah whilst performing the Hajj.

A further example of a symbol would be for the Buddhist—the dharma-chakra which represents the eight-spoke wheel. This symbolizes key teachings of the Buddha, reminding the devotee of concepts on craving and pain, impermanence, emptiness, karma, enlightenment, and the possibility of nirvana. In Judaism the ancient representation of the seven-branch candelabrum called the menorah represents God's eternal presence and light among the Jews. It reminds them of the covenantal relationship they have with God and their responsibilities as his chosen people. In Chinese traditions, central ideas concerning harmony and balance can be represented through the symbol of the yin and yang, reflecting light and darkness, male and female, as opposites that function to balance energy and create peaceful co-existence.

SACRAMENTAL SYMBOLS

In the second description of symbol there is sacramental symbolism. In many traditions, there will be specific symbols that are believed to make present what they symbolize as sacred or divine through some form of direct physical immersion or consumption. These are referred to as *sacraments*.

This can be seen, for example, through Christian baptism as the outward sign or symbol of Christ's sacrificial death and resurrection. Being baptized "into" Christ, the believer identifies death to self and resurrection to new life through the sacramental washing away of their sins.

In Native American tribal systems, there is the pipe ceremony of lighting and inhaling tobacco and calling the ancestors to witness the sincerity of prayers, or an action. Inhaling the tobacco smoke connects the participant to the spirit world and thus acts

YARDENIT, ISRAEL—SEPTEMBER 30: Baptismal site at Jordan River shore. Baptism of pilgrims in Yardenit, Israel, on September 30, 2006.

© Zvonimir Atletic, 2013. Used under license from Shutterstock, Inc.

as a channel of communion. In Sikhism, there is also the sacrament of drinking Amrit, or holy nectar, whereby an initiate drinks this holy substance as part of their baptismal ritual. Amrit means "immortalizing nectar" and those who drink this substance are considered to have partaken of a sacrament and to have tasted immortality.

SYMBOLIC METAPHOR

The third category of symbols is known as symbolic metaphor. By definition, a metaphor is a term or phrase that is applied to something to which it is not literally applicable in order to suggest a resemblance. In the context of symbolic metaphorical representation, religions have widely used this means of communication to describe the sacred and intangible. Examples of this can be found in the context of using scripture as the living word, or the word of God as an inner means of contact with the sacred. Logically, how can an inanimate object such as a written text be alive? The underlying concept is that the gods (as in the Hindu Vedas) or God (as in the Abrahamics and Sikhism) "breathed" inspiration into the original hearers of the revelation, and through the words codified in scriptures, still breathe life into the present reader or recipient of the word. This inspires the recipient/devotee and they gravitate towards the spiritual. But how can a spirit deity breathe? What exactly is the breath of life? In this context it is the life-giving force of the supernatural revelation and the spiritual life that is imparted to the devotee to invigorate them.

Another example is that Christians often speak of God as father, which is a symbolic metaphor that rests on an analogy between fathers and God. In and of itself, the analogy does not assume that God is one's natural, biological father but rather is like a caring, authoritative parent.[22] Following along these lines is the analogy of the mother figure, which is a powerful metaphor for some of the attributes of the goddess in the religions of Hinduism. Mother becomes a metaphor for the nurturing divine presence, the feminine manifestation or shakti. The goddess manifestation represents the holy one who cares for her devotees as a mother cares for her children.

Other symbolic metaphors include the ancient analogy of the sun as a metaphor for deity. Egyptian and Aztec cosmologies, together with images in Hinduism as expressed within the ancient Hindu wedding ritual, believed there to be a likeness between the life-giving function of the sun and that of the divine giver of life and fertility.

To further illustrate this use of metaphor depicting the sacred there are the analogies of fire as both the

transforming and the destructive power of the holy, and light is used to symbolize truth and eternal wisdom. There is also the use of concepts of the expansive sky as a symbol for the infinite and incomparable.[23]

RITUAL

Ritual is by definition a formalized pattern of observance conveyed through ceremonial acts. It incorporates repetitious actions such as stylized gestures, words, chants, prayers, and often includes the use of a specific symbol at the centre of the devotional act. In this context, all religious traditions assign the first use of a specific ritual to a sacred time, person, or event within their mythos and history to establish validity and authenticity. Rituals are, therefore, sacred, repetitive actions which establish patterned structures of respectful observance; function is to ensure accurate continuity of the memory, memorial, or commemoration of the many and varied events and beliefs within the respective religious systems. Further, as part of the procedure, the whole process of celebrating or observing a ritual is undertaken with the recognition that the participants are aware of their limitations and finitude and approach the private or public ritual with humility, respect, awe, and often fear. The reason for this devout approach is that rituals are perceived to be ways of communicating with the metaphysical according to the cosmology of the community.

Ritual itself functions to crystalize a significant myth or particular important belief based on scriptural teaching or tribal tradition. The believer, either as a lone individual or group participant within a religious group, will act out or commemorate a pivotal belief or event and thus be "reminded" of its spiritual significance, thereby receiving empowerment through the enactment. The ritual itself functions to reaffirm the core beliefs and values within the respective cosmologies as it is also linked symbolically with those who have gone before them in their belief tradition, and this in turn reinforces individual and community identification in the past, present, and future.

In order to understand the organizational complexity of rituals it is necessary to identify the categories under which all these repetitious, but sacred devotional ceremonies can be classified. For the purposes of analysis these can be defined as (1) rituals of worship and commemoration directed towards the sacred—these will include the observance of pilgrimage; (2) rituals of conduct such as in fasting and observance of things that are prohibited or *Taboo*[24]; (3) rituals of purification; (4) rituals of initiation; and (5) rituals of life passage—or recognition of significant life events. Each of these classifications will act as part of the complete circle within the cosmology as each one will incorporate elements of the others. In other words, each one will find authority and validation within the others and thus they are complimentary in function and uphold the entire respective religious tradition.

MYTH

Myths originate in the ancient art of storytelling in times long before written language systems were devised and they were regarded as sacred or divinely inspired in the minds of many of the listeners. These stories speak of origins and they offer accounts of creation, the existence of God or gods, heroes, or other exceptional beings.[25] They are usually set in the context of a golden age, a primordial setting, or a heavenly realm. The myths establish the basic cosmology of the ancient religious system and the majority of existing religions in our own time still embody some of these great artistically interpretive stories.

The myths will contain concepts of good versus evil, heroic figures, the origins of right relationships, and cautionary tales of consequences incurred because of disobedience. Some of the ancient stories will also speak to the role of the human being living in obedience to a deity or to God; the origin of death; survival of the soul or consciousness after death; the reason for suffering be it disobedience or ignorance; and the destiny of humankind, together with the

© Jeff Whyte, 2013. Used under license from Shutterstock, Inc.

fate of the world, thus making them *apocalyptic* in nature. Other myths will explain the origin of rituals, sacred spaces, pilgrimages, the role of religious hierarchy, and the function of a king.

In the study of mythic traditions it is also quite clear that myths can adapt and incorporate other similar myths from other neighbouring cultures or from past times. In this way there is a process of syncretism that occurs whereby ancient creation myths can have familiar antecedents as their foundational core. This is very much in evidence in some of the Akkadian and Babylonian stories, which then will find some similarity within the creation myths of the ancient Hebrew traditions encoded within the Hebrew Bible. This can also be observed in some Vedic myths where similar basic traditional ancient sacred stories are syncretized and manifested in various Hindu religious beliefs.[26] There are also interesting comparisons within indigenous North American traditions where the trained scholar will identify lines of demarcation between pre-contact or pre-conquest/invasion myths and the mythic stories that develop after contact, or after contact, conquest/invasion.[27]

SCRIPTURE

Developing out of the mythic belief tradition, many communities who had created and developed a system of written language included a variety of these ideas as the basis for their specific sacred codes. This then formed the foundation for religious teaching and authority and was invested with an aura of ancient, sacred identity. These stories concerning the divine were reworked or edited and then encoded in some form of scripture, and thus formed codes of conduct and religious beliefs based on existing ancient precedents.

For other cultures living within the tradition of orality, existing without a written text, their sources of reference still retained the authenticity of the sacred story through the verbal provenance and continuity provided by those who were trained to retell and keep the myths alive and relevant. These *keepers of the myth*, also known as historians, elders, or shamans, have traditionally borne the responsibility of continuity and identity for the tribal group. The myth keepers embody and transmit the sacred stories to the present generation; through their traditional continuity of passing the specialist knowledge on, together with those who follow them in the sacred custodial role, they hand down this knowledge to the following generations.[28] In addition to this, the stories are passed on through the arts of visual representation such as art in painting, carving, sculpture, metallurgy, and even textiles, and through song and traditional dancing.[29] In this context, the enduring aspects of religious art function to provide another description of scripture. It can also be interpreted as that which is foundational cosmology identified through traditional stories retained by the tribal system and the keepers of the myth.

Analyzing the construction of scripture it therefore becomes clear that religions will possess a body of oral or written authority which is considered to be more than ancient myth. In essence, scripture emerges as the codification of mythic stories, codes of conduct, and central guiding tenets of the specific religion which incorporates a worldview or cosmology. This material is regarded as sacred, embodying the continuity of tradition through orality or textuality. There are guardians of the original sources, although this is not always the case in tribal contexts where there may have been considerable cultural trauma due to invasion by another group and even physical displacement. Nevertheless, despite the physical and emotional conditions that the group may encounter, the primary functional role that scripture plays is to act as the recognized source of inspiration and guidance for the whole religious system of believers within its orbit. It is accepted in this way because it is believed to be the enduring, divine revelation or ultimate book(s) of enlightenment.

The authority of any scripture comes from consensus of the particular group in question. The basic steps to the "text" becoming authoritative are (1) through tradition whereby a community retains a certain story or writing in general use; (2) over the gen-

erations the writing is used as a source of inspiration and authority; (3) this acceptance over the years elevates it to a position of special spiritual value; (4) the writing then acquires an aura of holiness due to its perceived ancient identity; (5) the sanctity afforded this scripture renders it inviolate and no changes or deletions of the scripture are allowed. In the context of written scripture the text develops into a specific and set apart body of sacred revelation, and for religions who adopt the doctrine a divine completeness and inerrancy. To amend or alter the existing writing becomes an act of desecration and blasphemy.[30]

PAYING TRIBUTE TO THE MAKERS OF RELIGION

From an analytical perspective, what is interesting to note from a review of the archetypes is that each one embodies and manifests a complex construction of not only religious concepts but also artistic expression. Each archetype is intricately constructed and illustrates the religious realities of emotional and creative expression, manifested in and through the various mediums of physical art forms. This means of religious illustration comes through every expression of what we consider to be physical and metaphysical religious reality. For example, consider the sensitivity and insight of the artist, wordsmith, scribe, artisan, musician, composer, singer, goldsmith, silversmith, stonemason, and builder, who through their skill explored, demonstrated, and described the intangible sacred in and through tangible forms. Each mode of expression has contributed to the fabric of religion and attests to the organizational complexity within these archetypes of religion.

There is a creative quality within religious archetypal construction that takes observers from the mundane world and transports them to realms of significance outside their own selves. Consider the words of the famous Persian Muslim mystic Al Ghazali (1058–1111):

> Now the rational soul in man abounds in, marvels, both of knowledge and power. By means of it he masters arts and sciences, can pass in a flash from earth to heaven and back again …. His five senses are like five doors opening on the external world; but, more wonderful than this, his heart has a window which opens on the unseen world of spirits.[31]

This heart or, sensitivity, or consciousness, is a quality that all religions will acknowledge despite their varying perspectives and doctrinal belief systems. Our species creates through perception and expression because it is our basic nature to do so. The late Steve Jobs (1955–2011), cofounder, chairman, and chief executive officer of Apple Inc., and a practicing Zen Buddhist, described creativity as follows:

> Creativity is just connecting things. When you ask creative people how they did something, they feel a little guilty because they didn't really do it, they just saw something. It seemed obvious to them after a while. That's because they were able to connect experiences they've had and synthesize new things. And the reason they were able to do that was that they've had more experiences or they have thought more about their experiences than other people.[32]

CONCLUSION

Our religions were formed because we connected the dots, sometimes quite beautifully and sometimes hideously. Nevertheless, human creativity is a religious reality. It is part of our capacity to see behind ordinary reality and arising out of dreams, hopes, longings, and great artistic expression, we create a window into another dimension. In the words of the famous and influential Canadian artist, Emily Carr (1871–1945),

> I think that one's art is a growth inside one. I do not think one can explain growth.
> It is silent and subtle. One does not keep digging up a plant to see how it grows.[33]

Religion and reality go hand in hand with many aspects of the creative impulse and art is not confined to expressions within secular culture. The fact of the matter is, art is one of our earliest manifestations of conceptualizing the greatness that lies within us and around us. From this perspective, creativity is at once both earthly and mystical.

© Javarman, 2013. Used under license from Shutterstock, Inc.

GLOSSARY

Apocalyptic: Forecasting the ultimate destiny of the world; prophetic; foreboding tales of imminent disaster or final doom; terrible.

Archetype: A universally understood symbol, term, or pattern of behaviour, a prototype from which others are copied, patterned, or emulated; often used and identified as present in myths and storytelling across different cultures; considered to have been present in folklore and literature for thousands of years, including prehistoric artwork; contains the idea of a holy book or source of authority containing divine or enlightened influence.

Hierophany: An event in which one sensorily experiences a manifestation of the sacred; a physical manifestation of the divine; through physicality, can be seen, felt, heard, smelled, and tasted.

Keepers of the Myth: Also known as historians or elders, and shamans, bear the responsibility of continuity and identity for the tribal group; the sacred stories are transmitted through oral storytelling, rituals, art, song, chant, and dance.

Myth: Describes a genre of narrative that attempts to express a specific culture's sense of reality as expressed in their epic stories of truth and the supernatural.

Myth (The) of Eternal Return: The devotee literally relives an hierophanic encounter through physical and emotional identification; through participation and enactment they became part of the original mythic experience; is identified through the rituals of pilgrimage and ceremony.

Numinous: the holy and nonrational aspect of human communication with the *wholly other*.

Pilgrimage: A journey to a sacred place or shrine; a long journey or search, especially one of exalted purpose or moral significance; believed to be a life-transforming spiritual event.

Phenomenology: The study of appearances and patterns.

Profane: Marked by contempt or irreverence for what is sacred; nonreligious in subject matter, form, or use; secular; sacred and profane music; not admitted into a body of secret knowledge or ritual; uninitiated. By its very nature, the profane is a fleeting and impermanent sphere when compared to the sacred.

Reductionism: Argues that religious experience or motivation can be reduced to or explained by fixing it within the context of historical, psychological, or sociological terms.

The belief that complex data and phenomena can be explained in terms of something simpler and more easily identifiable as a root cause; rejection of the metaphysical; emphasizes only logical and physical causes.

Two main branches of thought: (1) *naturalist/eliminative* reductionism centred within the realms of science; and incorporates theories of cognition, evolution, and the resulting interpretation of evolutionary psychology along with philosophical justification for each aspect of emotional and religious reality; (2) *cultural reductionism* pertains to the spheres of influence within politics, structure of hierarchy, and social control that create boundaries, law codes, identification of self, religious structures, and the interpretation of religious experience.

Ritual: A formalized pattern of observance conveyed through ceremonial acts; incorporates repetitious actions such as stylized gestures, words, chants, prayers; often includes the use of a specific symbol at the centre of the devotional act.

Sacred: Dedicated to or set apart for the worship of God or gods, or sublime force; worthy of religious veneration; made or declared holy; dedicated, set apart, or devoted exclusively to a single use; worthy of respect; revered; of or relating to religious objects, practices, or specific rituals; considered to be of lasting value in life and in concepts of true reality, reason, and purpose for being.

Scientific determinism: All events, all physical life, all nature, are governed by universal physical laws. This interpretation denies the existence of chance or probability.

Scripture: Stories and teachings concerning the divine, incorporating codes of conduct; regarded as sacred with many of its early stories believed to date from early history; believed to be codified and written in some permanent form of record; now accepted that it can be transmitted in a culture of orality through word, song, ritual, and art.

Shadow (The): Dark or murderous side of human nature; identified by narcissism, cruelty, and aggression.

Speciesism: Prejudice or discrimination based on species; defined as discrimination against animals; based on the assumption of human superiority.

Symbol: A representational sign, which by conversion or stipulation, stands for or suggests something else by reason of relationship, association, convention, or accidental resemblance.

Taboo: Prohibited, forbidden, or disapproved of; prohibition resulting from social or other conventions; ritual restriction or prohibition, especially of something that is considered holy and not to be touched; or unclean and prohibited from use or contact; term originates from the religions of the South Pacific.

Tawaf: Relating to the Hajj; circumambulation of the Ka'ba.

ENDNOTES

1. Marked by contempt or irreverence for what is sacred; nonreligious in subject matter, form, or use; secular: sacred and profane music; not admitted into a body of secret knowledge or ritual; uninitiated. By its very nature, the profane is a fleeting and impermanent sphere when compared to the sacred, which is considered of lasting value in life and in concepts of true reality.

2. Dedicated to or set apart for the worship of God or gods, or sublime force; worthy of religious veneration; accepted as holy. Considered to be of lasting value in life and in concepts of true reality, reason, and purpose for being.

3. One of the defining marks of the twentieth century has been the triumph, especially in the social sciences, of the theory of determinism. The theory holds that all or most of a man's life is determined for him by factors beyond his control, be they the environment, heredity, or a host of other external forces that play upon him. The concept of free will, when it is considered at all, is relegated to an insignificant place in the makeup of the human person. http://www.chesterton.org/discover-chesterton/chesterton-briefs/scientific-determinism/
Note also that in scientific determinism every event is governed by universal laws. This interpretation denies the existence of chance or probability. Since the second half of the twentieth century, however, there has been a growing acknowledgement in the scientific community that not all natural laws are deterministic; some of these laws may be inherently statistical in nature. This line of argument could constitute an argument for indeterminism, based on the theories of quantum mechanics. http://www.enotes.com/determinism-reference/determinismhey apply to all events and objects.

4. Mircea Eliade, *The Sacred and the Profane: The Nature of Religion*, (New York: Harcourt, Inc., 1959), p 11.

5. Ibid.

6. Mircea Eliade, *The Myth of the Eternal Return*, (Princeton, NJ: Princeton University Press, 2005). This process can easily be identified through the pilgrimage ritual observed within nearly every documented religion in the world.

7. Matthew Alper, *The God Part of the Brain*, (Naperville, IL: Sourcebooks, Inc., 2006), pp 92-101.

8. Ibid., p 92.

9. William Wordsworth, *Lines Composed a Few Miles above Tintern Abbey, On Revisiting the Banks of the Wye during a Tour. July 13, 1798*. http://www.poetryfoundation.org/poem/174796

10. plato.stanford.edu/entries/phenomenology/

11. http://www.ochs.org.uk/lectures/importance-religion-1-religion-and-reductionism

12. Ibid.

13. Erich Fromm, *The Art of Loving*, (New York: HarperCollins Publishers, 2006), pp 31-32.

14. Ibid. 32.

15. Erich Fromm, *The Anatomy of Human Destructiveness*, (New York: Picador, 1973), p 58.

16. Ibid. Fromm cites R. B. Livingston, 1967.

17. Rudolf Otto, *The Idea of the Holy*, (Oxford: Oxford University Press, 1958), pp 60-65. Otto identifies the direct and indirect means of expression, and the way the numinous is expressed within art.

18. Carl G. Jung, *The Portable Jung*, (New York: Penguin, 1976), pp 139-162. Jung developed the concepts of the extraverted and the introverted personality, archetypes, and the collective unconscious and identified the indispensible, but aggressive, narcissistic shadow self in the human psyche.

19. Carl Jung, Psychology and Religion (1938) in *The Collective Works of Carl Jung*, Vol. 11: Psychology and Religion: West and East, (Princeton, NJ: Princeton University Press, 1975) p 131.

20. Ritual circumambulation (counterclockwise procession) of the Ka'ba.

21. There are other versions as to where the throne of Allah is situated but the dominant belief is above the Ka'ba. He can also be situated over the Dome of the Rock (Masjid Qubbat As-Sakhrah), in Jerusalem, where it is believed Abraham was going to offer up his son Ishmael as a sacrifice. It is also taught that the Prophet Muhammad ascended into the seventh heaven situated over Jerusalem, to meet with Allah at a significant time in the development of Islam. Other Muslims believe that Allah is everywhere.

22. Roger Schmidt et al, *Patterns of Religion*, (Belmont, CA: Wadsworth Publishing Company, 1999), p 13.

23. Ibid.

24. Prohibited, forbidden, disapproved of.

25. Robert Elwood, *Myth: Key Concepts in Religion*, (London: Continuum International Publishing Group, 2008), p 1.

26. William A. Graham, *Beyond the Written Word: Oral Aspects of Scripture in the History of Religion*, (Cambridge: Cambridge University Press, 1987), pp 67, 157, 163.

27. The references to conquest/invasion are noted to reflect the perspective of indigenous people's perspective on the events of white settlement in their lands.

28. Walter E. A. Van Beek, *The Dancing Dead: Ritual and Religion among the Kapsiki/Higi of North Cameroon and Northeastern Nigeria,* (Oxford: Oxford University Press, 2012). This book conducts an in depth analysis of some tribal transmission systems.

29. John W. Friesen, Virginia Lyons Friesen, *Canadian Aboriginal Art and Spirituality: A Vital Link,* (Calgary: Detselig Enterprises Ltd., 2006). A comprehensive overview of aboriginal art and communication placed within the context of spirituality.

30. James C. Livingston, *Anatomy of the Sacred,* (Upper Saddle River: Prentice-Hall, Inc., 2001), pp 128-136.

31. Al Ghazzali, *The Alchemy of Happiness,* Claud Field, translator, 1909, www.sacred-texts.com/isl/tah/index.htm

32. Steve Jobs, *Wired*, February 1995. http://edudemic.com/2011/10/creativity-steve-jobs/retrieved October 10, 2012.

33. Emily Carr, http://www.joyofquotes.com/self-discovery_quotes.html

CHAPTER 6

Mysticism

DEFINING FOUNDATIONAL EXPERIENCE

The study of mysticism is one of the most popular and intriguing aspects of religion being studied today. The reason for this is that as a phenomenon, it can be identified in almost every religious tradition in the world throughout millennia. Fortunately, this complex and often confusing array of supra-conscious experiences has resulted in detailed written and oral accounts and these speak to many facets of the process itself. The resulting documentation comes to us from varied sources including practitioners of mysticism, their devotees, those within the respective religions, and commentators in and outside of the religions. As a consequence, what the enquirer has to work with in the process of analytical methodology, or simply just making sense of it all, is a tremendously diverse, complex, contentious, and often paradoxical system of definitions and classifications. Indeed, during the twentieth century, with the classification and basic sorting of both primary source material and resulting analyses, it became evident that there were "many different interpretations and conflicting theories"[1] regarding this phenomenon. This data bank indicated that there existed a multitude of experiences defined as mysticism. The reality is that mysticism exists in varying experiential realities because the phenomenon will routinely conform to some sort of foundational reality in the faith tradition of the mystic, whilst at the same time, presenting an additional insight to further heighten awareness and comprehension.[2] In other words, this comprehension is based on foundational faith perspectives but then branches out in deepening degrees of cognition, thus enabling the devotee to grow in wisdom and comprehension. What we do know resulting from academic study is that mysticism is not merely exhibited through excitable, hysterical, psychosomatic, and sometimes psychotic expressions of human need, that offer a brief emotional high. In fact, contrary to this misinformed perspective, what becomes clear is that there are profound and lasting manifestations of enduring deep spiritual insight which have stood the scrutiny of thousands of years, attesting to something ethereal but at the same time, tangibly solid, contributing to cognitive insight and influence. The reality is that much of what reaches us today through the records attests to the existence of the mystical phenomenon presented in the flow of profoundly moving, insightful, and life-changing expressions. These experiences display deeply developed, mature cognition, infused with selflessness, the enlargement of patience and fortitude, a purity of spirit, and altruistic love, if perhaps somewhat alarming in demonstration.[3]

ADDRESSING COMPLEXITY AND CONFUSION

To comprehend the scope and depth of this remarkably complex phenomenon, consider the following. There are the four basic typologies that we have previously addressed, but mysticism has classically been categorized into three definitive streams of religious thought and tradition. These can be identified as (1) the Eastern mystical traditions, arising out of the Indian Tree and South East Asian; (2) the Western mystical traditions, developing out of Judaism, Christianity, and Islam; and (3) the Nativistic or Tribal synthesis, manifesting in many hues and complexities, including the practices of shamanism, possession states, and *altered states of consciousness*. But this is the simple explanation! Research indicates that there are multiple diversities within these stereotypical categorizations because categories break down again into other forms of mystical practices which are specifically adapted to each of the specialized individual cosmologies. The reason for this is that each of the streams contains ideas or concepts that can be found within one or both of the other streams. As Walter T. Stace (1886–1967)[4] wrote, presenting a by now famous hypothesis regarding the "core of mysticism"[5]

> … although certain mystical experiences may in certain respects have different characteristics in different parts of the world, in different ages, and in different cultures, there are nevertheless a number of fundamental common characteristics.[6]

Noting the above paradoxes it becomes clear to anyone studying mysticism that there is no one answer or definition for the phenomenon. The problem is that any simplistic classification system can only address certain identifiable signature themes and cannot provide a complete description of the streams. To understand mystical traditions, one must study each one in its singular context, look at the root cosmology, identify any syncretism that may have occurred, understand how this adaptation has influenced the mystic and how in turn the mystic has influenced the evolution of cognitive interpretation. This methodological perspective takes into serious consideration that mystics seem to possess a special interpretative insight that can add a dynamic of interpretation to their specific religion which invigorates and changes it.

For this reason, it is necessary to locate and present themes, beliefs, concepts, and practices specific to each group but, at the same time, focus attention on the fact that mysticism and mystical practices have "threads" of connection.[7] In the words of the Jesuit priest and author, William Johnson (1925–2010), who studied mysticism and these connections,

… there is a human question which psychology never asks and which leads people to religion; namely, what is at the deepest realm of the psyche? What is the basis or centre or root of all? Put in Jungian terms I might ask: "When I go beyond the ego, beyond the personal unconscious, beyond the collective unconscious, beyond the archetypes, what do I find?" And in answer to this all the great religions speak of a mystery which they call by various names: the Buddha nature, Brahman and Atman, the divine spark, the ground of being, the centre of the soul, the kingdom of God, the image of God….They use different terms; but all, I believe are pointing towards a single reality.[8]

These threads of significance regarding the mystical experience, exist to express a common human motivational desire which is based on the religious reality that people need to connect with something or someone greater than themselves in a profoundly transformative experiential inner life. This need is manifested in the development of a supra-consciousness, or higher state of consciousness,[9] which leads the seeker away from the superficial or undeveloped religious state and into a deeper perception of the ideas embodied within their specific perception of religious reality. It will differ in depth of comprehension from the regular interpretations of transcendence as it manifests a deeper comprehension of what is perceived by the mystic to be reality.

This deepening consciousness is reflected also in conformity to an experiential description which displays an awareness of a much wider consciousness that comprehends a Universal reality, state, or universal One.[10] In other words, at some point in the mystical experience there is the awareness of the sublime; of Someone or something much greater than limited human perception. This encounter has a profound influence on the understanding of reality, the self, and others and has often been linked to the dynamic of revelation, interpretation, communication, insofar as it will add a dimension to existing religious cosmologies. For an example of this, consider the observations of philosopher and psychologist William James (1842–1910), in his seminal work, *The Varieties of Religious Experience*.[11] James argued that there were four basic characteristics identifiable in profound mystical experience. These were (1) ineffability in that they defied expression or description in words—they could only be experienced within one's consciousness; (2) they embodied a noetic quality as they were special states of perception into the depths of truth; (3) they were transient and could not be sustained for more than an hour or two at maximum. Often, however, although the sharpness of the experience faded, the perception and memory retained led to deepening cognitive states in life as a process of ongoing mystical development; (4) passivity or the passive state occurs wherein the mystic feels that his or her will or consciousness is taken up and held in communion with a superior power.[12]

James also stressed that although mystical states were subjective in nature and only binding on the one who had experienced the event, the encounter itself could act as a window into a wider world of meanings. This broadened perspective opened up "the possibility of other orders of truth"[13] and absolutely overthrew "the pretention of non-mystical states to be the sole and ultimate dictators of what we may believe."[14] The understanding and interpretation imparted through the mystical experience and perspective challenged atrophied religious systems by adding a new expressiveness and a new connection.[15] It was this mystical experience that often had the ability to infuse new perspectives into a religion by adding a super-sensuous meaning to ordinary data and in so doing contribute to the respective cosmology's revitalization.

COMBINING INTROVERTED SUBJECTIVITY AND OBJECTIVE AWARENESS

The process behind the journey lies at the very core of the mystical encounter in that it is a subjective experience through which the encounter projects the devotee into an overwhelming embrace with a force which engulfs the conscious self within it. It is often described as a merging into some greater stream of metaphysical existence of mind and/or spirit. Through this, however, a paradox arises because it is the mystic who is experiencing and cognitively sorting the incomprehensible, while beholding the event, even during the process of being overcome with the "otherness" of this encounter. This makes it an introverted, subjective cognitive process. Paradoxically once again, what makes it even more intriguing is that the mystic is being conducted through the experience while objectively observing in some way the sensation of encounter and oneness with their Ultimate, even while being overcome. What this all means is that during the process, even while the person is engulfed in the ecstatic state whether this is a placid or effusive experience, they are conscious on some level. It is this form of consciousness that provides them with the ability to later, in the separate, independent, and intellectually conscious state, process the ineffable experience to the point of some intelligibility. This is the process of information retrieval and cognitive sorting of the experience to increase enlightenment and to communicate this to others, if the experience is possible to explain even to a limited degree. The fact is that even when the mystic claims to have experienced pure consciousness there is still subjectivity because the encounter can be identified as an encounter and processed as such through the cognitive state. The self still beholds the self, even when the claim is for pure ineffable transcendence; if this were not the case there would be no "memory" or recollection of the event having occurred in the first place and consciousness would not be heightened during physical life.

To more clearly illustrate this paradox, consider the following coding criteria identified through psychology,[16] where mystical experience is divided into the two forms of subjective and objective perception. The forms of mystical qualities or experience can be identified as: (1) ego, (2) noetic, (3) communicable, (4) affective, and (5) religious.

1. **Ego**: refers to the extent to which consciousness of the self is maintained.
   There are two parts to this experience of consciousness.
   a. The *loss of self* whereby consciousness will be present but consciousness of self is not experienced; thus there is the loss of self-identity. This is referred to as *the void*. As being "awake" but seemingly merged into a higher stream of awareness.
   b. The *presence of self*. In this state of consciousness the awareness of self-identity is maintained as full self-conscious observation of the event occurs.

2. **Noetic:** refers to the revelatory dimension of the experience and to the extent that it reveals and affirms fundamental concepts within the cosmology.
   a. The experience can be objective in that it reaffirms the authoritative "truth" of specific beliefs within a religious system.
   b. It can be subjective and personal, a valid "gift" or an insight given to the mystic. It will provide personal insight and guidance.

3. **Communicable:** refers to the degree to which a mystical revelatory experience can be made comprehensible to the self and to others.
   a. There is the incommunicable classification whereby the experience itself is felt but defies classification. This will be interpreted as inexplicable but will still be explained in the context of *ineffability*.
   b. The second aspect of the communicable quality is that the experience can be defined with the use of words and relayed to others.

4. **Affective:** this experience pertains to the experience itself in the way it can be either an emotionally negative or a positive event.
   a. The negative experience can engender feelings of fear, guilt, depression, and even despair. Can be classified as the *diabolical*.[17]
   b. The positive or benign experience which creates states of joy, ecstasy, peace, comfort, and reassurance. Promotes growth in "faith."

5. **Religious:** pertains to whether the one experiencing the event perceives it as either sacred or profane.
   a. As a sacred event it will evoke feelings of reverence, awe, devotion, love, and mystery. It is beyond scientific, empirical research or explanation. It is a supra-sensitive glimpse into another reality that cannot be quantified and must be treated with great respect.
   b. As a profane event it is more problematic to explain as the person who does not believe or comprehend the experience will not appreciate the gift or revelation. The experience itself, that of the mystical quality of the event, will therefore not be acknowledged as different from any other religious experience. It will, therefore only exist on record as something to be observed or studied scientifically. There will be no mystical engagement in the event and thus will have no spiritual energy that can be discerned or defined.[18]

Whatever the category or quality of the phenomenon, what is evident is that there is an identifiable state which exists as the individual attains a vision or revelation of ultimate reality. It is a folding of time and dimension whereby one form of reality folds into and through the other. In addition to this, it is also the experience of Ultimate reality which flows through the mystic, causing the mystic to flow through the reality of an unfolding truth, whether that truth is objective or subjective.

What is also apparent from this study is that the mystical experience has as its unique defining characteristic, a non-temporal, non-spatial, pure consciousness that is devoid of all content, including awareness of self, yet the self still observes. This experience is also characterized by ineffability, paradoxicality, sacredness, positive effect, and a sense of objectivity.[19]

To explain this experience further, within in a systematic paradigm, the theologian and scholar of comparative religions, Rudolf Otto (1869–1937), authored a seminal work on mysticism entitled, *The Idea of the Holy*.[20] Otto is held to be one of the most influential thinkers concerning religion during the first half of the twentieth century, *and* his work on mysticism is considered to be a lastingly erudite treaties on the subject. In *The Idea of the Holy*, Otto fashioned the now famous definitions:

> *Numen/Numinous* (creature feeling).
> *Mysterium tremendum et fascinans* (fearful and fascinating mystery).
> *Mysterium* (the Wholly Other, experienced with blank wonder, stupor).
> *Tremendum*: awefulness, terror, demonic dread, awe, absolute unapproachability, "wrath" of God; overpoweringness, majesty, might, sense of one's own nothingness in contrast to its power, creature-feeling, sense of objective presence, dependence; energy, urgency, will, vitality.
> *Fascinans*: potent charm, fascination, attractiveness in spite of fear, terror,[21] weird, monstrous.[22]

From these definitions, it is evident that encountering the otherness which constitutes a mystical experience creates emotional, human responses within a mystical state. Not every state would be experienced, but suffice it to say, Otto observed that there was the possibility of a depth and wealth of emotional interaction that could occur during the event of altered consciousness in a mystical encounter.

It is these concepts which, from a scholarly perspective, form the general construction of the phenomenon known as mysticism. Such a basic understanding, however, only provides the researcher with a general understanding. Once again, the labyrinth of mystical otherness presents more paths of enquiry.

ANOTHER ASPECT OF THE LABYRINTH: THE DIABOLICAL

Throughout the mystical encounters documented and observed through our histories, there is also another aspect of the phenomenon that religions acknowledge. This is the manifestation of an alarming experience which William James dubbed the *diabolical*. In many cosmologies this manifestation is regarded as negative and destructive. In other traditions, it is accepted as part of encountering the spirit world. Whatever the tradition's explanation, it is a force that should be noted.

William James explained it in terms constructed by psychology and noted that there was a clear difference between a positive experiential mysticism and that of *diabolical mysticism*.[23] He wrote that there were two halves to mysticism, one being the religious form of positive encounter and the other half which

> … has not accumulated traditions except those which the text-books on insanity supply. Open any one of these and you will find abundant cases in which 'mystical ideas' are citied as characteristic symptoms of enfeebled of deluded states of mind. In delusional insanity, paranoia, as they sometimes call it, we may have a diabolical mysticism, a sort of religious mysticism turned upside down.[24]

The problem with James's explanation is that he does not seriously consider the evidence which is clearly recorded and identified in the various religions' encounters with this other side of the phenomenon. The experiences are not merely psychotic episodes or even simply schizophrenic in nature. From the perspective of a religious/supernatural experience, these events are considered extremely serious in their very essence. Once again, Rudolf Otto provides an insightful explanation insofar as he was able to contextualize this occurrence from a Religious Studies approach. Otto defined alarming experiences using the terms *tremendum* and *fascinans* and each one of these descriptions indicates often cathartic emotional response markers.

If one takes these markers, considers the significance of Otto's descriptions, and then studies the cosmologies of the religions where they occur, it becomes evident, that despite what the detached observer may think, the encounters are considered very powerful, ominous, and often terrifying events for the believer. Thus, in studying beliefs such as spirit possession, hauntings, and ominous events, it is prudent and respectful to hold one's own beliefs and prejudices in abeyance and observe the events as impartially as can be achieved.

DEFINING DIFFERENCES

Upon the commencement of analyzing the various fields of mystical experience, particular differences must first be noted within the religious traditions. These differences pertaining to mysticism relate to a central belief in God, known as monotheism or theism, in contrast to types of the same phenomenon that have at their centre an atheistic cosmology. Theistic beliefs are obviously clearly represented in the Abrahamics, but they are also present in Sikhism and a certain type of Hindu tradition known as Advaita. In other traditions, polytheism, or the belief in many deities, will associate visits from one or several deities, as manifesting through an ecstatic and/or possession trance, or cause the devotee to journey to the spirit world for an audience with spirits and ancestors, and sometimes even to fight demons. The Abrahamics accept that in altered states one may sense or encounter the closeness of God but these traditions may also harbor beliefs in malevolent spirits and ghosts, in demons, and also possession states. Atheistic mystical traditions are located within Buddhist, Jainist, and certain Chinese traditions such as some types of Taoism and definitely the majority of Confucianist streams. At the same time, although atheistic, they will harbor beliefs in ghosts who can be angry or benign, spirits, even superior spirits who are considered gods, together with demons and ancestral spirits. In certain types of Japanese and Chinese traditions, beliefs in ancestral reverence is central with no need for distinctive worship of an omnipresent deity figure, but will encompass ancestral spirit worship, spirits in nature, demons and angry ghosts, together with possession trances. In nativistic tribal groups there will be belief in the ancestral spirit realm, the spirit world, spirit guides, possession trances, angry and friendly ghosts, and in various animal spirit forms both benign and malevolent, known as trickster spirits, together with a transcendent and distant Creator god. Other Hindu traditions, with ancient tribal roots to animistic and ancestral worship traditions, will also believe in possession trances, demons, ghosts, and localized deities who can be both beneficent and/or malevolent.

It is in all these contexts that mysticism in its many modes will manifest and, according to whether it is considered beneficial or disturbing, will be designated by these communities as a contact with the other realm. The mystical state itself, according to the cosmology, will be regarded as uplifting and inspiring, or set through with chilling power that must be obeyed, contained, and often appeased.

CENTRAL RELIGIOUS COSMOLOGICAL ORIENTATIONS AND MYSTICAL EXPERIENCES

In order to proceed further towards an understanding and appreciation of the mystical experience it is necessary to consider the many routes of meaning that have developed over millennia. For this reason, seven central cosmological orientations will be analyzed: (1) Hindu mysticism, (2) Buddhist mysticism, (3) Taoist and Confucianist mysticism, (4) Nativistic/tribal, shamanism/mysticism, (5) Hebrew and Jewish mysticism, (6) Christian mysticism, and (7) Islamic mysticism. A basic overview of these mystical traditions will therefore now be considered.

Hindu Mystical Systems

To appreciate some of the Hindu mystical systems it is necessary to address the authority and cosmologies they cover. The following material, therefore, is provided to simply give the reader a basic understanding of the complexity of the development of mysticism over thousands of years.

To commence the study of mystical Hinduism, it must be noted that Hindus possess a complex variety of authoritative mystical traditions. Hindu scriptures are extensive, and incorporate many different views of spiritual reality and the processes of achieving *mukti or moksha* which means liberation from samsara through enlightenment and is generally linked to one or other form of the mystical path towards that experience. In addition to these ideas is the central practice and/or belief in *samadhi*, which is function of conscious experience that lies beyond waking, dreaming, and deep sleep and allows for absorption of the object of meditation. This state of consciousness is often referred to as "one-pointedness of mind."[25]

At the root of Hindu mysticism lies the sacred scriptures that form the basis of diverse mystical traditions. These scriptures are divided into two classifications: (1) *shruti*, or that "which is heard," and (2) *smriti* or that "which is remembered."[26]

Shruti is held to be the primary revelation which was "heard" or sensed by the ancient rishis or seers. The seers "heard" the truths while in deep meditation and transmitted these truths to their followers through the cultures of orality and tradition upheld by the Brahmin, or priestly caste. These revelations and prescribed rituals were gradually encoded into a collection of scriptures that are recorded as:

Veda-samhitas: Four in total
    Rig-Veda (containing 1,028 hymns)
    Yajur-Veda (sacrificial formula)
    Sama-Veda (containing 1,549 mantras)
    Atharva-Veda (spells, curses, charms, with 731 hymns in 20 books)

Brahmanas (Brahmin Books which correspond to each Veda)

Aranyakas (Forest Books—philosophical speculations on sacrifice)

Upanishads (Sitting Near the Teacher. Final part of shruti. Philosophical monologues on the nature of cosmic reality; debates between opposing schools of thought. Emphasizes self-denial, asceticism to find truth. Concerned with finding truth that lies behind all physical/material reality, which would be interpreted as Brahman [Nirguna Brahman—God without attributes]).[27]

Smriti is the second section of the scriptures and signifies "that which is remembered" in the context of interpreting shruti and applying it to later ages. Smriti is not held to be revelatory in nature but its truths serve to illustrate and expound upon the authority of the shruti material. These books are:

Puranas (18 books containing legends. Addressed to the ordinary person. They stress devotion to a specific divinity as the way to moksha. Speak of Shiva, or Vishnu or the divine feminine creative power known as Shakti.)

Mahabharata (Great Stories of King Bharata's family. Includes the revered and always popular *Bhagavata Gita* containing the story of Lord Krishna.)

Ramayana (story of Rama, a prince who overcame the demon Ravana with the help of Hanuman the Monkey God.)

Manusmriti (Laws of Manu—foundational laws and customs: codification and operation of the four-caste system in Hindu life.)

Vishnusmriti (Laws—both criminal and civil, castes, duties, witnesses, inheritance, funerals and obligations, impurity, women, transmigration of soul, etc.)

Tantras (Looms, weavings: deal with rituals, beliefs, yogic meditation. Explained popular gods and how to bring their powers to the devotee by ritual and yoga.[28])

From this overview of the Hindu scriptures certain beliefs can be identified. First, at the centre of this extremely complex and diversely theistic and polytheistic system lies the concept of the One as identified in the Upanishads. This one is Nirguna Brahman, God/Brahman who is beyond the reach of intellectual consciousness. Nirguna Brahman is without qualities and its/his nature or essence cannot be defined. As the unmanifested source behind all things, he can only be ineffably sensed through dedicated study, intensely reflective thought, rejection of maya or the illusionary physical world, and deep meditation which all act as corollaries to the general ascetic practice of renunciation. This ancient concept can be identified in the Vedas, which are the oldest source of Hindu scriptures and developed in great depth within the Upanishads.[29] Later, this form of mystical regimen evolved into what is generally known as Advaita Vedanta which was developed through the teachings of the eighth century c.e. scholar and mystic, Shankara. Through Advaita Vedanta,[30] which incorporates *non-dualism,* followers are to seek liberation/release by recognizing identity of the Self (Atman) and the Whole (Brahman) as one stream of being. It is believed that concentrated study of the Vedas will provide the foundation for truth along this path. The path itself is one of long preparation and training, normally under the direction of a guru and aims at serenity of mind and body. It will also involve jnanamarga or the path of knowledge of scriptures, renunciation of worldy activities, and meditation on the unity of atman and Brahman as being one and the same, hence non-dualistic, whilst still concentrating on the essence of Brahman in order to merge into oneness through assigned yogic practices.

The whole concept of Advaita Vedanta is based on a refined, scholarly, and disciplined path of asceticism. Although it is considered by its devotees to be the superior mystical path, one that is situated in the serenity of meditation and withdrawal, it is still regarded, however, as the elitist path by many Hindus who themselves seek a more basic mystical experience. This different and more immediate path is termed *Bhakti.*

The Bhakti form of mystical alignment is to be found within the popular concept of Saguna Braham and is defined by its poet saints who hailed from South India.[31] The many forms of this tradition will accept the principle of Nirguna Brahman but will focus on Saguna Brahman or God/Brahman with attributes and will be located within religions that are classified as Vaishnavite (worship of Vishnu, his avatars and the Shakti feminine force) and Shaivite (worship of Shiva, his avatars and Shakti feminine force). Due to the centrality of Vishnu and Shiva, the respective followers will often relate to these gods as being the very essence of Saguna Brahman. Bhakti is a widely popular expression of mystical piety and, in its many religious traditions, emphasizes the following concepts:

- The adoration of God through intense and passionate loving devotion to him.
- Involves *prapatti,* or complete self-surrender.
- All action must be performed for God's sake.
- Such devotion leads to the realization of God, the union of the soul with him.
- The chief quality of both Vishnu and Shiva is boundless grace.
- The embodied life in this world, with all its ills, is the means which God has appointed for union with himself; therefore he is owed limitless devotion.
- Listening to the praise of God and reading the sacred writings.
- Singing the praise of God.
- Remembering God's name which should be repeated in all circumstances, regularly and continuously. It is believed that all difficulties are destroyed by this practice if it is done in love.
- The remembrance of God's name leads to the loss of self in rapture.
- Repetition of the divine name (Brahman) brings deliverance from sin.
- There are nine forms of bhakti enumerated: it is said that each of these will lead men to the goal, if followed with sufficient fervor.[32]

In such states of worship and adoration, Bhakti mysticism provides the ordinary person with the ability to encounter his or her god in an uplifting and accessible devotional exercise. Although there is strong emphasis on morality, piety, and renunciation, it is more "user friendly" because of the writings of the sants/saints and their emphasis on love directed towards the specific god, which opens the door to a relationship based on personal, emotional devotion. The process itself is guided by a personal guru or spiritual director who is herself (Ananda Bhairavi)[33] or himself (Ananda Bhairava), believed to have personally already attained god-realization or being one with God. As an outcome of this, the guru is held in such great reverence and obedience that he/she is traditionally regarded as God because the guru is regarded as a means of union with God himself.[34]

To complete the analysis of Hindu mysticism, there are devotees who are known as *saktas*. This tradition is identified by its worship of the Mother Goddess, who embodies the feminine creative power of the divine and is placed within the *tantric* classification, which is derived from the sacred texts known as Tantras.[35] The tantric system was originally focused on the married householder's conjugal relationship and evolved a series of practices and techniques, through yogic meditation, ritual, and sexual engagement that was believed to balance the mind and spirit. The tradition affirmed engagement in daily life, which is still considered by many practicing Hindus to be the path to enlightenment that experiences the transcendent through the imminent. The female energy was, and still is, considered to be the life animating force, which when coupled with the transcendent but inactive male force creates life itself—both physical and spiritual.[36] Observance of these practices is still considered to possess important spiritual, salvific, astrological, or magical benefits in the Tantric traditions of the Indian religions.

Tantricism was further developed by other mystical groups within Hinduism, including the ascetic sadhu sect known as the *Aghori* who are known for their extreme violations of typical Indian social mores. As part of their tantric system of mysticism they focus on the worship of Shiva in his avatar manifestation as Lord Bhairava and Shiva's shakti manifestations as Kali or Durga. They believe that by obliterating social taboos they will achieve heightened perception through altered states of consciousness because God is manifested in everything without boundaries. This will lead them to liberation and oneness with their deity. To accomplish this goal of mystical awareness they eat human flesh from the cremation grounds, consume urine and feces in religious rituals, smear their bodies with ash from the cremation pyre, and use human skulls as food and drink receptacles; they also use human bones for other religious rituals. This group is also distinguished from other tantric devotees by their heavy daily use of ganja (marihuana) and alcohol. Their form of tantric enlightenment leads them to understand the illusory nature of all conventional categories and frees their perception from illusion or maya. In other words, the Aghori mystics utilize a type of shock value system which destroys all societal boundaries, and brings them to a state of holiness and liberation. Many Hindus utterly condemn these practices, but there are other Hindus who hold the Aghori in high esteem, consulting them to foretell the future, provide charms and rituals, curses, healings, and guidance.

BUDDHIST MYSTICISM

In order to gain an appreciation for the variety of mystical forms and practices identified within Buddhism, it is necessary to present the three basic roots of mystical tradition identified through the following branches: (1) Hinayana also known as *Theravada*, (2) *Mahayana,* and (3) *Vajrayana* or Tibetan Buddhism. As a consequence, the three streams presented will only address specific identifying protocols as they pertain to mysticism in its variance. Of note, however, is the fact that although each of these major streams of Buddhism embody within their own religious structures many different schools of thought and devotion through discipleship, they still retain at their core the dharma of the Buddha, the four noble truths, the skandhas, impermanence, emptiness, reincarnation, and nirvana. From all mystical perspectives, the central aim is to achieve detachment from the physical, grow in compassion and balance within the consciousness, and finally achieve liberation or nirvana which is synonymous with moksha.

Development of the Traditions

As previously noted, Buddhism developed out of the matrix of Hinduism, through the teachings of an Indian reformer named Siddhartha Gautama (563-483 B.C.E.), also known as Shakymuni. Siddhartha is considered to be the ultimate Buddha (one who attained full enlightenment) and the historical development of the philosophy[37] dating back to the fifth century addresses the special enlightened nature or, as a contrast, the supramundane essence of their founder.[38] In addition to this, and as a consequence of its Hindu antecedents, Buddhism shares certain root ideas on mysticism regarding illusion, enlightenment, transmigration, nirvana, and the possibility of cessation of suffering. However, the philosophy, which is now referred to by many as the *Tradition*, was originally atheistic in outlook and this original form can be identified as Theravada. It was only, however, over the course of a few centuries following the death of Siddhartha, that certain Buddhist groups, identified as the Mahayanists, felt the need to reintroduce conceptual forms of deities and include within their beliefs the compassionate and saving role of the *Bodhisattva* as a particular inspiration for the laity.[39] What this means is that the earliest Buddhist traditions are completely devoid of deities within their interpretations of the mystical or enlightened meditational experience. They are atheistic in their cosmology and undertake meditation, leading to focused concentration and altered states through visualizing and nurturing Buddha nature or Dharmakaya, which is the truth body within them.[40] This leads to the true understanding of emptiness or *shunyata*, and the concept of impermanence and detachment. Concentrating on these teachings, meditating Buddhists endeavour to achieve deep trance states through which they may gain true enlightenment on the path to nirvana either in this lifetime or after innumerable rebirths. There is no visualization of specific Bodhisattva-type superior entities within Hinayana tradition, which is also referred to as *Theravada*, and means *Way of the Elders* or *Doctrine of the Elders*.

On the other hand, there will be other traditions, known as the *Mahayanist* school, that focus on visualizing glorious Buddhas and/or Bodhisattvas, in order to aid them on their mystical paths. This potentially offers them the prospect of a personal encounter, full of wonder or encouragement, with the hope of a more auspicious reincarnation, or inspire them to achieve liberation in their lifetime.

Mahayana is referred to as the *Greater Vehicle* due to its more widespread popularity throughout most of East Asia and now North America.

Another Mahayanist sect, considered to be the most widespread Buddhist school in East Asia, is named *Pure Land Buddhism*. Pure Land originated in India but found popular acceptance in China, Japan, Korea, Vietnam, Thailand, and Myomar, and it concentrates on the form of a particular salvific Buddha named Amitabha or Amida Buddha.[41] Known as the Buddha of Boundless Light, this Buddha, in Pure Land cosmology, represents the closest equivalent to a devotional monotheism that can be identified in Buddhism as a whole.[42] For many within the Pure Land sect there exists the belief in an unlimited after-death lifespan, dwelling with Amitabha, in his realm of infinite light if they concentrate on him and live out his dharma for ten consecutive rebirths.[43]

On the other hand, to illustrate how contradictory or paradoxical Mahayana sects can be regarding the path of mysticism, *Soto Zen Buddhism* developed out of the need to return to primitive Buddhist belief and practice.[44] It presents itself as deist insofar as there is a belief in an impersonal force, somewhat like Nirguna Brahman. On the other hand, the sect does not seek out this force or even the answers to subjective questions. It believes that metaphysical questions cannot be resolved, such as the nature of God, the afterlife, reincarnation, or nirvana, because as such, the questions only impair mindfulness. Soto Zen focuses only on the here and now, together with right practice as elucidated in the Eightfold Path taught by Buddha. Through rigorous hours of meditation, Soto Zen teaches that a sense of deep mindfulness, and the inner experience of intuition or *prajna*,[45] leading to or out of *samadhi—or full consciousness—*can be achieved. One is enabled to be deeply conscious of the present moment and merge or be absorbed into all things.

Vajrayana or Tibetan Buddhism is arguably the most elaborate form of Mahayana that has evolved over the centuries.[46] In the seventh century C.E. Buddhist missionaries from India began to press northward to a new region in Central Asia—the isolated Himalayan mountains of Tibet. What the Buddhist missionary monks encountered in the region was an indigenous shamanistic religious practice called *bon* (pronounced "pern") which focused on possession trances, altered states of consciousness, and the worship and/or appeasement of many spirits, both benign and malevolent, together with animistic beliefs and worship of natural phenomenon. The shamans communicated with the spirit world and the people generally offered animal sacrifices.

The first missionary monks[47] from India enjoyed only limited success. It was not until the monk Padmasambhava, who was himself a tantric practitioner, reintroduced Mayahana into Tibet in the eight century C.E. that the tradition began to successfully establish itself. It did this through converting the shamans to Buddhism and as Mayahana Buddhism contained a strong element of tantricism inherited from its Indian tradition, a syncretization occurred whereby elements of tantricism and altered states fused into the Tibetan evolution of Buddhism, or *Vajrayana*.[48] This specific type of Buddhism, created in Tibet through the interaction between Indian Tantricism and Tibetan culture, was and is still often termed *Lamaism,* referring to *lama*, or one who has reached the highest pinnacle of tantric expertise and is regarded as a spiritual master.[49] In addition to this, in some instances, even female adepts can be regarded as incarnate bodhisattvas, and are trained from an early age to assist others less enlightened in the path of Vajrayana so that the followers may experience and comprehend "the clear light of bliss."[50] In addition to all this, there is a specific form of Vajrayana that is still practiced, albeit discretely, which focuses on sexual practices and disciplines. This is a very esoteric form of tantricism which has its origins in early Buddhist tradition when it is thought that some monks rejected the strict celibacy required under the teachings of Siddhartha. Most of its male traditional practitioners today are either wandering holy men known as yogins or laity as most monks observe the traditional abstinence requirements.

Vajrayana mysticism centres on methods of visualization including deity yoga which means meditating on one of the many visual forms of deities or Bodhisattvas that embody specific qualities or powers that the practitioner wishes to experience. This ritual projection of divine powers will then be incorporated into the physical body and also absorbed into the consciousness. There is also the use of *mantras* or sacred words, which are in themselves considered to possess great power and can be used in a variety of ways, including some which can manifest as supernatural powers, such as levitation and clairvoyance.[51]

Chinese Mysticism

Within this category there are three core religious systems that can be identified as central to mysticism: (1) Taoism,[52] (2) Confucianism,[53] and (3) Buddhism. As Buddhism was a later chronological addition to Chinese cosmology,[54] and the main ideas within the Buddhist system have been previously discussed, suffice it to say that the Chinese ideas on this tradition will retain the basic Mahayanist themes, but will also include, in the particularly Chinese way, the worship of ancestral and other spirits.[55] It will also include in its popular varieties found with its many branches, ideas that are shamanistic and also animistic as Chinese Buddhism integrates a general culture of the supernatural that it acquired from Taoism and to a degree, even Confucianism.[56] Of note also is the fact that there is an enduring Christian[57] representation in Chinese culture which, by virtue of its very different approach to mysticism, will try to avoid (although not always very successfully) ideas regarding supernatural elements that may manifest. As the whole Chinese system is very complex, the general Christian tradition will be addressed separately under Christian mysticism.

The Taoist cosmology has its beginnings in ancient roots dating back to early tribal cosmologies, settlements, and civilizations; and as such, Taoism as it evolved, incorporated, reflected, and sometimes adapted the enduring ideas of its early antecedents. Archaeological excavations of settlements in the Yellow River Valley have provided evidence of written language existing around 2000 B.C.E., together with material evidence establishing the existence of musical instruments, silk, ceramic, and bronze metallurgy. What has also been established is the centrality of ancestor veneration keeping the deceased happy and closely bonded to their living descendants. This was done in order to please, pacify, and also placate the spirit of an offended or angry ancestor.[58] Dating back to the earliest dynasty, the Shang (c 1751–1123 B.C.E.), there are artifacts that come to us today establishing the use of oracle bones to foretell the future and discern current events. Another integral part of these early cosmologies was the belief in demons and ghosts who caused misery for the living and charms that deflected evil, together with incantations, gongs, and firecrackers were used to keep them at bay. There was also the popular use of shamans and local mediums, prayers, incense, exorcisms, and spirit walls acting as blockades that were placed on door posts or located in various parts of surrounding areas around homes. Further, entrenched beliefs in animism, with the flow of forces and nature spirits that permeated the physical world, meant that offerings were required to establish communication between humans and spirits, which again called for the expertise of a sensitive such as a mystical practitioner, medium, and/or shaman.[59] Interestingly enough, to varying degrees, these beliefs and ritual practices continue to this day. It is out of this social matrix and constellation of cosmologies[60] that Taoism evolved and established itself as one of the central influences in Chinese mystical reality. Indeed, so powerful was the entrenchment of ancient cosmologies that Taoism, with its varying concepts of the Tao, developed out of this and also to a degree influenced its contemporary philosophical tradition of Confucianism, which in turn also influenced Taoism!

Daoist ideas regarding mysticism find their foundation in their sacred text the *Daodejing*, which is believed to have been written by a hermit mystic, prophet named Lao Tzu, was in full harmony with the universe through his realization of cosmic truth and its power[61]—the force of the Tao. The *Daodejing* can be read in many ways as follows: philosophical, ethical text; political and military stratagem; scientific attitude towards the cosmos; or a utopian tract. It is however, "primarily a cosmological interpretation of the universe and it provided instruction on how to live in perfect harmony with the universe."[62]

The Tao cannot be described, named, or known; it can only be intuitively perceived. It is transcendent, yet immanent, and although not part of the universe, creates, orders, and flows through it. It

is this very essence that the mystic tries to perceive or sense through concentration on the Tao. The mystical experience is described as progression to a higher consciousness in an ecstatic state, in which a person is completely unconscious of outer things, and absorbed in the knowledge of the Transcendent. In later developments, Taoism also incorporated ideas of immortality and the man who had achieved this high state of consciousness was believed to transcend even physical death. Even though the corpse might be laid within the tomb it was merely an illusion because the real physical body had become ethereal and had entered the Sacred Island of Paradise.[63] For some monks/adepts this is still considered to be a functioning dimension of their tradition.

In addition to this highly esoteric and refined path, however, there is also the Taoism of popular culture. This form of mysticism still incorporates all the ancient ideas about mediums, shamans/monks, ancestors, spirits, curses, possession states, altered states of consciousness, fortune telling, and the Tao which manifests through animism.

In Confucianism, the Tao was and is interpreted as primarily the way of life for men and women, not as it was interpreted in Taoism as the supreme Reality or force. Central to Confucian mysticism, is the concept of *imperturbability of mind*,[64] which is a much desired condition of inner quiet and calm. It is therefore through proper actions that one accumulates righteousness and becomes sincere and fully real, by being on the right path as this path bestows a quality of being which belongs intrinsically to Heaven but is realized "in a state of spontaneous harmony with the law of his being."[65]

Once again, however, there is a different and more complex aspect to Confucian mysticism in so far as it will, just like Taoism, also contain the ancient beliefs of shamanistic traditions, and will keep as a central observance, ideas about luck, fortune telling, the ritual of ancestor worship, and the placation of spirits human, animal or ghostly. All these will be considered part of their mystical reality.

Nativistic/Tribal Mysticism

When discussing the tribal systems an unavoidable problem arises due to the many complex and differing rituals that can be identified. The reality is that there are so many different groupings of cultural clusters in the world that one comprehensive perspective of mystical practice is impossible to formulate. To appreciate some of the complexity consider the fact that there are approximately

3,000 tribal systems remaining in Africa; 750 in the United States; different groupings in the Maori New Zealand traditions that retain many tribal practices but have assimilated into urban society. There are also approximately 500 tribal systems among the Australian indigenous peoples, and an estimated 600 dialects that are living languages within those clan systems. In addition to this, the numbering of tribes in the Amazon rainforest indicates that there are 400 identifiable tribes, each with their own language and culture. The final census, however, has yet to be completed as there are many unidentified tribes still to be contacted. In China there are 55 minority groups, not including the Han whose population form the majority representation, but who themselves have varying traditions within their cultural systems. In addition to this, and to make the task of explaining mysticism even more challenging, consider the fact that on the Indian subcontinent there are a total of 645 district tribes under of "Scheduled Tribes," referring to specific indigenous peoples who are classified separately from that of the mainstream Hindu population.

What can be generally agreed upon through the extraction of information from the data at hand, is that there are certain identifiable perceptions and experiences, or patterns, that form the basis of the general tribal understandings of mysticism. At the centre of this mystical tradition lie the beliefs and practice of shamanism, which is a generally hereditary office. The shaman is central in a tribal system due to his/her ability to enter into altered ecstatic states in and through which the spirit doctor/shamanic intermediary contacts the unseen.[66] These intermediaries function as experts

in supernatural healings, exorcisms, séances, ghosts, curses, together with the lifting of them, in the worship of various spirit beings, coupled with leadership in central tribal rituals. In addition to this, there are others who are not considered to be shamans, but whose trance states make them prophets or mediums and who are commonly believed to be vehicles for spirit possession from ancestors, ghosts, totemic spirits,[67] and sometimes nature spirits to convey messages to the people.[68] In addition to this, in most encounters with the unseen, there is the customary use of drums, songs, dances, rhythmic chants, and quite frequently, according to the tribal grouping, hallucinogenics of various kinds in order to create the desired emotional receptivity. These shifted perceptional responses can be manifested through dream states and states of altered consciousness for the shaman, medium, or leader of a particular ritual and also for the participant who has sought their special touch.

ABRAHAMIC MYSTICISM

In the Abrahamics there is an identifiable common monotheistic thread. Further, what is contained within this thematic commonality is a consensus that there is some form of supersensory communication between the created/human personality and the Creator of that personality—God. The Abrahamics, although differing greatly in their perspective on the encounter and explanation of God, possess central concepts which shape and identify their religious experience as contact with their one true Creator. Although perceiving or believing in different ways that one may approach this salvific being due to their major variances in belief about accessing this great God of Abraham, each of the traditions hold that God is *transcendent* yet *immanent, omnipotent, omniscient, omnipresent*, and beloved in an intimate, awe-filled relationship. God as Creator is thus supremely different and set apart from God's creation, yet at the same time, through grace and love interacts with his followers. It is by and through this reciprocal relationship that God grants salvation, forgiveness of sins, love, and enlightenment to those who seek him and it is this encounter which lies at the very heart of the interactive experience identified as mysticism. This is the quality of a mystical experience that delves more deeply into a close relationship with God; it is a possibility open to the earnest seeker, although experienced in varying degrees according to each of the three cosmologies. Through the practice of mysticism, the seeker will embrace the reality of God through a supra-consciousness known as *perceiving God*.

Jewish Mysticism

As previously discussed, Judaism is the oldest of the Abrahamic traditions. The religion comes to us today having developed over thousands of years and as such contains certain longstanding ideas on mysticism. In the development of ancient Hebrew and then Israelite traditions there were pivotal ideas and teachings concerning the Prophets of Israel who encountered Yahweh in a mystical way. Indeed, central to the formation, development, and preservation of the Jewish perception of God (Yahweh) has been a collection of sacred writings referred to as the Hebrew Bible or Tanakh. The Tanakh is derived from the acrostic TNK which stands for: T—Torah (Teachings, also called the Pentateuch), N— Nev'im (the Prophets), K— Ketuv'im (Writings); and together these writings form the core authority for Jewish identity to this day. Within the category of the Nev'im there are nineteen books which are acknowledged to be prophetic record. These prophets were mystics and were described or referred to by a number of terms due to the nature of their ministry and calling. They were called prophets, seers, watchmen, men of God, messengers, and servants of the Lord. According to I Samuel 9:9, the prophet was in earlier Israel commonly called a *ro'eh*, or one who perceives that which does not lie in the realm of natural sight or hearing. Another early designation of similar etymology was a *hozeh*, or "one who sees supernaturally" (II Samuel 24:11).

A later development was that the Israelite seer became more commonly referred to as a nabhi' (I Samuel 9:9). This popular name is related to the Akkadian term 'nabu', "to call or announce," either passively, one who is called" (by God), or actively "an announcer." Also the term can be construed to mean that the prophet is the passive recipient of a message manifest in his condition as well as in his speech, and is "one who is in the state of announcing a message which has been given to him" (by God). The text would introduce the revelation by stating, "The Word of the Lord came to me" or "The Word of the Lord came to …" As a mouthpiece or spokesman for God, the prophet's primary duty was to proclaim God's message in the historical context of what was happening among God's people and it was their prophetic duty to admonish, reprove, denounce, threaten with the terrors of judgment, call to repentance, and bring consolation and pardon. The activity of rebuking sin and calling for repentance consumed more of the prophets' time than any other feature of their work. It was from this established revelatory experience that the concept of revelation, interpretation, and communication developed in such a broadened context that the altered states became synonymous with the mystical experience as the centuries passed.[69]

From this established mystical tradition, in its many forms and hues throughout the centuries, Judaism developed. This is a contentious issue, however, because for many scholars who dispute the validity of the prophetic mystical stream in the Tanakh, the practice of mysticism did not begin until between the second to the sixth century c.e., with the development of *Merkavah*—meaning *chariot*—Mysticism, or *Mysticism of the Divine Throne* and was developed in Palestine and Babylon.[70] In this early form of mysticism the mystic made a visionary journey through the palaces of the seven heavens. The final goal of this journey was the privilege of beholding God, who was seated on his glorious throne in the seventh palace of the seventh heaven. These practices were highly esoteric and rigorously guarded by the rabbis who practiced this mystical discipline; thus the ordinary layperson was barred from the experience. What does remain of this tradition is a corpus of literature recording the early esoteric traditions as well as mystical reports of the chariot journey through the heavenly realms and the descriptions of the throne of glory. This material collectively is known as Hekhaloth literature (which means *palace*).[71]

During the second half of the twelfth century c.e., two mystical currents developed, one through the Ashkenazi Hassidim[72] in Germany and the second, known as Kabbalah, in Provence and the Iberian Peninsular.[73] Kabbalah became a powerful movement and it is still a popular means of mystical expression in Judaism today with a central text entitled the *Sefer ha-Zohar* or "Book of Splendour" which is held to be the main Kabbalistic work. Although traditionally said to date back to the first century c.e., the Zohar in its present form is most likely the writing of the thirteenth-century writer Moses de Leon (c.1240–1305) who compiled the Zohar from a combination of his own ideas and contemporary Kabbalistic elements.[74] The text itself is the elaboration and interpretation of scripture verses from the Torah often in the form of obscure mystical allegorizations.[75]

As the heart of Kabbalah lie teachings concerning the tree of life and the ten sefiroth which represent characteristics of the divine Ein Sof—God. There are ten names given to the mystical "emanations" or essences of God and each are considered to be revealed aspects or lights of the hidden deity—regarded as the faces of God directed towards the world. In and of themselves, they do not say anything about the deepest nature of the hidden life of the deity, but form the side of God that is turned towards the world which is knowable and can be experienced by humans.[76] Each sefiroth must be encountered separately, and in a progressive growth of understanding. This forms the mystical experience which is encountered through deep prayer and meditation on the individual sefiroth and the essence of Ein Sof himself.[77]

Judaism Tree of Life

The most recent development within Jewish mysticism is Hassidim, which is not to be confused with the earlier Ashkenazi movement in the twelfth century. What makes this development of such interest is the fact that it brought mysticism to the ordinary person who was often from the more disadvantaged groups within the Jewish social system. Initially it was a movement of protest and alienation that developed in Poland, Ukraine, Lithuania, and Belorussia against the rigidity of the rabbinic ruling class. The popularity of the movement and its demographics served to illustrate the growing social gulf between the unlettered poor, who had no funds to contribute to mainstream Judaism, and the wealthy and scholarly elite. The upper echelons of society, such as the scholarly elite, exhibited a deepening contempt for the masses whom they referred to as *am ha-arets,* which means the people of the land; flowing out of this, the Jewish elite actually believed that an illiterate Jew was not capable of true piety. This tension is believed to have contributed to the emergence of a new mystical movement known as *Hasidism.*[78]

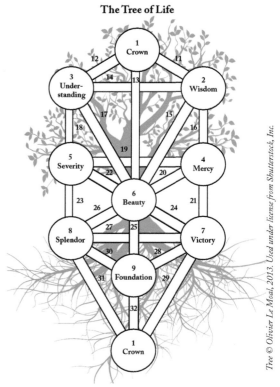

The Tree of Life

Tree © Olivier Le Moal, 2013. Used under license from Shutterstock, Inc.

According to general Hasidic tradition, the man credited with bringing mysticism, and therefore a direct contact with God to the people, was an impoverished and supposedly illiterate rabbi by the name of Israel ben Eliezer (ca. 1700–1760), later referred to as Ba'al Shem Tov (Master of the Good). What is known of Ba'al Shem Tov is that he was a mystic who was knowledgeable of practical Kabbalah, which was the side of the tradition that dealt with magic and its practical applications. The Besht (anagram composed from the name Ba'al Shem Tov) sought a direct mystical experience of God known as *devequth,* or cleaving to God. Due to the fact that the Besht did not stress or even practice a rigorous study of the Torah and Talmud, his movement, initially consisting of a small group of mystics, gradually spread to the uneducated populace, both men and women, where it developed into a powerful mystical community. The emphasis of this movement was on cleaving to God through meditative and ecstatic prayer, special concentration or meditation, inspiration derived from the twelfth-century Ashkenazi Hasidim, and from special sources of Kabbalah which emphasized concentration on letters, words, names, and sentences from traditional prayers to the sefiroth. The motivation behind these practices for the common, uneducated person, as well as their spiritual leaders, was to live in a constant state of *devequth*, so that one's whole physical and emotional life could be lived in the glorious presence of God.

The movement went through many adaptations but still exists in the form the tsaddikim and their communities. Each community of hasidim will follow a charismatic spiritual leader known as a rebbe or tsaddik and will place great emphasis on his inspired, mystical, and practical leadership using traditional esoteric practices.[79]

CHRISTIAN MYSTICISM

Christianity has its doctrinal roots in mysticism, and an emotional interaction with God was a central part of its early teachings. These concepts can be clearly identified in the Gospels as follows: the Synoptics (Mark, Matthew, Luke) all present Jesus as a mystic and a miracle worker of exceptional quality. Of note is the fact that nearly one-fifth of the entire gospels are devoted to Jesus' healing and discussions surrounding his power because Jesus is recorded as asserting that the source of his power was the Holy Spirit. Further, in John's Gospel, which is considered to be the Trinitarian Gospel because it presents the concept of God the Father, God the Son, and God the Holy Spirit, there is the presentation of a mystical worldview and purpose. This gospel depicts the strongest and most consistent portrayal of the mystical Jesus as healer, discerner, and raiser of the dead, who is God the Son or the Word made flesh.

John, the Mystic

John's Gospel is also referred to as the "mystical handbook" of the Christian Church as the content speaks to an intensely intimate relationship between Jesus and God and exhibits all the signs of mysticism. Jesus constantly referred to God as the Father, who was always with him. Jesus was himself taught by the Father, he heard truth from the Father, what he spoke and declared was what he heard from the Father and he received his authority from the Father.[80]

After the death and resurrection of Jesus Christ, the church developed its belief in the power of the Holy Spirit and in the mystical states. The gift of the Holy Spirit to the believers at Pentecost was and is seen as the fulfillment of Jesus' promise to send the *Paraclete* (Holy Spirit) to his followers. The

Holy Spirit would be given as the guide for believers until Jesus returned. The gift would involve supernatural mystical powers of prophecy, dreams and visions, the power to heal, and the power to preach or bear witness to who Jesus was. Thus, mysticism was a central tenet of early Christianity and was seen as a gift given to males and females, freemen or slave, and was to be experienced by Jewish Christians and Gentile Christians alike. Paul, as the apostle to the Gentiles, was also a recipient of the gift of the Holy Spirit and displayed many mystical attributes. It is recorded that he too expected all believers to receive this mark because they had become children of God, through Jesus Christ.

Further evidence of this concept is to be found in many of the early records of the acetic third, fourth and fifth century wilderness dwelling *Desert Fathers* and *Desert Mothers*,[81] the teachings of the *Church Fathers,* and in the written works ascribed to the notable and theologically influential male and female mystics in the early Middle Ages through to the twentieth century. In this material it is the norm to find the orthodox doctrine of Jesus as divine.

There were, however, elements that were not orthodox in faith and these can be identified as an enduring system of Gnostic traditions from the mid to late second and then third centuries C.E. These different interpretations of Christianity in their rejection of certain elements of Christ's divinity or humanity have also presented different perspectives and experiences of mysticism which bear more similarity to pagan mystic cults and mystery religions than they do the traditional New Testament mystical profile.

Whereas traditional Christian mysticism had presented an open account of the Holy Spirit and the mystical encounter with this Person, the Christian Gnostics dealt with mysteries and levels or degrees of understanding which were considered secret. The Gnostic tradition stressed initiation into divine mysteries and taught that as such, anyone who had gone through the process of the revelation was the possessor of esoteric teachings, or hidden knowledge that was not accessible to most human beings. These groups were many in number and formed no single body or consensus of creed. In many ways, these were the successors to the Egyptian, Greek, and Roman mystery religions and, due to their code of secrecy, no extensive record of their practices remains. What we do know is that they produced cosmologies and cosmogonies (the creation of the world or universe; a theory or account of such creation) that differed greatly from the account found in the Jewish scriptures.[83] Some denied that Jesus the Christ actually bore a physical human body, and thus he could not have experienced a literal death and resurrection. Others denied his divinity, whilst others denied his humanity. In addition to this, the Gnostic interpretation of the Holy Spirit was very different to that of the orthodox. The traditional belief system as presented in the New Testament acknowledged the immanence of the transcendent God through the agency of the Holy Spirit who indwelt, comforted, and sanctified the human believer. In contrast to this, the Gnostic interpretation emphasized that the Holy Spirit was Sophia, the Goddess of Wisdom, and that it was not until the Spirit descended upon the man Jesus at his baptism, that he became the instrument through whom Christ spoke. In addition to this, the Spirit, or Sophia, had left him before the crucifixion because the divine cannot die or be associated with sin. This meant that the Spirit had only a brief and tenuous association with matter and humanity, which in turn rendered the central teachings of permanent indwelling for the Christian believer, and salvation from sin, through the sacrificial atonement of the physical and divine Christ, null and void.[84] The Gnostic beliefs, therefore, clashed with core Christian beliefs and was for the most part rejected by the emerging orthodoxy of the New Testament.

In studying mainstream Christian mysticism it is the individual accounts and interpretations of the various writers which provide insight into their special perspectives. The mystical tradition of Christianity presents an active system which can be identified through the classifications of: (1) early church, (2) early Middle Ages, (3) Franciscan[85] (from St. Francis of Assisi), (4) English Medieval, (5) German and Flemish, (6) the two Catherines,[86] (7) Spanish, (8) French seventeenth century, (9) Protestant, and (10) Modern.[87] What is fascinating to note is that in spite of persecution leveled against them by opponents (often within their own churches), and despite traditional sectarian, cultural, and time differences, they all routinely explained a particular state of conscious union with God known as *orison*.[88] In this state, the consciousness is fully awake and aware as regards to God, but the necessity or drives within the self and the physical are unimportant and shrink to nothing. In other words, the self beholds the beloved God and is wrapped up in union within his presence; all else pales in comparison. In essence, this experience is at the root of all interactive, worshipful mystical encounters, and it is known as participatory engagement.

ISLAMIC MYSTICISM

Islam, as a cosmological system, stresses total obedience and love for Allah, which is demonstrated through submission to his revelations, received by the Prophet Muhammad. In general Islamic thought the Five Pillars of Islam provide a structure for the manifestation of the obedience through observance and submission and, for the majority of Muslims, is at the very centre of their experience of Allah. There were and are, however, those who have always sought a closer, experiential encounter with the transcendent that would bring into their very being a sense of Allah in immanence and presence. These people belong to Islamic mysticism and are referred to as Sufis from the Arabic word for wool, which is *suf*. As Muslim ascetics distanced themselves from worldly attachment, they are believed to have adopted course woolen raiments as the symbol for their path. This in turn led to the mystics being termed *Sufis*.[89]

Historically, it is also clear that there were monotheistic ascetics in the Arabian peninsula who predated seventh-century Islam and who were also considered to be holy men and referred to as hanif mystics, so the tradition itself is of ancient lineage. A primitive Sufism, as part of the tradition that spilled over into Islam, had an early presence in the religion and it is out of this tradition that an identifiable mystical Islamic movement evolved.[90] One of the greatest early mystics who reflected this earthy, raw, and powerful tradition was the renowned eighth-century Rabi'a al-'Adawiya (717–801)[91] who was known to practice extreme austerities but to always be filled with love for Allah.

The main development of Sufism arose out of a desire for more than what mainstream established Islam was teaching. It voiced a need felt by many to devote the whole self to Allah and to experience a direct connection with him. Historically, in the broader context, this movement was originally a counterculture protest against the worldliness of the Umayyad (661–750 C.E.) and Abbasid (724–961 C.E.) Caliphates.[92] It encouraged the rejection of wealth and class distinctions and based

itself on the simpler lives led by Muhammad and the first Caliphs, and many of the male ascetics assumed the life of poor wandering dervishes called *faqirs*.

The Sufi mystics also contested certain features of Orthodox Islam that they regarded as orthodox legalism due to the mainstream tenets of orthopraxy (right ritual practice) and orthodoxy (stringent emphasis on right teaching and theology), which they perceived as working to stultify emotional Islamic faith—*iman*. They were against the intellectualism of theologians and proclaimed the importance of intuitive mystical experience of Allah, known as *ma'rifa*. This encounter, delivered through a mystical experience, was indescribable by human language and this led the movement to use paradoxes and riddles, dancing, music, and rhythmic chanting inducing altered states, in order to express the unfathomable nature of Allah.

Sufism encouraged a desire for inner, personal experience of the divine, through a deep meditational process known as *tariqa* (the inner way of meditation, which is the path). This, they claimed, contrasted with *shari'ah* the outer path (the outer path of law). Although not fully dismissing *shari'ah*, the Sufi perspective was and is that observance of "outer" Muslim law is only a first step to help sever attachment to earthly things. There were other Sufis who were inspired to open violation of the law in order to indicate that they had transcended it. There was also a tendency to erase separation between the mystic and God, in direct opposition to a primary orthodox Islamic teaching which maintains a clear separation between the believer and Allah that cannot be breached. This blurring of orthodox Quran'ic theology sometimes led to accusations of blasphemy and Sufis found themselves in conflict with orthodox leadership.[93]

At the heart of this ancient mystical belief system is the Sufi emphasis on *fana,* which is the complete denial of self as part of the process toward true realization of God and merging into Him.[94] Still a central configuration in the Sufi tradition, *fana* can be attained by constant meditation and contemplation on the attributes of God. It is taught that when Sufis succeed in purifying themselves entirely of the earthly world and lose self in the love of God, they have "annihilated" individual will and "passed away" from their own existence to live only in God and with God. This is somewhat different from mainstream Islamic thought. The reason for this is that while all Muslims are instructed to believe that they are on the pathway to God, eventually becoming close to Him in Paradise, after death and the Final Judgment or Day of Doom, Sufis believe that it is possible to become close to God and to experience this closeness through *fana* whilst still alive.

Sufism, however, recognizes, as does mainstream Islam, that there exists barriers that the mystic must always be aware of. The barriers came by way of the *nafs,* or soul, which also means self, psyche, or ego.[95] In its unrefined state, "the ego (nafs) is the lowest dimension of man's inward existence, and can mean an animalistic and satanic nature which incites one to sin." This part of one's nature varies to differing degrees within humans, but it is a force to always be reckoned with. The other two parts to the nafs are (1) the self-accusing nafs—the voice of an awakened conscience; and (2) the nafs at peace, which represents the ideal state for the ego where one is strong in faith and actions and satisfied with the will of God through submission.

CONCLUSION

The encounters, traditions, and experiences of mysticism, as this chapter has demonstrated, are enormously varied and often contradictory. Nevertheless, what can be adduced from the many perspectives presented is that there is a reality behind the mystical search—a common thread of need, no matter the cosmology. The fact is that mysticism as a phenomenon is an integral part of religious experience. Whatever the religion, no matter how diverse in development, the mystical experience functions as an integral and enduring aspect of human need in the encounter with physical and metaphysical realities.

GLOSSARY

Advaita Vedanta: Hindu concept of liberation/release by experientially recognizing identity of the self (Atman) and the whole (Brahman). Concept of non-dualism pertaining to Nirguna Brahman, or God without attributes. Process of liberating knowledge requires long preparation and training, which is usually under the guidance of a guru. It requires rigorous training through knowledge of scriptures, renunciation of worldy activities, and the inducement of direct identity experiences to "realize" the identity of Atman and Brahman as one.

Altered states of consciousness (ASC): All religious traditions will accept that there are certain spiritual experiences which are distinctive in the way that the devotee experiences a change in perception. These are marked as existing outside of the normal religious experiences. A variety of religious traditions will accept that there are religious specialists who can enter an ASC for the purpose of contacting the metaphysical spirit realm. These specialists are able to gain knowledge, insight, teaching, and guidance which they then utilize in the physical world. NOTE: Mystics who claim to enter an ASC will attest to enlightenment from God, the Universe, Buddha, etc. The testimonies and claims of mystics and spirit meditators regarding this ability are generally met with great skepticism among the majority of scientists in Western society. Other researchers, especially those in the field of parapsychology, maintain that proponents of Western scientific materialism must recognize the value of studying ASCs because there are many kinds of supra-consciousness.

Animism: The religious belief that natural phenomena, including animals, plants, and sometimes even inanimate natural objects, possess a spiritual essence or mana. This force can be communicated with, feared, and observed. It is often worshipped in its manifestations.

Bodhisattva: One who achieves enlightenment but vows to postpone nirvana and Buddhahood until all can be saved. They therefore undergo samsara for the sake of others in order to save them by bringing them to enlightenment.

Daodejing: Sacred text in Taoism; believed to have been authored by the sage Laozi. According to the text, Laozi is considered to be a mystic and a hermit.

Desert Fathers and Desert Mothers: Hermits, ascetics, and renunciates. Lived mainly in the Scetes desert of Egypt at beginning around the third century C.E. They abandoned the pagan cities

and Christians fleeing the chaos and persecution of the Roman Empire's Crisis of the Third Century. They were often sought after for wisdom on guidance by both males and pilgrims and records of these events date back to the fourth century C.E.

Devequth: Mystical experience of cleaving to God in Hasidism.

Diabolical: An emotional experience based on a delusional state. A "sort of religious mysticism turned upside down," according to William James. The person encounters a sort of ineffability which controls the individual. In this state the recipient may hear voices, see visions, obtain teachings, and receive commissions and missions. Have an unbalanced sense of importance, which is often accompanied by paranoia and persecution complexes. It will be negative and destructive in character, often providing the rationale for violence, killing sprees, and hatred.

Fana: Sufi mystical state. The complete denial of self, the realization of God and union with Him. Attained by constant meditation and contemplation on the attributes of God, coupled with the denunciation of human attributes. When the Sufi succeeds in purifying himself entirely of the earthly world and loses himself in the love of God, it is said that he has "annihilated" his individual will and "passed away" from his own existence to live only in God and with God.

Hasidism: In Judaism, term used to designate one whose spiritual devotion extends beyond the technical requirements of Jewish religious law. Describes a sect of Jewish mystics founded in Poland about 1750 that was and is characterized by religious zeal and a spirit of prayer, joy, and charity.

Immanence: Theories of divine presence, in which the divine is seen to be manifested in or encompassing the material world.

Imperturbability of mind: Confucian concept which denotes a condition of inner quiet and calm.

Mahayana: Known as the greater vehicle; is the more widespread demonstration of Buddhism due to its greater openness for the laity, the concept of accessible Buddhas and Bodhisattvas. In this tradition, there are many different sects.

Mana: Spiritual force or energy that is believed to permeate nature and natural phenomenon.

Mantra: Sacred word or syllable used as an object of concentration and embodying some aspect of spiritual power. Used in prayer, meditation, or incantation.

Nafs: In Islam refers to the soul, ego, or self. There are three levels or states of nafs: the evil, base part to our nature; the conscience; and the soul at peace.

Omnipotent: God who is infinite in power and authority over all things. No power or force can ever stand to overcome His divine nature as author and ruler of all things.

Omnipresent: An attribute of God by which He is present everywhere at the same time.

Omniscient: Pertaining to God who perfectly and eternally knows all things which can be known, past, present, and future. God knows how best to attain His desired ends.

Orison: Christian mystical state. The mystic's consciousness is fully awake and aware as regards to God, but the necessity or drives within the self and the physical are unimportant and shrink to nothing as they are permeated with the presence of God and interaction they have with Him.

Prajna: Wisdom, understanding, discernment, insight, or cognitive acuity. It is one of three divisions of the Noble Eightfold Path which are virtue, concentration, and wisdom.

Sadhu: Hindu holy man, a renunciate; a wandering ascetic who lives in caves, temples, or forests. He will revoke all ties to family, sexuality, and material attachments. Can be found in India and Nepal.

Samadhi: A conscious experience that lies beyond waking, dreaming, and deep sleep. This state of consciousness is often referred to as "one-pointedness of mind." Pursued through deep meditation and yogic practices.

Sefer ha-Zohar: Held to be the most authoritative Kabbalistic work, written by Moses de Leon.

Shakti: In Hinduism, the primordial cosmic energy; considered to represent the dynamic forces that move through the entire universe. Is the concept, or personification of divine feminine creative power, referred to as The Great Divine Mother. Believed to manifest through female embodiment and creativity/fertility and also considered to be present although hidden in masculine nature.

Tantricism: Instructions from the scriptures (Tantras) on how to honor the feminine divine. Series of practices and techniques, through yogic meditation and ritual, aimed at balancing the mind and focusing it on spiritual concepts. These practices are believed to possess important spiritual, astrological, or magical benefits in the Tantric traditions of the Indian religions. The female energy is considered to be the life animating force, which when coupled with the transcendent but inactive male force creates life itself. Linked to sexual practices which join the male and female. Popular with married couples.

Therevada: The earliest form of Buddhism. It is known as the *Way of the Elders* or *Doctrine of the Elders*. It represents atheistic Buddhism, with no need for gods. Emphasis in on enlightenment alone, which is usually believed to be something only the ordained monks and some nuns can achieve.

Transcendent: As pertaining to God, who exists above and independent from all other things in heaven and earth. God created all things, yet exists above and independent from them. All things are upheld by His mighty power, yet He is upheld by Himself alone.

Vajrayana: From the term *vajra*, which refers to the indestructible substance of the religious tradition. The term is sometimes translated as "adamantine" or "diamond." Thus it can be referred to as the *diamond vehicle*.

ENDNOTES

1. Ralph W. Hood, Jr. et al, *The Psychology of Religion,* (New York: the Guilford Press, 2009), p 331.
2. Ibid., pp 333, 335.
3. William James, *The Varieties of Religious Experience,* (New York: Random House, 1994), pp 300-301.
4. Walter Terence Stace was a British civil servant, educator, and philosopher who wrote on Hegel and Mysticism. He was appointed Stuart Professor of Philosophy at the Princeton University in 1935, and was president of the American Philosophical Association 1949-50.
5. Walter T. Stace, *The Teachings of the Mystics,* (New York: Mentor Books, 1960), p 14.
6. Ibid.
7. William Johnson, *The Inner Eye of Love: Mysticism and Religion,* (London: William Collins Sons & Co., Ltd., 1978), p 32.
8. Ibid.
9. Kenneth Walker, "The Supra-Conscious State," *The Highest State of Consciousness,* (New York: Anchor Books, 1972) ed. John White, pp 15-16.
10. Rudolf Otto, *Mysticism East and West: A Comparative Analysis of the Nature of Mysticism,* (Wheaton, IL: The Theosophical Society of America, 1932), p 7.
11. William James, *The Varieties of Religious Experience.*
12. Ibid., pp 414-415.
13. Ibid., pp 461, 465-467.
14. Ibid., p 466.
15. Ibid.
16. Ralph W. Hood, Jr., *Dimensions of Mystical Experiences: Empirical Studies and Psychological Links,* (Amsterdam: Rodopi B.V., 2001), pp 77-78.
17. William James, *The Varieties,* pp 464-465.
18. Ibid. See the complete descriptive table on pp 77-78. I have paraphrased and included specific concepts from a Religious Studies context. I have used Hood's basic analytical paradigm as a construct and have added from my discipline.
19. Ibid., p 74.
20. Rudolf Otto, *The Idea of the Holy,* (London: Oxford University Press, 1958).
21. *Rudolf Otto's Concept of the "Numinous,"* www.kenyon.edu/Depts/Religion/Fac/Adler/Reln101/Otto.htm
22. Rudolf Otto, *The Idea,* p 40.
23. William James, *The Varieties,* p 464.
24. Ibid.
25. Samadhi is also a central part all the Indian Tree traditions and man SE Asian cosmologies that practice deep meditational disciplines, including yoga, which would bring them into blissful contact with their Absolute reality or god. http://self-knowledge.com/109718.htm
26. Robert E. Van Voorst, *Anthology of World Scriptures,* (Belmont, CA: Wadsworth/Thomson Learning, 2003), pp 27-34.
27. Ibid., pp 28-29.
28. Ibid., pp 29-30.
29. Sidney Spencer, *Mysticism in World Religions,* (Middlesex: Penguin Books, Ltd., 1963), pp 18-29.
30. Advaita Vedanta is the term used to describe the philosophical concept of non-dualism.
31. Ibid., p 48.
32. Ibid., p 49.
33. There are some female gurus, especially in the Shakti devotional stream.
34. Ibid., pp 50-51.
35. Mary Pat Fisher, *Living Religions* (6th ed), (Upper Saddle River, NJ: Prentice-Hall, 2005), pp 84-85.
36. Willard G. Oxtoby, *World Religions: Eastern Traditions* (3rd ed), (New York: Oxford University Press, 2002), pp 55-56.
37. The original reform movement was atheistic in philosophy. It rejected the idea of Nirguna Brahman and Saguna Brahman, together with worship of the gods, or any form of dependence upon these entities to achieve enlightenment and Nirvana.
38. Paul Williams, *Mahayana Buddhism: The Doctrinal Foundations,* (London: Routledge, 1989), pp 150-152, 18-20.
39. Ibid., p 20.
40. Buddha taught that everything people need to achieve enlightenment is within themselves; thus there was no need for any god.
41. Mary Pat Fisher, *Living Religions,* pp 161-162.
42. Paul Williams, *Mahayana Buddhism,* p 251.
43. Ibid., p 253.
44. Bradley K. Hawkins, *Introduction to Asian Religions,* (New York: Pearson-Longman, 2004), p 320.
45. D. T. Suzuki is considered to be a leading expert on Zen and wrote extensively on intuition and the inner experience.
46. Mary Pat Fisher, *Living Religions,* p 154.
47. There is some issue regarding whether the first monks were Theravadan or Mayahanist.
48. Sidney Spencer, *Mysticism in World Religions,* pp 93-96.
49. Mary Pat Fisher, *Living Religions,* p 155.
50. Ibid.

51. Ibid., p 156.
52. Taoism was developed between 600 B.C.E. and 300 C.E.
53. Began c. 551–479 B.C.E. with the life and teachings of Confucius.
54. Buddhism was introduced during the Han Dynasty (206 B.C.E.–220 C.E.).
55. Livia Kohn, *Early Chinese Mysticism: Philosophy and Soteriology in the Taoist Tradition*, (Princeton, NJ: Princeton University Press, 1992), pp 81-82.
56. Ibid., pp 10-11, 113.
57. Christianity was first introduce into China in the seventh century C.E., but did not gain a wider representation until the nineteenth century.
58. Sidney Spencer, *Mysticism in World Religions*, p 97.
59. Mary Pat Fisher, *Living Religions*, pp 177-178.
60. Bradley K. Hawkins, *Introduction to Asian Religions*, p 198.
61. Livia Kohn, *Early Chinese Mysticism: Philosophy and Soteriology in the Taoist Tradition*, pp 43-44.
62. Ibid., p 45.
63. Ibid., pp 98, 111-112.
64. Livia Kohn, *Early Chinese Mysticism: Philosophy and Soteriology in the Taoist Tradition*, p 115.
65. Ibid., p 116.
66. Sidney Spencer, *Mysticism in World Religions*, p 10.
67. Roger Schmidt et al., *Patterns of Religion*, p 65.
68. Sidney Spencer, *Mysticism in World Religions*, p 12.
69. Ibid., pp 170-172.
70. J. H. Laenen, *Jewish Mysticism*, (Louisville: Westminster John Knox Press, 2001), pp 18-19.
71. Ibid., p 21.
72. Developers and teachers laid the foundation for a comprehensive theology with esoteric and mystical overtones. This was transmitted through the generations emphasized an occult religious outlook in Ashkenazi Judaism.
73. J. H. Laenen, *Jewish Mysticism*, p 43.
74. Gershom Scholem, *Major Trends in Jewish Mysticism*, (New York: Schocken Books, 1961), pp 156-204.
75. Ibid., p 158.
76. Edward Albertson, *Understanding the Kabbalah*, (Los Angeles: Sherbourne Press, Inc., 1973), pp 57-58.
77. Gershom Scholem, *Major Trends in Jewish Mysticism*, p 157.
78. J. H. Laenen, *Jewish Mysticism*, p 216.
79. Ibid., pp 220-221, 228, 232.
80. Steven Fanning, *Mystics of the Christian Tradition*, (London: Routledge, 2006), p 16.
81. General dates place the contemplative desert ascetics, living in contemplative, secluded environments, around the early part of the third century C.E. contemplative-life.org/desert-fathers-mothers.html
The Apophthegmata Patrum (Sayings of the Fathers) is the name given to various collections popularly known as Sayings of the Desert Fathers. The material dates from the fourth and fifth centuries and illustrates the spirit of early desert spirituality. See also: *The Life and Regimen of The Blessed and Holy Teacher Syncletica*.
The Church Father Origen (185–254 C.E.) is considered to be the first systematic theologian of the Christian church and wrote extensively on mysticism and the scriptures. See: Laura Swann *The Forgotten Desert Mothers*, (New York: Paulist Press, 2001), p 184.
The writings of Bishop Augustine of Hippo (354–430) were influential in the development of European medieval mysticism. See: Paul E. Szarmach, *An Introduction to the Medieval Mystics of Europe*, (Albany, NY: State University of New York Press), p 24.
83. The Nag Hammadi Library is dated around the late second century C.E.
84. www.spurgeon.org/~phil/creeds/apostles.htm.
85. St. Francis of Assisi.
86. St. Catherine of Siena and St. Catherine of Genoa.
87. Evelyn Underhill, *Mystics of the Church*, (Cambridge: James Clark and Co., Ltd., 1925), pp 9-239.
88. Evelyn Underhill, *Mysticism: A Study in the Nature and Development of Spiritual Consciousness*, (New York: Dover Publications, Inc., 2002), pp. 184, 243, 254.
89. Theodore M. Ludwig, *Sacred Paths of the West* (3rd ed), (Upper Saddle River, NJ: Prentice Hall, 2006), p 209.
90. http://www.sufiway.org/history/origins_of_sufism.php
91. John Renard, *Seven Doors to Islam*, (Berkley: University of California Press), p 110.
92. Mary Pat Fisher, *Living Religions*, pp 388-389.
93. R. C. Zaehner, *Hindu and Muslim Mysticism*, (New York: Schocken Books, 1969), p 181.
94. Mary Pat Fisher, *Living Religions*, p 389.
95. R. C. Zaehner, *Hindu and Muslim Mysticism*, pp 57, 149.

CHAPTER 7

Death with Meaning:
The Reality of Coping

Coping with, and explaining, the inevitability of death has been a major identifying factor in the way that our species relates to finitude. No matter how rich, powerful, beautiful, influential, gifted, or famous a person may be, the end result is exactly the same as for people who live within the confines of a more mundane existence. We all end up dead! The cold, hard fact is that despite all our pretentions, perceptions, and illusions pertaining to entitlement and human worth, death is the final adjudicator. Death is not impressed or cajoled by our perceived notions of importance and worth. The great equalizer is relentless in its process and comes for us all.

In our modern materialistic societies questions pertaining to the true meaning of life and existence can be triggered by the trauma of death; but in most cases, after a period of emotional healing, these issues will again be shelved or forgotten. As a consequence to this, there is often no real ongoing discussion because the whole process of dying and physical dissolution is so painful and/or offensive that we never seem to get over the initial hurdles of fear and grief. We might have a multitude of unspoken or unresolved questions but we push them back until the next event of death. Psychologically, these questions then abide within a dark abyss of repressed emotions which we quite naturally avoid during the process of ordinary living and survival. The reality is that we push the sharp recognition of finality into a hiding place, and "view death as somehow shameful or dirty; one only full of meaninglessness, horror and useless struggle."[1] Needless to say, avoidance of the inevitable does not prepare us for the final reckoning that each one of us faces. For this reason modern secular society is often acknowledged to be a death denying one, as can be seen from the introductory preface to an influential book entitled, *Intimate Death: How the Dying Teach Us How to Live*. This book was written in 1995 by a prominent psychiatrist named Marie De Hennezel, who dealt frankly with the open discussion of death thus encompassing the issues raised by *thanatology*.[2] The preface reads as follows:

> How should we die?
> We live in a world which dreads the question and which turns away from it.
> Earlier civilizations looked death straight in the face …. Never perhaps has our
> relationship with death been so poor as in these times of spiritual barrenness,
> where human beings, in their haste to exist, seem to sidestep the mystery. They
> do not realize that in so doing they rob the love of life of an essential source.[3]

In contrast to this, and to the credit of our species, there does, however, exist a broad range of explanations, clues, perceptions, and beliefs addressing this unpleasant subject and these are to be found in a broad range of representations and philosophies. Not surprisingly, within this corpus of knowledge, the perspectives presented in the context of religions reflect concepts of life, death, afterlife, and the consequences for a life lived with or without reflection on the purpose of existence. Historically, what the sum total of this evidence attests to is the fact that the topic and relating discussions is as old as humankind and even predates Homo sapiens.

Sadly, however, the simple reason for many people's unpreparedness or ignorance in dealing with death is that within our death-denying cultures we do not wish to pursue answers because it would mean confronting some of our greatest fears. Indeed, in our modern environments we appear to be increasingly distancing ourselves from facing death. These degrees of separation are manifesting through a cultural and emotional atmosphere of remoteness and can even be identified in many different aspects of how we treat the preparation of the body and how we engage in funerary rites. Two examples of this growing separation from the reality of death can be seen in the ways we accept the often very synthetic and unreal cosmetic preparation of the body and also in funerary rituals that bear more resemblance to a generic protocol than a personal ritual of farewell, with many services "growing more impersonal and remote."[4] As George E. Barker writes in his work *Death and After Death*

> So skillful is the mortician's art that we can scarcely visit a funeral parlor and
> look upon the face of the corpse without hearing the inevitable comment, "how
> natural he looks!" ….The very language of death is [also] often evasive or euphe-
> mistic. To hear some tell it, 'people do not die anyone, they only pass away or
> depart or expire or sleep. The family does not buy a grave; it invests in a memo-
> rial estate.[5]

The reason for our unpreparedness in facing the biting reality of death is that it takes specific coping skills on the part of the dying person and often those supporting the person to face it. Unless we have access to "old" knowledge through traditional culture within our families, or core belief patterns, death will be viewed as an isolated, often remote incident—even something completely out of the norm. If one lives within a culture of avoidance where there is a void or even a code of silence in operation regarding the meaning to life or the mystery and significance of death, one's ignorance and anguish will be compounded because one does not have easy access to cognitive negotiation skills. In other words, the trauma is worsened because we do not have the emotional and rational tools to navigate the misery. We must all endure the pain of bereavement but this does not mean that each of us will embrace the unique significance of a life lived, or the spiritual power and comfort derived from transcending death with hope or assurance. This is exactly what religions offer insofar as they present the hope of various forms of transcendence and the affirmation of life perhaps lived on another plane of existence.

In reality, however, there are no glib answers or magic words that can be pronounced to remove the sting of dying and death. To face the event of death always needs courage—indeed often heroic bravery. For instance, consider the suffering seeker or enquirer contemplating hope of survival in some form after death or on the other hand, simply and with stoic resignation, accepting total obliteration. It might also be abstractly useful or even comforting in some way for one to contemplate one's own death but then consider for a moment, visualizing for oneself, the death of a loved one, or even plural deaths of loved and cherished members of family and friends. The thoughts become highly uncomfortable, and rightly so. Also, how does one cope with the trauma of grief that often endures for years? The reality is that as full realization draws near, the emotional pain may, and often does, become overwhelming. Due to the enormity of these realities, secular society will quite naturally close itself off because it does not comprehend or even possess the necessary coping skills. Sadly, through this process of evasion, we in many ways render ourselves totally hapless in the face of despair and separation.

From the perspective of developing insight and strength in dealing with death the noted psychoanalyst Carl Jung recognized the need to develop spiritual coping skills. Jung emphasized that it was imperative that people grasp the significance of mortality and immortality and consider death not as an end but a transcendent beginning. In other words, from Jung's perspective, it was necessary for us to adopt the concept of soul and its journey through life, together with our transition into death and immortality. Jung wrote:

> Death is psychologically as important as birth and, like it, is an integral part of
> life …. As a doctor, I make every effort to strengthen the belief in immortality,
> especially with older patients when such questions come threateningly close. For,
> seen in correct psychological perspective, death is not an end but a goal.[6]

In this context, consider the following two simple examples which serve to illustrate the extremes of explanations pertaining to the meaning of life and death. The first one is an eloquent statement coined by a famous American science fiction writer and contributor to the Star Trek series, named David Gerrold (1944–). He extolled "Life is hard. Then you die. Then they throw dirt in your face. Then the worms eat you. Be grateful it happens in that order."[7] For many people this philosophy is a popular, if rather dismissive, summation of the cost and significance of living and dying. Indeed, for many thoughtful persons facing the death of a cherished loved one this observation strains the senses. Whilst presenting as a very pithy and realistic sequence of events for many during their lives and then during the dying and ultimate death process, it is devoid of respect, compassion, and acknowledgment of the significance of life and its ultimate physical ending. Of course, this process of decay obviously applies to the traditional burial process but for those who opt for cremation, the description of dissolution through the burning or rendering down of the physical remains is just as harsh. Whatever means by which the disposal occurs, this is a rationally stark appraisal of life and death. At this point, perhaps pitched into the darkness of a depressive state, one could be tempted to ask, "What is the point of thinking about the significance of life if this is all there is? It's just misery, with some fun interspersed to break up the monotony!" As the great mystic, scientist, and philosopher Blaise Pascal observed when commenting on the starkness of existence without a faith belief, "The last act is bloody, however pleasant all the rest of the play is: a little earth is thrown at last upon our head, and that is the end forever."[8]

This second observation reflects another perspective which was articulated by the famous Nobel Prize Laureate Thomas Mann (1875–1955) in his work *The Magic Mountain, A Novel*. This approach is perhaps a more gentle yet definitely perceptive explanation for the mystery surrounding death and the meaning to life, to which many can assent. Mann wrote:

> The only healthy and noble and indeed . . . the only religious way in which to regard death is to perceive and feel it as a constituent part of life, as life's holy prerequisite, and not to separate it intellectually, to set it up in opposition to life, or worse, to play it off against life in some disgusting fashion—for that is indeed the antithesis of a healthy, noble, reasonable, and religious view . . . Death is to be honored as the cradle of life, the womb of renewal. Once separated from life, it becomes grotesque, a wraith—or even worse.[9]

THE NEED FOR ACKNOWLEDGED SIGNIFICANCE

Existing between these philosophical perspectives lies the reality of our routine human encounter with the practicalities of dealing with death and disposal of the remains. Historical evidence attests to the fact that our species has routinely buried, cremated, embalmed, mummified, desiccated, and sometimes naturally baked, frozen, or even freeze-dried mortal remains.[10] To accompany these behavioural patterns, we have also routinely created and sanctioned an honoured place, or sacred space, in which to either deposit or disburse the remains and to attach sanctity to that practical process.[11] Further, and in addition to these patterns, the whole procedure was customarily imbued with religious or spiritual significance which was interpreted as exhibiting affection and/or respect for the deceased. Extending out of this were particular rituals designed to escort the dead through to the next world.

Another observable and verifiable concept of enduring ritual enactment can still be identified in remaining patterns of behavior in present day funerary sentiments. The enduring legacy of protocols surrounding ideas regarding respect for the dead in these ancient religious customs and sentiments was so widespread and influential that even in our modern secular cultures there remains the enduring expectation that final respects should be paid. Sociological research describes modern secular funerary ritual as some quasi religious rite which still retains part of a significant, if undefined or even loose code of bereavement behaviour for many.[12]

To make sense of this ritualistic behaviour one must consider the fact that at the root of all religious funerary rituals and ingrained belief patterns is not only the obvious acknowledgment of death but also the incorporation of explanations in order to ease through the inevitable. In fact, all religions contain within their systems the explanations for the process of dying and most will teach some sort of concept of social renewal, regeneration, and perpetuation of a cosmic order. There will also be a distinctly identifiable belief in a variety of modes of transcendence which incorporate a belief and perception of survival into a hereafter; indeed, it is a broadly observable fact that all societies see death as a transition for the person who dies. Thus, in the context of religions, what is embodied in their belief codes is a structure of hope for continuance in some form. This enables those left behind in the physical realm to undergo the mourning process with a degree of shared cosmology and encouragement through which bereavement can be faced individually and as a group. The religious hope, linked closely to a belief in an afterlife, coupled with a strong survival instinct even in the face of death, enables the living to conceptualize or imagine a line of continuation for the deceased and for themselves when it becomes their turn to die.

In addition to this, these deeply intertwined feelings of attachment, incorporating respect, solemnity, grief and care, also acknowledge significance of the death of an animal friend. This inate grieving process can be identified in the ways that many of us dispose of a beloved animal friend or pet and grieve deeply for them. There are final resting places even for animals, be they large or small, with many people still burying their pets in designated sacred or revered places such as pet cemeteries (but not of the Stephen King ilk as in *Pet Sematary*) or even in a protected area on their property. Many people will also often have their small and medium sized pets cremated and will go to considerable financial expenditure to purchase urns for the remains which are then kept in a significant place in their homes. Larger animals, either pets or animal celebrities as noted by a culture or community as worthy of commemoration, can be submitted for taxidermy. For examples of this tradition, consider the case of Emperor Napoleon's beloved horse, Le Visir, or movie star cowboy Roy Roger's faithful horse, Trigger, or even Australia's famous racing horse Phar Lap.

What can be seen from the reality of physical disposals is that there is significance and loyalty attached to the deceased. An inner and deeply intense motivation leads us to express gratitude and mourning in the way we accept responsibility for the body and look for a suitable ceremony to commemorate a loved one's death. In our care for the remains we display feelings of love and loss, and of caring for our loved ones' physical shells. These means of disposal are identified with not only the practical aspects of dealing with unpleasant decay but also with the pervading concept that the mortal remains should be dealt with lovingly, respectfully, and protectively. The question arises as to why we would care about the reverential or respectful disposal of distressing physical decay in the first place. Why is it so significant for us to show love, reverence, or respect? Why do we observe ritual surrounding decaying matter that in its own mass knows nothing of our lavish demonstrations of sorrow and respect? Why do the majority of us care? Why do we wish to protect the corpse and provide it with a safe final 'resting' place? The reasons are many and often very complex, in that we feel protective, with keen awareness of our recently severed bonds. Sometimes we think that these demonstrations will in some way ameliorate our pain or even please the spirit of the deceased. We may spend lavishly on funerary tributes, flowers, large gravestones and expensive coffins, but what good does that really do anyone? The fact is that despite all the proffered answers or theories, the reasons for our funerary protocols are complex and often not fully explored or acknowledged. Truth be told, many of our outpourings of grief and actions of empathy also spring from an unspoken sense of guilt or perhaps regret regarding our conduct toward the deceased when they were alive. We may regret unresolved issues or harsh words, perhaps even neglect or cruel treatment we might have visited upon the live person now departed. We can also feel remorse in the case of a traumatic bad or sudden death which might also cause a tinge of fear of angry ghosts or traumatized spirits. For example, consider the proliferation of mediums or movies concerning angry, unavenged ghosts and/or the supernatural.

Recognizing our universal speciel need to acknowledge the dead and conduct a fitting disposal of their remains has at its root an intensely emotional variety of psychological triggers that are not easy to present unequivocally. From an academic and often scientific perspective there endures a plethora of unanswerable questions as to our speciel behavioural patterns regarding death. What can, however, be generally assumed is that any interpretation of our rituals and disposal systems function as mechanics for dealing with raw, but often enduring grief, coupled with shock and fear. Whatever lies at the root of our personal grieving mechanisms, there is the need to find some comfort within our pain and a sacred and/or respected disposal ritual provides continuity in functioning to close the emotional door on one very unpleasant and deeply frightening part of the grieving process. To assist us in this process we use ritualistic behaviour and it is estimated that between 50 and 99 percent of ritual disposals among cultures are still conducted under the canopy of some form of organized religious tradition.[13] From a practical and also an emotional perspective this is done in order to find a modicum of continuity and comfort within an established traditional system. This does not mean we will necessarily fully embrace a particular religious creed, but many of us will definitely turn to a defined spiritual and ritual protocol in order to pay our respects to the deceased. In more ancient times, this need to pay respects was part of entrenched religious belief systems that addressed the rituals needed to conduct the deceased to the other side and even perhaps assuage the anger of a departed spirit, thus providing the living with some protection and peace. Prayers offered for the rest and peace of the deceased were not merely parting farewells, but sincere wishes that the spirit would quite literally rest in peace. In these ways, order, significance, and meaning contribute to physical closure and emotional acknowledgment and encouragement of the deceased's separation from the living.

INTERPRETING MATERIAL MARKERS—BUILDING EDIFICES

For the cynic, it is often difficult to discern whether displays of grief and/or devotion are undertaken out of sincere private/public sentiments or merely for display, gratification and influence. It is easy to observe that sometimes these rituals are merely contrived moments of public relations and are simply blatantly orchestrated incidents of propaganda. These multifarious motivations can easily be identified through how our species has constructed material markers in the building of ornate tombs and monuments to display significance or save face in order to deposit the remains of often maniacal and despotic rulers. Many of the spectacular mausoleums are monuments to frivolity, pride, cruelty, or even misguided urges to lavish love on decay. Generally, these have been erected at the cost of untold suffering and upon the broken bodies of slaves and conscripted labourers. The enduring message was, however, that no cost or sacrifice was too great for the departed in question. In addition to this, the funds for the majority of opulent tombs as far as archaeologists, anthropologists, and historians can construct, were derived from enormous compulsory tax burdens levied upon the ordinary populace, plundering, or painful, sacrificial giving on the part of those who really would have benefitted reversely from bequeaths of charity bestowed as parting gifts from the revered deceased. Sadly, the reality is, however, that no expense or physical cost was spared for the despotic, the spoiled, and sometimes criminally insane. The saving of face, continuance of perceived honour and power, or the display of wealth in material funerary goods, together with solemn yet lavish rituals pertaining to the deceased, have customarily been the components of burials for rulers, leaders, and the rich and famous.

A central motivating factor behind the construction of all these buildings of commemoration has always been to preserve the memory of the enshrined dead leader and to maintain a message of enduring power and continuity. The concept behind this display was and is still to provide a subtle message of stability, continuation, and permanency for the regime, dynasty, or surviving family members and for the people they control. In addition to this, encouraged and validated by the respective existing religious or state rituals, official burials sanctioned the site as revered and set apart, thus emphasizing the need to sanctify the resting place, and protect the remains.

The repositories often also functioned in the various belief traditions as essential portals for the conveyance of the soul into another realm. Examples of this survival cosmology can be identified in many diverse cultures. By way of illustration, consider the chieftain burials that included their chariot and horses, excavated in Russia, and which date back to approximately the third millennium B.C.E.[14] Also dating from the third millennia B.C.E. are the royal gravesites found in the Sumerian city-state

of Ur, which was located near the Persian Gulf. In addition to this, there is the evidence taken from the famous and well-documented Egyptian mummification rituals and pyramid systems. Later, there was also the great Chinese tomb complex dating to 1000 B.C.E., in the province of Xinjiang[15] and then, at a later date, the famous and exquisite funerary terracotta sculptured army of warriors, chariots, and horses depict-

ing the armies of Qin Shi Huang, the first Emperor of China. The terracotta sculptures were buried with the emperor in 210–209 B.C.E. for the purpose of protecting the emperor in his afterlife. Along with his army, the Chinese emperor also had buried with him a collection of terracotta officials, acrobats, strongmen, and musicians whose only purpose was to serve and entertain their great master in his celestial realm, thereby basically keeping him company.

The belief behind these grand constructions, only erected for the noble, rich, and famous, was that the tomb acted as a portal for the soul through which either to survive or make entrance into a holy realm. The prevailing belief was that in such a location the deceased would still enjoy all the comforts of home and the benefits of superiority over lesser beings such as sacrificed subjects, slaves, dedicated servants, and animals![16] Sadly, in many cases the souls of often truly horribly despotic leaders were believed to reside in full majesty, holding sway over his/her minions in a privileged afterlife, in which the subjugated would exist eternally content with the purpose of serving the ruler.[17]

SIGNIFYING SIGNIFICANCE: SHRINES, MEMORIALS, AND GRAVESITES

On a more benign and personal note, in other cases there were and are shrines and final resting places—gravesites—constructed to reverence the corpses, remains, or ashes of beloved spiritual leaders, celebrated, accredited heroes such as soldiers or martyrs, and also for ordinary loved ones. These commemorative places become shrines in memory of a noble sacrificial action made by a courageous person which empowered or saved a community, or a nation, or simply to those who merely enriched the lives of family members.

In the context of notable leaders, warriors, or martyrs, the purpose of these revered focal points was and is to function as a rallying point for a communal ceremony either religious or secular. The whole protocol surrounding this act of memorial remembrance is to engender solidarity within group memory through identification with a significant act, and to reaffirm heritage, identity, and loyalty.

Examples of shrines in their many secular/religious aspects are war memorials, or cenotaphs which function on both a local and national level.[18] These memorials serve to enforce national or local identity and foster emotive association with their gallant and courageous departed warriors. They also stand as reminders to the living of the gratitude and the debt owed to such gallantry. These edifices also reinforce a subliminal and often an overt message of responsibility on the part of the surviving community towards future generations. The dead live on in the hearts and memories of those they died to save and thus acquire lasting transcendence. There are also the moving memorials to the unknown soldier, where the identity of the remains remain unidentified but function to represent all those lost and unaccounted fallen soldiers who were never buried or repatriated.

At the core of these permanent memorials lies the human identification with suffering and trauma. In addition to this, the memorials serve as educational vehicles through which to evoke an empathetic response and an awareness of suffering in the consciousness of future generations.[19] The per-

The Canadian War Memorial

manent shrines function as vehicles through which to confront death on a mass scale and to convey meaning, even if the meaning is remembrance of senseless destruction and the reliving of sorrow. They pay homage to the nobility of the human spirit as it faces the misery of rampant carnage and horrific acts of war. In this way, there is an endeavour to create meaning out of slaughter, as the suffering of the gallant dead is honoured for the accomplishment of peace and safety for those who continue and live in relative peace. In this context, the shrines act as purveyors of cultural transcendence in that they offer "a kind of immortality" by establishing a collective memory of noble acts within the cultural memory of a society.[20]

The psychological mechanism behind this commemorative act functions through the use of reverential rituals and commemorative observances. In this context, it provides in the minds of the living a conscious immortality of the dead, if only for the brief time of ritualistic behaviour.

Another function of the shrine is to be identified in the often spontaneous makeshift constructions of roadside tributes or localized impromptu memorials somehow linked in location to the deceased. These shrine types draw attention to traumatic, tragic, and often violent deaths but do not mark the final resting places of victims whom they honour.[21] Essentially, what the sites do is mark a centrally significant place where strangers and/or those closely affected by the event can rally to pay homage through a quasi religious/secular ritual to the deceased or missing person. In some ways they function as a protest against senseless death, also acknowledged as "bad death," and function as a means by which to express vulnerability, anger, sorrow, horror, and outrage. Simply put, these shrines act as forms of grief therapy in that they express group bonding among strangers brought together through commonly shared grief.[22] Thus the makeshift shrines become the embodiment of sociopsychological group solidarity and identification through various tokens of love expressed by a company of strangers, who in the face of death, respond in various ways to a mutually experienced event. In this way, these hallowed places become manifestations and vehicles of group therapy through which mutual grief, experienced by strangers, drawn together by the shared association of empathy and sorrow, assist to focus or voice outrage in the midst of a shared traumatic social loss. In addition to this, the temporary shrines stand not only as tributes to those who have died to signify public places of mourning and memory[23] but they also express deep sympathy for the survivors, family, and griev-

ing parents. The placement and purpose of the shrine is also to turn a site where earlier there was only tragedy and pain into a space of love and memory. In this way, there is a psychological ownership of the place and through the actions of commemoration, the area undergoes a symbolic cleansing through which it is transformed into a secular but at the same time, spiritual or religious, place of sanctuary and significance.[24]

Another intriguing dynamic behind these shrines is that they often break through normal social patterns of separation as in social hierarchy, privilege, culture, wealth, or celebrity status. For example, the striking and very visual public tribute to Diana, Princess of Wales, was a spontaneous and genuine outpouring of love made by people of all races and classes. This was culturally surprising especially in such a class-stratified and enduringly segregated society as the United Kingdom, where a stringent cultural separation between privileged royalty and commoner is the norm. Diana was, however, perceived or carefully culturally constructed to be the "People's Princess" and the common people demonstrated their emotional "ownership" of Lady Di through the unprecedented massive display of flowers and tributes made to her by the British public.[25] Thus mutual human grief, protest, identification, outrage, and even despair were all presented swiftly and with growing momentum, outside her home at Kensington Palace, and then at Buckingham Palace and other palaces, in the form of flowers, trinkets, and message tributes.

In examining the phenomenon of Lady Di's transformation into the tragic victim of publicity and media hype, an interesting fact emerges. Diana, Princess of Wales, was transformed through a process of prose, publicity, and sentiment into the public persona of the quintessential, fragile, and beautiful English rose. Through the genuine tragedy of her death the princess was mourned and celebrated and by the psychological process of public grief, was set within the memory and history of a society. The princess thus achieved a type of immortality known as *cultural transcendence*[26] whereby she was transformed through popular culture into an iconic enduring public figure.

A further example of the significance of temporary shrines which embody our acknowledgement of tragedy and heroism can be seen in the spontaneous makeshift tributes after 9-11. Cultural, *mythic,* and *ancestral transcendence*[27] are easily recognizable in our collective need to demonstrate solidarity and respect through the placing of deeply emotive tributes in the face of overwhelming grief and shock. The deep significance of the 9-11 shrines is that although the victims and heroes were physically destroyed their memories, contributions, and family ties were emphatically affirmed to acknowledge that they did not die in vain. Group solidarity, family kinship, and the promise to keep the deceased living in memory were also acts of defiance against the manifestation of devastation. Family and tribe are once again united against the assailant in acts of commemorative validation and affirmations of honour. The makeshift shrines functioned as channels through which the immediate survivors and all empathetic strangers came together to comfort one another and immortalize the significance of the victims and heroes of the 9-11 carnage.

It is this ratification of life's significance that can also be identified in the way we construct permanent markers to mark bodily "resting places" known as graves, or specific markers and depositories of cremains. The need to mark significance is also established protocol or ritual that is frequently practiced in the case where the cremains have been scattered or the bodies never retrieved. This is done through commemorating the memory of a loved one with the planting of a tree, plant, plaques, and even benches in particularly significant spots or gardens, as tributes to those they name. What can generally be identified through all of these rituals is that for the ordinary person, confronted with the responsibility of disposal, there is generally the need to honour, using some form of memorial marker, the final memory of the departed. Thus the role of the permanent marker functions to demonstrate respect, devotion, family solidarity, and often and most enduringly, deeply profound love and remembrance.

ACADEMIC THEORIES FOR BEHAVIOURAL PATTERNS

Theories or explanations abound, however, that seek to further plumb the hidden depths and complexities of our confrontations with death and the resulting shock of the encounter. Thus our grieving mechanisms and the struggle to make sense of life have been strenuously dissected to understand the origins of our formal and personal displays of grief and mourning and sometimes our general fear of the unbounded power of the dead. Some of the early anthropology theorists, such as E. B. Tylor, propounded the idea of the "Doctrine of Survivals," which contained a theory called the "Doctrine of Souls." Tylor argued that primitive man was "deeply impressed by two groups of biological problems"; the first being what was the difference between a "living body and a dead one." Tylor believed that through inference, the second observation was that the primitive concluded that there was a live being and a phantom being as the second self and that this evolved into "civilized" man's idea of a personal soul or spirit. [28]   Later theories addressing the resiliency or even origins of religions addressed ideas pertaining to the evolution of religious protocols developed out of our primitive conjectures regarding the difference between the life force and the stillness, menace and primal fear of death.   In this context, the noted anthropologist, Bronislaw Malinowski, argued that "Death, which of all human events is the most upsetting and disorganizing to man's calculations, is perhaps the main source of religious belief."[29]   It was later argued that our rituals were routinely— even if we no longer analyzed them as such—part of the process of appeasing the departed through showing grief in order to ensure their favour and protection, as well as to reaffirm social or cultural transcendence.[30]   Whatever the argument proffered or reason accepted, the fact exists that there is a mental and physical process that can be observed in all cultures surrounding death.   As Michael Parker Pearson observes in his work, *The Archaeology of Death and Burial,*

> Whether we weep for the dead because we fear them or we fear the dead because we weep for them, the dead are universally a source of fear, especially during the corpse's putrefaction. With the passing of time, the deceased may come to be venerated, and fear and veneration go hand and hand. Places of the dead such as tombs and graveyards may also provide a material locus for feelings of dread and fear. The separation of the corpse from the living is one means by which fear of the dead is controlled. Many ethnographic studies allude to strategies designed to sever connections with the deceased.[31]

Arising out of a broad spectrum of archeological burial evidence, and from our previous discussions about death protocols, it is apparent that our ancestors did attach great store to appeasing or encouraging the departed to journey to the other side through prayer and ritual. What is also fascinating to note is that evidence of these enduring sentiments is still easily identifiable in many funerary rites, both religious and secular. Our ceremonies will still include prayers for the dead, rituals surrounding their safe passage and ease into the hereafter, or in general express a hope that the deceased will "rest in peace." These sentiments can be voiced without the mourner even having to accept belief in continuance, but at the same time, presenting a wish that the dead will be happy and perhaps, on a subliminal level, also contain the hope that the dead won't come back to frighten them! Routinely, these rituals are all undertaken to comfort those participating in the disposal and help them feel that the deceased was given a "nice sendoff." These observances are identifiable coping mechanisms that we routinely utilize either consciously or subconsciously within both secular societies and religious communities to this day.

COPING MECHANISMS—LOVE, GUILT, OR DISPLAY

In our secular age, these coping connections are not always clearly apparent or even meaningfully recognized. Rituals surrounding death and the disposal of remains do not have to be overtly religious in their basic beliefs or observances but they will, as custom permits, still require addressing death, emotional pain, and the ever practical disposal of the remains. Indeed, so deep is our need for meaning or even the demonstration of love in the midst of grieving, that it can render us deeply vulnerable to secular materialism. Sadly, in our very status-minded or superficial societies, we think or are encouraged to think, that an expensive ritual will be of more benefit or homage to the dead one, as if money can be the measure of love.[32] This sentiment can be identified in lavish funerals, mass, or national state displays of mourning, or long processions of those wishing to pay their respects to a dead body, when there paradoxically exists no belief in an afterlife anyway!

This outpouring of respect can also be seen in the way we have public and private viewings of the remains, and in the often opulent and wasteful misuse of money either in lavish ceremonies or tomb construction. Psychologically, we can reason that it shows respect to the remaining family; it can also be utilized as a vehicle by which to perhaps assuage our guilt or regret for perceived or real acts of unloving or careless conduct towards the deceased when alive. These behavioural exhibitions seem irrational if one merely considers the physical and secular perspectives on death, but as with many concepts within our materialistic, secular cultures, we often think that an expensive funerary rite for the disposal of remains will in some way ameliorate our nagging conscience and in some way manifest love. Simply stated, from a rational, secular perspective, the dead person can no longer be apologized to and so our conduct is rendered no more than a shallow display of ostentation. Once a person is dead, he or she is dead, and there are no avenues by which to make amends. In this context, how then can any funerary ritual help one with a living and painful awareness of guilt?

The issue raised here is one that is keenly distressing when seriously considered; how can anyone apologize after the finality of death? Also, subconsciously or consciously knowing this, does this total finality, with its accompanying inability to make amends, lead someone experiencing deep grief to even greater despair and regret? The problem here is that no one possesses a blameless record regarding conduct towards another, especially under the extreme stresses of a protracted final illness or even in the ordinary tensions, or dysfunctions that occur within any sort of meaningful relationship. Sadly, it is a very deep, black chasm into which many of us look without any comfort. Once the person is dead there is no hope of reunion—the dead one is "lost" forever to those that grieve and there is no opportunity for apology.

Set against this secular backdrop, the plain reality is that our species has always faced the issue of encountering these aspects of grief and have had to navigate through unresolved sorrow and/or guilt. What is evident is that from the archaeological, anthropological, and sociological evidence to hand, together with surviving and enduring religious texts, the reality of death and the various ways of coping with death and bereavement have always been addressed to provide hope. The reality is that there is a consistent pattern of widespread religious traditions that speak to these problems in their specific cosmologies. Thus within their teachings there are provisions through which to make amends, repent, and/or seek comfort for our grieving consciences and turmoil as we cope with the sorrow of death. The reality is that as a coping mechanism, religions contain functions of funerary and prayer rituals, together with various beliefs in an afterlife, that can help both the living and those who have transitioned into another realm of existence through the process of death. In the religions, there is always the prospect of hope and healing—a prospect of survival through transcendence. Religions have simply explained that one must consciously accept and process dying as a transformative and transcendent power. It is from these teachings that people have drawn on religion/spirituality to gain energy for the final leap into the next realm.

COSMOLOGIES: PATTERNS OF PROVISION

If then, as the religions assert, death presents itself not as an end but as a beginning, how is it explained? According to the typologies, the explanations are many and diverse. Some cosmologies pertaining to death are very complex and culturally specific in their concepts of transcendence, while others are transparently simple offering concepts that speak to all cultures. Complex or simple, the traditional typologies are worthy of examination in order to extract their truths or perspectives regarding the meaning to life and death. As these views are presented, a tapestry of meaning and problem solving emerges which generates an overall respect for our ancestors' coping mechanisms as they sought closure through their religious beliefs. What is fascinating to observe is that within each existing typology there are many and various ideas about survival after death. These ideas then offer continuity to their own adherents within the broad familiar pattern of religious belief contained within their various traditions. In this way, religions offer a broad canopy of shelter for the bereaved and provide familiar rituals to carry the dead over into the other world thus providing a feeling on continuity and stability for those coping with bereavement.

OVERVIEW OF RELIGIONS

Judaism

Judaism has its antecedents in an ancient tribal religion with roots dating back to around 2000 B.C.E. The religion bases its faith tradition on an historical founder named Abraham, who received the revelation of monotheism directly from YHWH. As the religion has evolved through six identifiable developmental stages from that time until the present, beliefs in an afterlife have undergone conceptual changes throughout its history. Consider, for a moment, the six developmental stages associated with a tribe that became a nation: Hapiru Stage (2000 to 1300 B.C.E.); Israelite (1300 to 586 B.C.E.); Second Temple Judaism (586 B.C.E. to 70 C.E.); Rabbinic/Classical Judaism (70 to 640 C.E.); Medieval Judaism (640 to 1787 C.E.); Modern (1787 to present). In the context of belief in an afterlife, ideas can be identified through each stage with the result that there are now three main belief traditions regarding survival after death.

To appreciate the foundational and cohesive idea of a covenantal, reciprocal relationship with their God YHWH, as the central tenants of faithfulness and solidarity one must consider that this relationship is based on adherence to the Law of Moses, also known as the Torah. Observance of these laws and the resulting influence have created a specific people, who are bound together historically as Jews. Jews can be observant and follow the laws and resulting cultural traditions which are interpreted as binding religious tenets, or Jews can be secular and attach no religious value to the teachings but still identify themselves culturally. What has happened throughout the history of what society now identifies as Judaism is that Jews of all religious or non-religious persuasions still consider themselves a people with a long tribal history that is full of identity and attachment as a group. Within this cultural context there is solidarity and continuity based on an ancient system which still creates a people's Jewishness. So, there is comfort metaphorically in death within *the Bosom of Abraham* as part of a tribal, national, and small community-based system which believes that all who bear the mark of covenant will be allowed into a final place of rest and happiness.

Over the centuries of developing religious thought pertaining to beliefs on death and the afterlife three basic perspectives have become representational of Jewish thought and communities. The Jewish believer, therefore, can choose from three equally acceptable teachings on the afterlife. These three systems can be placed in a chronological order of development. First, there is the most ancient perspective which is annihilation where one only achieves immortality through one's descendants, one's good name, and good works that live on. One is therefore commemorated and lives on through family and community memory. Second, there is the general belief in a life after death, where the soul, according to the level of observance of the Jewish Torah, and righteousness developed in life,[33] receives recompense, undergoes purgatorial punishment in an interim state after death, is thereafter admitted into a heavenly interim state. Finally, they are resurrected on the Day

of Judgement to experience heaven which is known as *Gan Edan*. The concept of a permanent state of distress, referred to as Gehinnom, is not generally accepted as a place where Jews go because of their ancient covenantal relationship with God. This is, however, open to dispute as generally the Jewish tradition contains a variety of opinions on the subjects of heaven and hell and so there is no one limited perspective. Thirdly within Judaism, there is the belief in reincarnation, leading to final elevation upon full completion of the 613 commandments within the Torah; this idea is central to Kabbalistic mysticism[34] and has been extensively addressed from within the mystical tradition. What is evident from existing historical texts is that the concept of reincarnation has an ancient history dating back to late Second Temple Judaism and this has remained a central idea that is traced through Medieval Judaism right through to the present.

Christianity

Christianity's foundational beliefs are identified through the enduring teachings of an individual soul, spiritual rebirth, life lived in the physical and also the spiritual Kingdom of Heaven, and the bodily resurrection of the dead, together with judgement based on one's acceptance or rejection of Jesus Christ as God/Saviour. The central belief system's concept of immortality is based on the resurrection of Jesus and his promise to provide a place within the supernatural Kingdom of Heaven after death and in eternity, for those who loved and believed in him.

As Christianity began as a Jewish sect there are early and recognizable ideas taken from some Jewish thought; these include heaven and hell. In the *primitive church*,[35] also known as the early church, there developed various ideas about what occurred immediately after death and leading up to Judgement Day. The earliest ideas were very basic regarding life after death and then over time developed in complexity. Initially, the belief system conveyed the expectation that imme-

diately after death each person underwent a primary judgment where those who were saved went to dwell in spirit form with God under the altar of God[36] in heaven which was a heavenly interim state of conscious peace and happiness until the final Judgment Day. When Judgment Day arrived they would be physically resurrected into the fully realized Kingdom of God on a new and perfect earth where there was no death. For those who were not saved, however, the primary judgment placed them in an abode of the distressed spirits in a state known as Gehenna, which was a place of torment and burning. They were consigned to this state to await full recompense for their actions during the final judgement of the dead which would then result in a permanent version of hell.

Arising out of these straightforward beliefs there developed many different interpretations of life after death and this can be identified within differences between the Roman Catholic tradition and Eastern Orthodox systems on one hand, and those of mainstream traditional Protestantism that developed out of the sixteenth century C.E. Reformation. One of these major differences concerns the immediate fate of the dead. In the early Roman Catholic and Eastern Orthodox Christian traditions there developed the idea of a purgatorial chastisement for some sinners whose misdeeds were less severe than the overtly evil. These sins could be "purged" in a purgatorial realm as they awaited the physical final resurrection of the dead. This belief system arose out of Second Temple Judaism's concept of purgatorial punishment for many within the "fold" who were not yet worthy to enter into God's rest. The Roman Catholic idea also dealt with the same belief concerning the less righteous believers and those who were righteous but had lived before the time of Jesus Christ. This idea still held that the final Judgment Day adjudication was fixed but that lesser sins not repented of in life could be dealt with or expunged before the day of reckoning.[37] These ideas led to prayers for the dead, funerary and anniversary masses, and included some early ideas regarding baptism for the dead who had never heard the message of Christ's salvation.

With the advent of the Protestant Reformation in the sixteenth century[38] and its emphasis on *justification by faith*, *sola scriptura*, and the *priesthood of all believers*, a radical reversal in Christian popular religion began. These three tenets are considered to be the foundation for the Reformation and were emphatically taught by reformers and spearheaded by the Augustinian monk Martin Luther

(1483–1546). *Justification by faith* as taught by St. Paul in the New Testament letter to the Roman Church, emphasized that one could only be forgiven by Christ and that there was no way to earn forgiveness or to burn off sin by one's own endeavours. One's salvation rested solely on Christ's death and could not be earned by good deeds. *Sola scriptura,* or scripture alone, was the only source of authoritative guidance and the early teachings of Jesus about spiritual rebirth and entry into the Kingdom were the only means by which to live in a blessed state after death. The final point emphasized was that of the *priesthood of all believers*, which meant that all were equal in standing and vocation in Christ's eyes. No one was more worthy than another as everybody had sinned against God. Arising out of this realization was the reality that part of God's nature was that he showed no favour for the ordained over the laity. The good news was that it was one's salvation in Christ alone that was important and was the only requirement to meet God on the other side of the grave.

As Christianity had from its early beginnings been a religion that included both Jews and Gentiles, it always incorporated a mixed ethnic representation throughout history. As a consequence to this, it therefore now reflects a broad cultural hue and various philosophical and theological interpretations. However, despite this wide global mix and divergence on how or when one may obtain a tranquil state after death, the dominant ideas held by most groups are generally consistent. Reflected within Christian traditions is an emphasis on the Kingdom of Heaven over which Christ presides with those who love him being allowed to enter into his heavenly realm after death. The mainstream Christian idea is that Jesus is Lord over life and death and faithful followers will be saved from hell and will have a final resting place in heaven.

Islam

Similar to tribal concepts of allegiance within Judaism, Islam was built upon ancient ideas of identity and allegiance within a tribal system. Under the revelation given to Prophet Mohammad from Allah via the Archangel Gabriel, the beliefs within Islam overtook the tribal pagan ideas of many gods and varying teachings on the afterlife. During this process of religious change, Islam crystallized its

faith view. Through the twenty-three-year period of direct revelation to the Prophet, and certainly clearly identifiable in the Qur'an which was standardized during the reign of Uthman (r. 644–656), the third of the four immediate successors to Mohammad,[39] the following tenets became central for all Muslims: Allah alone is everlasting and everything else perishes; Allah ordains both life and death and is the author of both life and death; Allah, therefore, gives and takes away. Arising out of these ideas it became clear that if Allah defined the life span of every living thing, and if Muslims submitted unequivocally to his will, then death was in his hands and was no longer viewed as the result of the disruptive action of time and age. Life was transient, and the abode of that which perished, but under the will of Allah, death was but an entry into eternal life for the faithful.

Islam teaches that a human being is composed of a living soul (nafs) which is animated by a spirit (ruh).[40] The *nafs* represented the self, which is the soul or psyche. When death occurs it is believed that Allah and his angelic messengers extract the nafs. This event will differ for those who are righteous as the soul is gently taken from the body. In the case of sinners, who are those considered to be the polytheists and unbelievers, the soul is violently torn from the body cavity.[41]

Whatever the spiritual state of the soul, the Qur'an describes a twofold experience after death. Upon dying the deceased enters a realm of permanent separation from the living which is referred to as a partition or barrier. At some undefined stage shortly after death, in an interim state, the Judgment of the Tomb begins for all souls, whether righteous or wicked. Within this realm of existence a good soul, led by the angel Gabriel, ascends through the seven layers of heaven, to see what will eventually be its ultimate state of existence. The righteous are rewarded by a vision of Allah after which the soul returns to the grave where the tomb becomes a peaceful resting place and in which the dead person can feel the sweet breezes of heaven. On the other hand, for the wicked soul or for the person who has not properly followed Allah's commands in physical life, the interim state is one of horrific and disgusting punishment. A wicked soul is foul smelling and barred from heaven, and is instead given a vision of what awaits them on the final day of judgment, often referred to as the Day of Doom. From there the wicked person is then returned to the grave to await the final horrors of hell.[42] The living can still conduct intercessory prayers for the deceased for forgiveness of sins and a more comfortable experience within the grave.

Another commonly accepted tradition within the Judgement in the Tomb motif is the dreaded visit by two questioning angels named Munkar and Nakir[43] who appear shortly after internment to question the soul. If the deceased answers correctly and unwaveringly regarding the uniqueness of Allah and the identity of Muhammad as the Messenger of God, the soul is told to rest until the Resurrection of the Dead on the Day of Doom. On the other hand, if the deceased was a disbeliever he or she will answer incorrectly and will face as a consequence the punishment of the angels who will "smite" the faces and backs of the disbeliever and will say "Taste the punishment of burning."[44] This dreaded punishment is known as "the torment of the tomb" and from the moment of judgement a waiting period commences for individuals as they await the final Day of Doom at the end of time as we know it.

The Qur'an makes clear that all people are individually responsible for their past deeds and that they will be held accountable on Judgment Day. On that day each one will have to review their earthly life's record and for those who are heedless or unthinking the record will be the ultimate shock and humiliation. From this day on the soul will face either a realized and permanent bliss known as the Garden of Paradise or the ultimate torment of the Fire of Hell.

As a consequence of these final realities the observant Muslim, existing on the earthly side of the separation or barrier, is allowed to recite the Qur'an over the grave in order to provide the deceased with support and religious information. This is done so that the dead one can face the interrogation of the two angels Munkar and Nakir more fully equipped with added knowledge and preparation for the questions.[45] For the living relatives there is also the opportunity to conduct intercessory prayers for the deceased for forgiveness of some sins or for a more comfortable experience within the grave.[46] In addition to this, the efficacy of the Prophet in intercession, and the possibility of the influence of some saints, is incorporated into a supportive system of faith within some Muslim communities.

Hinduism

Hinduism, within the Indian Tree, falls within the classification of *dharmic religions,* and pertains to guidelines and rules of obligation or responsibility that are considered appropriate for human conduct on the path to liberation or *moksha.* It is considered to be a personal path to enlightenment and the eventual eradication of karma, thus allowing the atman to break free from the bondage of the cycle of samsara. This system incorporates moral and ethical values, appropriate actions and conduct within human society, but most particularly, through ritual or *puja,* towards deity, whether this be perceived as Nirguna Brahman as ultimate reality or Saguna Brahman through the personification of gods and goddesses.[47]

Originally, Hinduism contained no ideas about karma and rebirth, but instead emphasized that departed males from the upper three castes of the Brahmin (priestly caste), the Kshatriya (warrior/administrator caste), and the Vaishya (merchant/artisan caste) would join their forefathers after the appropriate last rites had been performed. The ultimate state of moksha, which in this context means heaven, would be enjoyed on the cool moon.[48] These beliefs still endure and can be identified through the continuance of the ritual of the *ancestor lists* and ancestor worship. The ancestor lists are kept for three generations but once the great-grandson of the ancestor dies, ritual oblations are discontinued and the ancestor is eliminated from the list.[49]

Belief in ancestral transcendence can also be identified in and through modern ritual observations. The belief is that without the help of living relatives performing particular rites at specific times, the departing soul would be incapable of acquiring the necessary body through which it could partake in the enjoyments experienced by the *pitrs* (fathers/ancestors). Therefore, during all ritual protocol, the living relatives were and are still required to perform specific required rites to ensure this transition. When a person dies, the family observes *shraddha* which is a ten-day mourning period. There is also an obligatory ritual ceremony that must be performed every month leading up to the first anniversary of the death. On the anniversary of the death, and each year subsequent to it, the surviving family members offer tributes to the deceased. This ritual requires that the family prepares the favourite foods that the deceased liked in life and these are then offered symbolically to the deceased. In addition to this, the family is required to offer these foods to eligible Brahmins and to cows and crows.[50] It is only upon completion of these offerings that the family members are allowed to eat the ritual meal. In addition, as part of the ancestral worship tradition, there is the Pitru Paksha (fortnight of ancestors) ritual, which is a two-week-long ritual observance. At this time, the family remembers all its ancestors and observes *tarpan* which consists of standing in water after bathing in a river or tank and offering water three times with appropriate chants. By observing these rituals it is believed that the deceased can enjoy all the comforts of the pitr realm. There is, however, one further link to belief in ancestor worship in this ancient system and that is a Hindu's duty to his ancestors to beget at least one son. This is required so that the surviving male descendent can continue to make offerings to the related ancestor. If this specific offering is not realized the ancestor will suffer and it is believed that the pitrs can resort to inflicting pain upon themselves in an endeavour to cause guilt in their living relatives in order to convince their descendants to have at least one male child.[51]

There are, however, other beliefs within Hinduism that reflect the integration of other traditions into the ancient Vedic religion; these reflect the view of reincarnation of the atman, and emphasis on karma, samsara, and moksha. In this form of traditional cosmology it is believed that one will reincarnate or be reborn in an appropriate form according to the karma one has created. This karmic process of cause and effect will include physical rebirth into human existence, encompassing being born with deformity or good health, in a state of wealth or poverty; or into the animal realm with all its resultant suffering. In addition to this, there is the concept of rebirth into heavenly worlds and horrific hells.[52] Arising out of this belief paradigm later ideas encoded in the Puranas and later Vedic literature speak of the existence of not one hell and one heaven but of many sun-filled worlds and many dark and demonic worlds.[53] The belief in heavens and hells is, however, in the ultimate sense of reality, believed to be relative or even immaterial because both stages are part of maya, or illusion. In the ultimate sense, the purpose of an afterlife is to remind souls of the true meaning to their existence and it functions neither to punish nor reward the souls, but to ultimately lead them to liberation through addressing karmic outcome.[54]

What can be ascertained from these beliefs and rituals, whether of the most ancient Vedic period or developing through the Puranas and other literature of later times, is that the belief system served to comfort the dying and support the living. These beliefs and practices are enduringly reflected in the customs of present-day Hindu society.

Buddhism

Buddhism is the second of the dharmic religions and has many similar religious concepts and themes to that of Hinduism, but at its inception began as a totally atheistic system of discipline and meditation towards enlightenment. What has occurred within the development of the Buddhist tradition, however, is that there are many different doctrinal branches and cultural interpretations.[55] These differences arise out of the two major "streams" within Buddhism—those of Hinayana generally referred to as Theravada Buddhism or Southern Buddhism and the later tradition known as Mahayana Buddhism or Eastern Buddhism. There is also a major tradition that developed out of Mahayana when it was introduced into Tibet, and this is referred to as Tibetan or Vajrayana Buddhism, also known as Northern Buddhism.

As a consequence of this impressive diversity, a challenge arises regarding the identification of a single belief system or core interpretation, pertaining to life after death. To appreciate this dilemma consider that some Buddhists will believe in the practical building of karma in order to achieve a prosperous new birth, whilst others will concentrate on meditation and asceticism for realizing enlightenment and liberation in order to enter nirvana. This state of nirvana is supposedly inexplicable but explained as stillness of mind, one without desire, without emotion or delusion, without aversion, and where there is peace as the self is extinguished. In addition to this, there will be other Buddhists who believe in a salvific figure, namely Amitabha or Amida Buddha, who can be petitioned for entry into rebirth in the Pure Land where this Buddha resides, along with all his devotees.[56]

What can be generally ascertained, however, is that there is a broad acceptance within Theravada, Mahayana, and Vajrayana of the central doctrine of the *anatman*, or no self.[57] What this means is that there is no enduring entity known as self that exists because it lacks substantive reality; in fact, the doctrine of impermanence or *anitya* illustrates that everything is merely a fleeting process of change.[58] Siddhartha Gautama taught that there was no atman or permanent self, but instead there existed a stream of being that every sentient being experienced. To explain this, Buddha emphasized the concept of a conglomerate Five Aggregates or Five Skandhas which he identified as (1) the material body, (2) feelings, (3) perception, (4) predispositions, and (5) consciousness. He believed that the five aggregates changed every moment and that the self was nothing but a stream of perishing physical and psychical phenomena that came together at birth, dissolved at death, and were not reborn together again. Arising out of this, Buddha taught that if we grasped this concept we could destroy all wants and cravings, be free from anxieties, attachments, and disappointments, and thus enjoy peace of mind and tranquility. This would lead to the burning off of karma, liberation from samsara, and the realization of nirvana.[59]

There is also a central belief in the realms or *Lokas* of rebirth into which the consciousness can be "born" and will be dependent on the outcome of karma. From these realms it becomes clear that rebirth is assured, but the type of rebirth is not, and will depend on one's actions manifesting through karma.[60] Thus the wheel of birth and death provides an intricate variety of possibilities concerning rebirth and within the concept of the samaric wheel there are incorporated thirty-one planes or lokas of existence.[61] This number will vary in classification and order according to whether it is Theravada which streamlines the lokas into five main groups, or Mahayana and Vajrayana that believe in six. For Theravada these realms are (1) hells, (2) animal, (3) hungry ghost, (4) human, and (5) heavenly. For the Mahayana and Vajrayana traditions these are (1) Deva or God Realm; (2) Asura or "Demi-God" Realm; (3) Human Realm—a middle realm thought to be the only one through which to achieve liberation; (4) Animal Realm; (5) Preta or "Hungry Ghost" Realm; and (6) Naraka or "Hell" Realm.[62]

These realms, together with clearly defined mourning rituals, show that Theravada, Mahayana, and Vajrayana traditions indicate an interval between death and rebirth. It is also believed that during the ritual mourning period the offerings made by the living create good karma and this good karma is then transferred over to the deceased in order to facilitate a more auspicious rebirth.[63]

Of all the texts endeavouring to describe the interval between death and rebirth, it is within the Vajrayana or Tibetan tradition that these ideas concerning an interim stage are clearly defined in an eighth-century work known as *The Great Liberation Through Hearing*, but more commonly known as the *Bardo Thodol*, or *Tibetan Book of the Dead*. The Bardo Thodol describes a three-stage journey between death and rebirth and it is read for forty-nine days, commencing from when the person is near death or newly dead, right through to the forty-ninth day after death when it is believed that the deceased's consciousness has reentered one of the six realms of existence.[64]

In addition to these ideas, in the Mahayana tradition it is also believed that a *bodhisattva*, as one who embodies compassion, may choose to reincarnate into any of the realms in order to aid the beings existing there. This concept of the beneficent bodhisattva can easily be identified within Mahayana Pure Land Buddhism with its emphasis on Avalokiteshvara, who is companion to Amitabha,[65] and in the Bodhisattva Jizo who moves through the six lokas extending compassion to the unborn child who died either through miscarriage or deliberate abortion.[66]

Buddhism, therefore, addresses broadly different cultures and provides a means of adapting central belief systems about life after death in order to accommodate a multitude of needs.

Jainism

Jainism is a very ancient, non-Vedic, indigenous Indian religion, with references to it found in both Hindu and Buddhist scriptures[67] and is classified as the third of the dharmic religions. Historically, what can be established regarding the tradition is that it emerged around 1000 B.C.E. and contained within it the reassertion of religious ideas and practices that predated the Vedas, including concepts and disciplines that could be of non-Aryan origins.[68]

As a tradition, Jainism identifies its first historical teacher as one, Mahavira (The Great Hero) who taught during the sixth century B.C.E. Jains hold to the belief that prior to the great Tirthenkara (Ford Maker) Mahavira, there were some twenty-three other Tirthenkaras who proceeded him dating back into the mists of time.[69] In the Jain belief system, Tirthenkaras (Ford Makers) were credited with having reached enlightenment but each chose to remain on earth in order to teach humankind the path to liberation from the samsaric cycle of life and death.[70]

The idea about enlightened teachers is a common factor within all of the Indian Tree traditions, but Jainism forms and adapts this staple of the typology by explaining the role of the Tirthenkara in its own unique way. Jainism explains that the universe is without beginning or end and passes eternally through long cycles of process and decline. At the beginning of each cycle, humans are happy, enjoy long life, and are virtuous and, as a consequence, have no need for religion. Sadly, however, these qualities decline and humans take on the burden of karma.[71] As a consequence to this they look to elders for guidance. This in turn leads to the creation of religion in order to steer people away from the growing evil in the world. In this context, the Tirthenkaras are revered as *Jinas* or supreme winners over their passions and thus are considered to be liberated jivas, or souls, who have taught and helped others on the path of liberation. As a consequence to this, they are held as great examples upon which the Jain can meditate and receive inspiration.

Like many Eastern religions, however, Jainism uses the concepts of reincarnation and deliverance but explains the consciousness in a divergent way. Jains hold that there is a soul, referred to as the *jiva*, which means a conscious, living being. For the Jains, the body and soul are two different things: the body is just a container and the conscious soul being is the jiva.[72] Each jiva is an individual entity which exists independently of all other jivas. Thus, there is no universal soul or consciousness into which all things flow, but in contrast, there are an infinite number of souls in the universe. It is believed that every living thing is a jiva and that some of these entities exist in embodied form and others in various forms of disembodiment, such as *siddhas,* who may or not be Tirthenkaras. This group of liberated souls possess almost god-like qualities, but are not considered to be gods as Jainism does not believe in God or gods.[73] The siddhas are not, therefore, worshiped and they have no interaction whatsoever with human beings but they serve as examples and hope of liberation within an inspirational context. Jains believe that every jiva has the possibility of achieving liberation from samsara, and can, through the process of reincarnation and the eradication of karma, eventually become a siddha. This is believed to occur when the jiva has been freed from all karmic influences and at that time then travels to the "supreme abode" or highest level of the universe. At this stage it then enjoys a disembodied, blissful state of existence alongside the other siddhas or liberated souls.[74]

In addition to the concepts of liberation and jiva, a major component of Jainst belief is the acceptance of karma and reincarnation. It is believed that after each physical death, the jiva is reincarnated into a new and different body and that this will be based on the karma accrued at the time of death. The new body may not be human or even animal, but could be plant life, an insect being, a water body, a fire body, or even clay or sand. In addition to this, the jiva can also reincarnate into varying hell realms as infernal beings according to the karma accrued.[75] It is, therefore, always important to focus the mind on spiritual matters in order to nullify, or at least dissolve some of the consequences of karma because the jiva is responsible for all its actions and will be held accountable to cosmic law. It is believed that the reincarnation process continues until the jiva is able to achieve liberation/deliverance, which in turn can only be gained when the jiva is free from all karma.

It is the building up of karma that makes the jiva attractive to more karma, thus imprisoning it within the samsaric process. This concept is explained through the ideas that the universe is permeated by karmic particulates that contain subtle matter. The particulates, or subtle matter, gravitate to the soul and the more karmic matter that is attracted and accumulated by the jiva the more it obscures the true nature of the soul. Jains believe that this material forms a coating that covers the soul and "grows" with every action based on desire and wrong action.[76] It is believed that every action and thought will result in karmic deposits and that both the destructive inclinations (actions that cause delusion and obstruct right conduct) and the nondestructive actions (those that produce pleasure and pain)[77] make the energy field surrounding the soul especially "attractive."[78] This in turn results in the concept of "coats of clay" whereby the particulates seemingly weigh down or trap the jiva within the cycle of samsara.

Liberation from this condition has two components: the first is to prevent the accumulation of any more karmic matter and the second is to cleanse the soul of the matter that it has already accumulated.[79] In order to do this, Jains adhere to the teachings of Mahivira which incorporates the practices of strict asceticism, renunciation, and adhering to the moral path. These precepts became encapsulated in what is known as the *Three Jewels*, which are right belief, right knowledge, and pure conduct.[80] As part of the *Three Jewels* concept there are three basic principles that Jains adopt to avoid accumulating karma and which are known as *ahimsa* (non-violence), *aparigraha* (non-attachment), and *anekantwad* (non-absolutism).[81] It is also believed that a life of extreme vegetarianism, together with a strict ascetic path (especially for monks and nuns), can lead the individual jiva to final liberation.

Sikhism

Sikhism emerged in the fifteenth century C.E. in northern India under the teachings and revelations of Guru Nanak (1469–1539). As the fourth of the dharmic religions, Sikhism also holds a central belief in reincarnation and it is believed that birth into a Sikh family and the Sikh faith is the result of good karma.[82] The aim of Sikhism is to provide the devotee with an attainable goal throughout the passage of life and some certainty in death and the beyond. This goal is based on one's own efforts as a practicing Sikh which are deemed necessary to provide the individual with the correct karmic path right up to the time of death after which the devotee meets God and undergoes an audience with Him. The Sikh will then be allowed to dwell either near to or far from Him, according to past efforts in this life.[83] In this context, therefore, it is upon the result of one's own efforts in this life that one's destiny after death will be determined and the record of one's deeds will be scrutinized in the presence of the Supreme Judge.

As part of this religious system, there is, therefore, the belief in both karma and samsara. It is also believed that karma from previous lives can be worked out in the present life and that present deeds can modify the rewards and penalties for former lives. So, although realistically many Sikhs will concede that they will probably have to undergo rebirth, there is still great emphasis placed up divine grace. If one has, through successive human rebirths, all within the Sikh community, come to a place of true liberation and holiness, death will lead to entry into the abode of *Waheguru* (Wonderful Lord), divine liberation, and the end of samsara. Integral to this key concept of belief in a blessed afterlife is the teaching that the soul belongs to the spiritual universe which has its origins in God and that the amount of good done and good karma accrued in life will store up blessings which will ultimately lead to union with God.[84]

As a core feature of Sikh belief in the transmigration of the soul, Sikhism believes that that the soul undergoes many rebirth eventualities before finally coming into birth as a human. It is believed that God is all-pervading, timeless, and in Himself unformed, and that He is in all things.[85] As a consequence of this, humans have also been part of all things, and have passed through all the lower forms of life and inanimate objects (such as rocks, stones, and trees) in order to be realized in the highest form which is human. Sikhism teaches that Waheguru places His divine spark, which is part of His very nature, within the human soul and this is seen in the way conscience and reason manifest within the human form. In the Sikh understanding, the human struggle to attain good karma involves rejecting the ego-centred life and embracing the inner life of opening to the divine *Sat Guru* (another name for God) within. It is only through this divine spark which resides in the human heart that Sikhs believe humans can live in the right way and be empowered to develop their spiritual faculties. Opening to the divine *Sat Guru* empowers the devotee to reject a selfish existence and live the life of holiness.[86]

In order to assist those who are dying on their final journey and to help them resolve spiritual issues, the *Akhand Path* (uninterrupted complete reading of the *Adi Granth*) is undertaken.[87] This ritual is conducted on special occasions such as joy, sorrow, or distress and is carried out over one set period of approximately forty-eight hours. Both male and female Sikhs are allowed to participate in the reading and it is regarded as a sacred prayer duty on behalf of a dying person.[88] As the person is dying he or she is also encouraged to chant the name of *Waheguru*, the Wonderful Lord.

The funerary ritual itself requires that the deceased's body be washed, dressed, and adorned with religious ornaments. The funeral ceremony is called *Antam Sanskaar* or *celebration of the completion of life* and hymns are recited by the congregation to induce feelings of detachment and at the same time hope for salvation.[89] The body is then taken to be cremated.

Confucianism and Taoism

The South East Asian traditions of Confucianism and Taoism[90] present challenges to the researcher insofar as they combine a mixture of atheistic philosophy, ancestor worship, folk religions, and a religious concept known as the *Tao* or *life force*. Together with this many-faceted system of practices, there exists the pervading belief in balance and harmony through forces known as yang (representing the positive/masculine) and yin (representing the negative/feminine) which were both held together through the *ch'i*, which represented the pure energy of the life force.

Of all Eastern philosophers, Master Kong, or Confucius as he is known in popular culture, was born in 550 B.C., and he is considered perhaps the greatest of all Eastern philosophers. The influence of Confucius has been so widespread that his teachings are still considered to be foundational to Asian cultures and his central works entitled *The Five Classics* (a collection of ancient Chinese writings) and *The Four Books* (a collection of Confucius and his disciples' teachings) functioned as the standard curriculum for Chinese education over many centuries.[91] In addition to this, Confucian ideas contributed to the systemization of Chinese beliefs about death and life after death, which included ancestor worship.

At the very core of Chinese traditional folk religion lay animistic beliefs in which gods and spirits inhabited natural formations and it was believed that the ancestral spirits were present both in the family home and at the gravesite of the corpse. These spirits of the dead were considered part of the real physical world which the living inhabited and as such required respect, loyalty, and ritual attendance.[92]

Incorporated into ancestral transcendence and concepts of survival after death, there were early and evolving beliefs that humans possessed a two-part spirit identity which was composed of the hun and p'o spirits.[93] The *hun* embodied the conscious personality that the person exhibited during life. The *p'o* spirit was the energy or vital animating force of the body. After death these two entities separated, and the hun which retained consciousness, intellect, and will was the subject of a specialized funerary ritual entitled, "summoning back of the *hun* spirit." It was believed that the hun then became an immortal being known as a *shen* who lived either in the celestial empire or in the blessed island of the spirits. It was to this spirit that living family members paid their respects and offerings and to whom the living sent their petitions for assistance as family members.

In contrast to this, the *p'o* spirit remained present with the body after death and transformed into a malevolent entity known as a *kuei*. Traditionally, it was believed that the *kuei* caused harm for family members, thereby causing great disharmony and stress.[94]

Against this cultural background, Confucius presented his philosophy as an integrated ethical code. Master K'ung avoided spiritual issues and can be categorized as an agnostic; at the same time, however, he believed in spirits and the supernatural but was not interested in them. As a scholar and philosopher, Confucious went against the folklore norm and refused to speak about either gods or any concept of heaven and also refused to ponder the meaning of death or the possibility of an afterlife. He argued that if one did not live appropriately and serve the living correctly, how could one appropriately serve ghosts. He also believed that to fully understand death one must understand life,[95] and that this was a long and meticulously difficult process within itself. As a sage or learned, cultivated man, he emphasized right and fitting behaviour which would be required for any situation including the ritually correct way that one was to conduct oneself in facing death. Giving such minute attention to detail, he provided people with meticulous coping mechanisms through which to navigate all of life's eventualities or possibilities.

In the context of grieving, coping, and right actions, Master K'ung taught that each funeral was to be given meaning by personal presence fused with ceremonial actions. In this way, grief, concentration, and ritual provided to those who were participating in the funerary obligation parameters of appropriate action. This ritual in and of itself also stipulated an appropriate period of three years' mourning and in this way demonstrated that all things come to an end and one must govern oneself accordingly.[96]

Also contributing to the development and systemization of Chinese beliefs, the Taoist tradition provides further perspectives on immortality through a calm acceptance of death, which is believed to be a return to the Tao. This, however, is a very simplistic explanation for a varied belief system and the scholar encounters problems in identifying a single, unified Taoist belief regarding afterlife and salvation. The reason for this is that Taoism was never the only religion within the Chinese system in that it existed alongside Confucianism and Buddhism, as well as with Chinese folk religions. Indeed, it often exhibited very similar beliefs to those of traditional folk religions insofar as ancestor worship and spirit beings were concerned. It also incorporated belief in magical incantations, and magic elixirs that would fend off death, or even avoid the event completely, thus gaining immortality. What is also evident is that each Taoist sect had its own beliefs and textual traditions, and these underwent changes over time. In addition to this, as Buddhism gradually became the major interpretive force regarding death and the afterlife, many of its ideas were adapted or developed by Taoism in order to define what Taoist beliefs were.[97]

What can, however, be identified as an enduring concept within the Taoist tradition is that it advocated an almost ecstatic acceptance of death. Examples of this approach can be identified in two sacred Taoist texts: the *Daodejing* (fourth century B.C.E.) which is traditionally believed to have been written by the philosopher Lao Tzu, who is commonly heralded as the founder of Taoism; and another early and substantial Taoist work entitled the *Chuang Tzu* (c. third century B.C.E.). In both works death was imagined as a return to the original powerful chaotic unity that was the beginning and end of all things.[98] Death was interpreted as a way of disappearing and then reappearing within the Tao which also renewed itself through a form of death and re-formation.[99] Death within the Tao was considered to be a form of moving away and then returning, in which one died in order to be renewed. Following through with this concept, it was also believed that if people alienated themselves from the flow of the Tao as the ultimate life force, they would then wither, suffer, and spiritually die. If one turned away from the renewing energy of nature one lost everything.

There were, however, others who did not meditate on returning to the Tao, as they sought immortality of the physical body. Taoists from specific traditions hoped that they would never die and would live forever in human form, whilst developing supernatural powers through specific esoteric rituals, which would place them in the realms of the immortals. These realms were generally located on earth, either on mountains or islands, or in other cases, places that were usually invisible to the human eye.

The diversity of beliefs within the Confucian and Taoist traditions leads the observer to the realization that there are many different views on survival after death within the Chinese systems. What, however, can be identified as a central body of enduring beliefs to this day can be summarized as

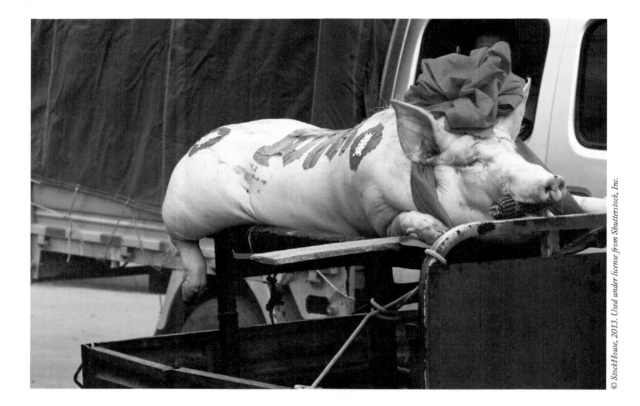

arising out of later traditional beliefs.[100] These ideas hold to the concept of (1) each person contains the masculine principle known as yang, and the feminine principle known as yin; (2) each person possesses a "higher" soul or yang soul, and also a "lower "soul" or yin soul; (3) the yin soul is more dense and clings to the body. It stays near the gravesite and is acknowledged at least once a year in the spring when families "sweep the grave" of their dead relatives; (4) the yin soul is viewed as more problematic, as it inhabits the realm of disembodied spirits and can cause problems for other spirits, together with hauntings and other unpleasant experiences for humans who have failed to placate it; (5) the yang-like soul, which is less dense, less malevolent, remains around the house where it must be remembered and appeased at the family altar, with daily incense, and food twice a month, and on New Year; (6) the living believe that offering their oblations to the ancestors will also benefit them as there is a reciprocal relationship whereby they themselves receive benefits from the dead,[101] thus there is an ongoing generational family connection based on harmony and respect.

INDIGENOUS TRADITIONS

Indigenous traditions are many and varied insofar as they represent thousands of tribal systems throughout the world. To analyze these individual systems would prove to be an overwhelming task within this chapter. What can, however, be established within these ancient beliefs in death and the afterlife is that they adhere to certain core concepts, whether it be ancestors, spirits and/or ghosts, or reincarnation of some kind.

Within many indigenous systems there is the belief in ancestors and ancestral transcendence. The ancestral spirits function as bridges between physical life, death, and life in the spirit world; thus it is imperative that a good relationship with deceased relatives be maintained. Just as within the tribal physical realm where cooperation is a necessity for survival, so too, reciprocity with the spirit world of the departed and also with other animistic spirit entities form the backbone of survival after death. There is a cosmology of interdependence through which one endures.

There are also specific rituals which are initiated by shamans in order to invoke the spirits and to also enter the spirit world. The power within these concepts is that survival in some form in another spirit realm can occur and can be accessed through bridging realities. Further, in some traditions, whether they be Australian, African, South American, or North American, there is the belief that the spirit realm functions to provide guidance in this life and a destination in the next.[102]

Another identifiable belief in an afterlife comes through the Arctic traditions which espouse reincarnation, such as the Naskapi or some groups of Inuit. In the case of the Naskapi who live in Labrador, near to the Arctic Circle, there is the belief that the whole world is filled with soul, or *Mantu*. In this tradition the physical world is real and animated by souls. Harmony must be maintained with all souls in order to survive and thus the shaman is essential in keeping communication flowing. The Naskapi believe that all souls between the times they reside in physical bodies, live among the stars. In this way, the four winds, rainbows, Northern Lights, and even the Milky Way become places where the spirits of ancestors exist until they return through reincarnation.[103]

In the context of Inuit traditions, beliefs concerning after-death survival are sometimes not specific but there is a definite unease regarding the spirits of the recently dead. Similar to the Naskapi peoples, many High Arctic peoples will also believe in reincarnation, ghosts, or that people go to another world. It is not unusual that a combination of all these beliefs will exist within a specific community.[104]

CONCLUSION

Having reviewed our species' ability to cognitively sort, and in some ways handle, the fragility of life and the finality of death, it becomes clear that there exists diverse coping mechanisms and belief systems that we have created over millennia. What is fascinating to observe is that we continue to adapt and find new ways of expressing our grief and governing our despair, even within secular and materialistic societies. We instinctively problem solve and address horror and we try to find meaning in a world that is so clearly full of suffering. Throughout our history and diverse cultures we have consistently found ways to face death and create realms of meaning, thus once again incorporating religion into our reality.

GLOSSARY

Adi Granth: The Holy Scriptures of Sikhism.

Ahimsa: In Jainism, means nonviolence.

Akhand Path: In Sikhism, means an uninterrupted complete reading of the *Adi Granth* for a special occasion.

Anatman: Buddhist doctrine of no soul or no self.

Ancestor list: In Hinduism, ancestor lists are kept for three generations but once the great-grandson of the ancestor dies, ritual oblations are discontinued and the ancestor is eliminated from the list.

Ancestral transcendence: Connecting the living and deceased through the biological chain of parent and progeny. Children keep a relationship alive through memory and ritual.

Anekantwad: In Jainism, means nonabsolutism.

Anitya: Buddhist doctrine of impermanence.

Aparigraha: In Jainism, means nonattachment.

Bad death: Used to describe untimely death. Applied to the deaths of a young warrior, a healthy child, or a person of special standing within the community. Can also refer to a suspicious death as the result of a malevolent act, murder, or curse.

Bardo Thodol: Also known as the Tibetan Book of the Dead. This is an eighth-century C.E. work that details a three-stage journey between death and rebirth. It is read for forty-nine days, from when the person is actually dying or already dead, right through to the forth-ninth day when it is believed that the deceased's consciousness has re-entered one of the six realms of existence. The stages are (1) Chikhai Bardo, the hour of death; (2) Chonyid Bardo, mental life after death, and (3) Sidpa Bardo, the process of rebirth into one of the lokas that appear.

Bodhisattva: A central concept in Mahayana and Vajrayana Buddhism. Refers to an enlightened being who, out of compassion, forgoes nirvana in order to save others and continues to reincarnate until all beings are brought to enlightenment.

Bosom of Abraham: Jewish term identified during Second Temple Judaism in a Jewish papyri which refers to the "Bosom of Abraham, Isaac and Jacob." Implies reaching rest and peace through observance of the covenant kept by all religious Jews. Also can be expanded to broadly incorporate any Jewish person as each one is considered to be a biological descendent of Abraham.

Chi: Animating force; refined life energy.

Cultural transcendence: the transformation of the social event of death. Part of the collective memory process of a community

whereby the deceased is kept alive as a social identity through memory and commemoration; kept "alive" through art, celebration, ritual and commemorative social memorials, celebrations, and popular memory.

Dharmic religions: Refers to the Indian tree systems of Hinduism, Buddhism, Jainism, and Sikhism. Guidelines and rules considering what is appropriate for human conduct; includes moral and ethical values, ritual and household duties pertain to deity and to human beings. Considered to be a personal path to enlightenment and the eventual eradication of karma, thus breaking free of the karmic cycle of samsara.

Five Aggregates: Buddhist concept defining the stream of being as identified in five skanhas or threads of being.

Heaven: Place of God's abode where the faithful will find final rest and peace. Also used to define the habitation of gods, goddesses, angels, saints, or venerated ancestors who are considered semi-divine. Set apart only for the holy.

Hun: Chinese concept of spirit. Refers to the embodied conscious personality that the person exhibited during life.

Jina: In Jainism, refers to those who have brought forth their highest true nature. The Tirthenkaras are revered as Jinas because they are considered to be "winners" over passion. It is from this term that the term *Jain* is derived.

Jiva: A Jainist belief that sees this energy as an entity which is a conscious, living being.

Kuei: Chinese concept of the malevolent part of the spirit that transformed from the p'o.

Mantu: Naskapi concept of world soul.

Moksha: Defined as salvation or liberation within the dharmic religions. In Hinduism, reaching moksha is synonymous with becoming one with God and attaining salvation. In the Hindu context, this means escaping the cycle of rebirth. In the Buddhist context, describes the ultimate state of enlightenment for the consciousness by which it is set free from all worldly attachments and cravings.

Mythic: Deeply profound and moving stories, visions, beliefs that transform death into a transition into another realm. Embues the hero and the martyr with mythic transcendence by which they are perceived to automatically achieve immortality through their actions or sufferings. Refers to a deeply ingrained perception of an afterlife.

P'o: Chinese concept of spirit. Refers to the energy or vital animating force of the body.

Primitive Church/early Church: Refers to a period of Church development dating from its inception in 30 c.e., until approximately the Council of Nicea in 325 c.e. which was convened by the Emperor Constantine.

Puja: In Hinduism refers to ritual in honor of the gods. Is conducted in home and temples.

Shen: Chinese concept of elevated spirit to whom living family members paid their respects and offerings.

Shraddha: Hindu ten-day mourning ritual conducted immediately after death within the family unit.

Tao: Chinese concept of the life force or life energy that permeates all things and to which all life returns.

Thanatology: Education regarding the reality of dying and death. Open and frank discussion which gives the dying person, and close ones who suffer with that person, social and emotional permission to face the reality of death. Systematic inclusion of the reality of death and dying into the process of living. To accept death and incorporate the event into a worldview, either religious or nonreligious, which will enlighten, encourage, and help people live their lives with purpose and face death with peace. To live with the reality of an end. To foster a broader perspective and appreciation of what it means to be alive.

Tirthankaras: Fordmakers; Jainist belief; enlightened human beings.

Waheguru: *Wonderful Lord.* The main and true name used for God in Sikhism.

Yang: Chinese concept for positive masculine energy of the soul.

Yin: Chinese concept for negative feminine energy of the soul.

ENDNOTES

1. Marie De Hennezel, *Intimate Death: How the Dying Teach Us How to Live*, (New York: Vintage Books, 1998), translation by Carol Brown Janeway, 1997, p vi.

2. Open discussion of death. See glossary.

3. Marie De Hennezel, *Intimate Death: How the Dying Teach Us How to Live*, (New York: Vintage Books, 1998), translation by Carol Brown Janeway, 1997, p vi. Francoise Mitterrand, introductory preface.

4. George E. Barker, *Death and After Death*, (Washington: University Press of America, 1979), p 7.

5. Ibid.

6. C. G. Jung, *Alchemical Studies: Collected Works of C.G. Jung*, Vol. 13, (New York: Princeton University Press, 1967), trans. R. F. C. Hull, para. 68.

7. David Gerrold quote: http://www.brainyquote.com/quotes/quotes/d/davidgerro136980.html

8. Blaise Pascal, http://www.brainyquote.com/quotes/quotes/b/blaisepasc400003.html#plPTQ5soU1PXfO8p.99

9. Thomas Mann, *The Magic Mountain, A Novel* (New York: Knopf, 1995), translated by John E. Woods, p. 1979.

10. http://www.mummytombs.com/mummylocator/group/kabayan.htm

11. William W. McCorkle, Jr., *Ritualizing the Disposal of the Deceased: From Corpse to Concept*, (New York: Peter Lang, 2010), p 6.

12. Tony Walter, *The Eclipse of Eternity: A Sociology of the Afterlife*, (New York: St. Martin's Press, Inc., 1966), pp 144-145. Walter describes a modern funeral with its strange mixture of intense emotion, ambiguity, and impersonal hypocrisy "with clergymen incanting words that no one believes," or survivors insisting on a religious rite of passage without any accompanying belief regarding an afterlife.

13. Tony Walter, "Secularization" in *Death and Bereavement Across Cultures*, (London: Routledge, 1997); Colin Murray Parkes et al, p 170.

14. David S. Anthony, *The Horse, The Wheel and Language: How Bronze Age Riders from the Eurasian Steppes Shaped the Modern World* (Princeton: Princeton University Press, 2007), pp 397-405.

15. http://english.peopledaily.com.cn/90001/90782/90873/7289260.html

16. Archaeologist, Sir Leonard Woolley, who discovered and excavated the possible tomb of Queen Pu-abi, discovered the remains and name written in cuneiform on a cylinder seal found close to her body. Woolley discovered the skeletal remains and artifacts of soldiers and serving ladies. The soldiers guarded the entrance to the pit while the serving ladies crowded the floor near to the entrance of the tomb. Finding no evidence of trauma on the bones, Woolley suggested that they might have taken poison. See: the Heilbrunn Timeline of Art History. The Metropolitan Museum of Art, http://www.metmuseum.org/toah/hd/urrg/hd_urrg.htm

17. Pharaohs, caesars, dictators, kings, queens, emperors, tribal chieftains, religious leaders, priests, some noblemen, and illustrious ancestors were believed to resume their dominant functions in the realm of the hereafter. Their minions were believed to join them on the other side and resume their servile existence, obeying and worshipping their superiors without release from domination.

18. Laura Wittman, *The Tomb of the Unknown Soldier, Modern Mourning, and the Reinvention of the Mystical Body* (Toronto: University of Toronto Press, 2011), p 7.

19. Ibid., pp 152-153.

20. David Chidester, *Patterns of Transcendence*, (Belmont, CA: Wadsworth Group, 2002), p 16.

21. In some instances, these shrines are transformed into permanent memorials. See Jack Santino, *Performative Commemoratives: Spontaneous Shrines and the Public Memorialization of Death*, (New York: Palgrave Macmillan, 2006), p 27.

22. Hege Westgaard, "Like a Trace: The Spontaneous Shrine as a Cultural Expression of Grief," in *Performative Commemoratives*, p 147.

23. John Belshaw, Diane Purvey, *Private Grief, Public Mourning: The Rise of the Roadside Shrine in B.C.*, (Vancouver, B.C., Anvil Press, 2009), p 13.

24. Jack Santino, *Performative Commemoratives*, p 27.

25. Floral shrines were also constructed at Spencer House, St James Palace, Clarence House, and Buckingham Palace, and there were numerous floral tributes in Victoria Embankment Gardens. There were also spontaneous tributes constructed in Paris immediately after her death, North America, and throughout most of the Europe.

26. Chidester, *Patterns of Transcendence*, p 16.

27. Ibid., pp 12, 16, 18.

28. One of the early theorists, E. B. Tylor (1901–1989), argued in his work entitled *Primitive Culture*, Vol. 1, (London: Gordon Press, 1974), p 429.

29. Bronislaw Malinowski, "The Role of Magic and Religion," in W. A. Lessa and E. Z. Vogt (eds.), *A Reader in Contemporary Religion*, (New York: Harper & Row, 1965), p 71.

30. Chidester, *Patterns of Transcendence*, pp 11, 16, 18.

31. Michael Parker Pearson, *The Archaeology of Death and Burial*, (Texas: A&M University Press, 2000), p 25.

32. Charles A. Corr, Clyde M. Nabe, Donna M. Corr, *Death and Dying, Life and Living* (Belmont, CA: Wadsworth/Thomson Learning, 2003), p 273.

33. It is usually accepted that only the most righteous ascend to a heavenly state immediately after death. One must undergo purgation in Gehinnom.

34. Eliezer Segal, "Judaism," *Life after Death in World Religions*, ed. Harold Coward, (New York: Orbis Books, 1997), pp 11-29.

35. Dated from 30 C.E. to just before the Council of Nicea in 325 C.E.

36. The Book of Revelation 6:9.

37. Terrence Penelhum, "Christianity," *Life after Death in World Religion*, pp 34-40.

38. There were earlier reformers dating back to the early fourteenth century, but it was Luther's teachings that brought the New Testament's teachings into the full public eye.

39. Jane Idleman Smith, "Islam," *How Different Religions View Death and Afterlife,* (Philadelphia: The Charles Press, Publishers, 1998), pp 132-133.

40. David Chidester, *Patterns of Transcendence,* p 180.

41. Ibid.

42. Jane Idleman Smith, "Islam," p 138.

43. Hanna Kassis, "Islam," *Life After Death in World Religions,* p 54.

44. Qur'an 8:50.

45. David Chidester, *Patterns of Transcendence,* p 232.

46. Hanna Kassis, "Islam," p 141.

47. Roger Schmidt et al, *Patterns of Religion,* p 213.

48. Klaus K. Klostermaier, *Hinduism: A Short Introduction* (Oxford: Oneworld Publication, 1998), p 40.

49. Ibid.

50. http://www.thatreligiousstudieswebsite.com/Religious_Studies/Phil_of_Rel/Life_after_Death/hinduism_life_death.php

51. http://www.esamskriti.com/essay-chapters/Significance-of-Pitru-Paksh,-Shraaddh-and-Tarpan-1.aspx

52. Klaus K. Klostermaier, *Hinduism: A Short Introduction,* p 41.

53. http://www.hinduwebsite.com/hinduism/h_death.asp

54. Ibid.

55. Roger Schmidt et al, *Patterns of Religion,* p 281.

56. Ibid.

57. This is somewhat confusing in Vajrayana as there is a more fully defined idea of the self as can be seen from the teachings within the Bardo Thodol, known as the Tibetan Book of the Dead, where one of superior spiritual enlightenment, known as a Bodhisattva, can be reincarnated and identified through a process of specific rituals.

58. Patrick S. Bresnan, *Awakening: An Introduction to the History of Eastern Thought,* (Upper Saddle River, NJ: Pearson Education, 2003), p 215.

59. Ibid., pp 220-221.

60. Christopher Jay Johnson, Marsha G. McGee, *How Different Religions View Death and Afterlife,* p 51.

61. Mary Pat Fisher, *Living Religions: A Brief Introduction* (2nd ed.), (Upper Saddle River, NJ: Pearson, 2009), pp 76-77.

62. Paul Gwynne, *World Religions in Practice: A Comparative Introduction,* (Oxford: Blackwell Publishing, 2009), p 141.

63. Ibid., p 144.

64. David Chidester, *Patterns of Transcendence,* pp 124-140.

65. Paul Gwynne, *World Religions in Practice,* p 49.

66. David Chidester, *Patterns of Transcendence,* p 231.

67. Mary Pat Fisher, *Living Religions* (6th ed.), p 116.

68. Bradley K. Hawkins, *Introduction of Asian Religions,* (London: Laurance King Publishing, Ltd., 2004), p 101.

69. Patrick S. Bresnan, *Awakening: An Introduction to the History of Eastern Thought* (2nd ed.), (Upper Saddle River, NJ: Prentice Hall, 1999), p 87.

70. Bradley K. Hawkins, *Introduction of Asian Religions,* pp 103-105.

71. Patrick S. Bresnan, *Awakening: An Introduction to the History of Eastern Thought,* p 87.

72. http://www.bbc.co.uk/religion/religions/jainism/beliefs/reincarnation.shtml. Retrieved February 28, 2013.

73. Ibid.

74. Ibid.

75. Ibid.

76. Robert S. Ellwood, Barbara A. McGraw, *Many Peoples, Many Faiths: Women and Men in the World of Religion* (7th ed.), (Upper Saddle River, NJ: Prentice Hall, 2002), p 108.

77. Mary Pat Fisher, *Living Religions* (6th ed), p 118.

78. Bradley K. Hawkins, *Introduction of Asian Religions,* p 103.

79. http://www.bbc.co.uk/religion/religions/jainism/beliefs/reincarnation.shtml. Retrieved February 28, 2013.

80. Bradley K. Hawkins, *Introduction of Asian Religions,* p 105.

81. Mary Pat Fisher, *Living Religions* (6th ed.), p 118.

82. W. Owen Cole and Piara Singh Sambhi, *The Sikhs: Their Religious Beliefs and Practices,* (Brighton: Sussex Academic Press, 1998), p 125.

83. Ian S. Markham with Christie Lohr, *A World Religions Reader* (3rd ed.), (Oxford: Blackwell Publishers, 2009), p 238.

84. Ibid.

85. Ibid.

86. John L. Esposito, Darrell J. Fasching, Todd Lewis, *World Religions Today,* (Oxford: Oxford University Press, 2002), p 311.

87. Ian S. Markham with Christie Lohr, *A World Religions Reader* (3rd ed.), p 253.

88. Ibid.

89. W. Owen Cole and Piara Singh Sambhi, *The Sikhs,* p 127.

90. NOTE: For the purposes of this study, only the Confucian and Taoist concepts will be addressed.

91. Buddhism and Christianity also play a part in the overall Asian cosmology. Zukeran, *Confucius,* http://www.leaderu.com/orgs/probe/docs/confucius.html

92. Kenneth Kramer, *The Sacred Art of Dying: How World Religions Understand Death,* (New York: Paulist Press, 1988), pp 90-91.

93. David Chidester, Patterns *of Transcendence,* p 99.

94. Ibid.

95. Harold Coward, *Life After Death in World Religions,* (Maryknoll: Orbis Books, 1997), p 107.

96. Kenneth Kramer, *The Sacred Art of Dying: How World Religions Understand Death,* p 88.

97. http://www.patheos.com/Library/Taoism/Beliefs/Afterlife-and-Salvation.html

98. David Chidester, *Patterns of Transcendence,* p 102.

99. Ibid., p 103.

100. Kenneth Kramer, *The Sacred Art of Dying: How World Religions Understand Death,* p 90.

101. Ibid.

102. David Chidester, *Patterns of Transcendence,* pp 70-71.

103. Warren Matthews, *World Religions* (7th ed.), (Belmont, CA: Wadsworth Cengage Learning, 2013), pp 20-21.

104. http://cronus.uwindsor.ca/units/hro/main.nsf/54ef3e94e5fe816e85256d6e0063d208/cdb98464b4c00954852571e0004a0e94/$FILE/Native%20Spirituality.pdf

CHAPTER 8

Evil and Suffering: Meanings and Explanations

© Carndens Design, 2013. Used under license from Shutterstock, Inc.

Unless one has totally retreated from reality, it is quite evident that there is evil and suffering all around us. We can identify it in the plight of the vulnerable, the sick, the anguished, the displaced. It screams to us through the tragedy of our disappearing and at-risk animal species, together with widespread environmental devastation, and our abuse of domesticated animals. It is also clearly represented through war and trauma—both in civilian and military personnel. Routinely, we cope with these harsh realities by distraction, denial, studied indifference, or even cultivated ignorance. This may seem a very harsh general observation, but the reality is that this is exactly what our world and its inhabitants manifest.

Set against this bleak physical, sociological, and emotional landscape one is driven to ponder whether everything around us is misery and tragedy? Obviously, the answer is most definitely no, but evil and suffering are experiences within life and our species regularly presents as the key instigators and perpetrators through which much of that misery manifests. This broad assertion must be corroborated with fact and so this chapter will address the ways in which cruel and corrosive tragedies display themselves and how we are often desensitized to these destructive dynamics—both tangible and subtle. In addition to this, we will discuss the evil and tragedy that befalls us through natural disasters and diseases. Arising out of these realities, we will then review the role of the world's religions in identifying these dynamics and explaining their meanings.

Having regard to these observations, consider the following statement presented by philosopher David Stewart, in his work, *Exploring the Philosophy of Religion:*

> The list of the sources of suffering is enormous and includes disease, war, famine, human cruelty to other human beings, psychological distress, and disappointment, to name only some. In attempting to sort out the various faces of evil, a distinction has frequently been made between natural evil and moral evil. [1]

Due to the sheer scope and complexity of evil and suffering the root causes of many of these inescapable realities initially present as incomprehensible. In many instances we cannot pinpoint the root causes of the event, but gradually become aware of its consequences only after the situation has caused sorrow and devastation. This is due to the fact that there are so many variables, patterns of intersection, and explanations, that the issues often confusingly morph one into another. This overlapping of variables inevitably becomes a morass of issues and trigger causes. In turn, these can become difficult to dissect and expose clearly; this in turn presents as a serious challenge to identifying or even finding remedy for some of the problems. Fortunately, however, due to the impressive contributions of our scholars and theologians throughout history who grappled with this reality, we can, to a limited degree, attempt to unravel and identify some identifying agents. Our ancient scholars, and many following in their intellectual paths, used two classifications to arrange the modes of delivery by which evil reaches us. Evil can be arranged through our analytical approaches, classifications, and examinations into two main categories—that of natural evil and moral evil. Natural evil refers to those events that bring suffering which are caused by nature; moral evil applies to those events causing suffering which we humans are responsible for. Utilizing these classifications of natural evil and moral evil it is possible to somewhat organize our often muddled comprehension into understanding the basic delivery systems through which evil and suffering are manifested and disclosed throughout all forms of life.

TOWARDS A BROADER UNDERSTANDING: THE CATEGORIES

In order to appreciate the scope and influence of the misery harboured within both classifications of natural and moral evil it is helpful to attach some sort of statistical percentage to the amount of evil harboured within each of the categories. Consider the following analytical observation made by philosopher David Stewart, who suggests that we can broadly estimate the amount of evil "attributable to natural causes and what amount is attributable to human perversity." Stewart presents a staggering ratio of a 60 to 40 percent weighting for moral evil set against natural evil. What is even more chilling is to further proceed with Stewart's extrapolations and consider, as he presents, a more critical but feasible estimated imbalance of a 90 to 10 percent ratio for moral evil set against natural evil.[2] Whether we accept or re-

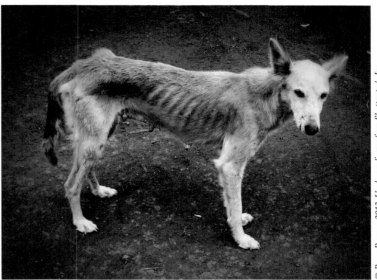

ject these generalized claims or models, the fact remains that upon even a cursorily analysis of events designated as evil, one fact is blatantly clear: our species deludes itself into thinking we play a relatively minor role as a major cause of systemic evil. What is evident from any historical survey of human conduct is that our species has played a major role in the delivery of suffering, destabilization, and death to many living beings, including our own kind. To prove this point, note that during "the past 3,400 years, humans have been entirely at peace for [only] 268 of them."[3] To comprehend this historical reality from another approach, this means that over the entire period of our species' recorded history we have only desisted from major mass murder events coupled with all the resulting horrific consequences, for roughly 8 percent of our historical record. If we then factor into this reality the resulting suffering manifesting as corollaries of war and its devastation, the permutations know no limits. There is no reign to the influence exerted upon natural evil through imbalance within the biotic systems. Arising out of these basic facts, natural evil and moral evil can now be more clearly comprehended in many aspects of life.

To offer a more concise explanation of the nature and function of evil, consider the two following observational points. The first observation is that natural evil raises questions about the order of nature and the human place within it, as to vulnerability and the impartial power and destruction within natural systems which all life experiences. The second observation addresses moral evil expressed through its broader range of delivery with our species acting as conduits for its malevolence. This aspect of evil raises questions about human nature and its conduct; further it presents the alarming reality of our active abetting in its delivery system.[4]

CONSIDERING NATURAL EVIL

For some reason, our species always perceives our planet's awe-inspiring and frequently terrifying natural functions as the major contributor to evil and suffering but this is an inaccurate assumption.

To be fair to those who have suffered a natural disaster or been in the midst of a violent natural upheaval of any sort, nature is indeed a callous and unstoppable force. What is evident and undeniable is that our interpretations are based on the keen awareness of the physical reality and vulnerability of life forms encountering the enormous power of the biotic web. For example, consider the acts of nature to which we are all exposed in varying degrees of susceptibility, location, proximity, and sometimes simple coincidence. The fact is that we are aware of our vulnerability to almost all other forms of life upon this planet, be it a bacterium, virus, angry animal, harsh physical environment, or tumultuous weather. In reality, however, nature is not intentionally cruel but simply manifests impartial physical laws which are the results of cause and effect or the outcome of imbalances introduced as contributing factors to upset its efficient operations. When nature runs quietly, smoothly, and without danger to our species, we think little of its complex and mighty power, but when the systems operate against us we deem these forces cruel or even evil. From a scientific perspective, it is easy to appreciate the multitude of ways the biosphere and nature maintain balance, regulate systems, or shift tectonic plates. Consider the life-threatening systems that surround us. There are hurricanes, tropical cyclones, typhoons, tsunamis, volcanic eruptions, earthquakes, major rain storms, snow and/or ice storms, blizzards, floods, monsoons, landslides, droughts, forest and bush fires, famines, plagues, diseases of all kinds, animal and insect attacks, and also animal suffering. Thus when we encounter the raw force of nature we imbue it with the persona of the enemy. In this context, we interpret it as a force that must be subdued and conquered wherever possible; so the feud with our biotic life-support system becomes an unrelenting and disturbing drama through which we interpret reality.

In contrast to this misconception, the reality is that much of what we attribute to natural evil has actually been caused by humankind's impact upon the environment. If one considers the ramifications of our ignorance through stupidity, violence, aggression, superstition, hatred, greed, lack of compassion, superstition, and prejudice, then the perspective takes on another vista. Next, factor in how we create unsanitary conditions through poor hygiene, squalor and environmental pollution. From these we can then clearly identify the outcome of many "natural" occurrences as being attributable to none other than ourselves, to our own conduct affecting them. Consider, for example, the cause of plagues and other diseases incubated by unsanitary conditions or sexual transmission. In addition to this, take into account the resultant suffering in the aftermath of natural disasters when human privation and vulnerability are preyed upon through unscrupulous exploitation by members of our own species who seek to profit through power, lust, or greed.

What can be observed from these realities is that natural events or catastrophes place us at the mercy of the mostly impartial power of the biosphere's self-regulation. As sentient beings we are often mistaken regarding the amount of power we really possess and do not truly comprehend the massive, raw energy of the planet that sustains us. Humans, like every other form of life, are always at the "mercy" of the environment even when we are deluded into thinking we are biologically, intellectually, or technologically superior and removed from its ultimate power. It is the nature of all life to die and the ways in which this fact is inevitability encountered speak to our susceptibility under the natural, physical laws of the biosphere. What arises out of a humble recognition of nature's firm hand upon us is the reality that natural evil, although extremely unpleasant and cruel, is part of the planet's life force. In this context, what we would designate as natural evil is in some ways easier to comprehend rationally because it speaks to the physical manifestations of an inexorably impersonal system. As a consequence to this, natural evil is often far more logical for us to identify due to the fact that we can overlook our personal culpability in destabilizing the environment. We can perceive the outcome of natural evil logically and yet still disassociate per-

sonal blame by emphasizing our *creatureliness* and vulnerability, and feeling sorry for ourselves because we are innocent victims of nature. Blindly and irresponsibly, we apportion cause and effect to the natural systems which we blame for our suffering, whilst systematically denying that it is our own species that often acts as a catalyst for some of the natural events that we consider evil.

COMPREHENDING MORAL EVIL

Set within our historical matrix, however, the staggering power and role of natural evil somewhat pales when compared to our own species' unrelenting influence through what we define as moral evil. What is interesting to note is that even though there may be cultural variance pertaining to codes of conduct or laws, there still exists an intrinsic value system inherent to all societies. These systems of moral organization require the identification and sorting of practical, ethical rules of interaction with regard to each other and to the environment. Thus it becomes evident that as a common speciel trait, we have created varying degrees of a moral value system easily identifiable throughout the written record of human history, with special definitions and emphasis on its importance relayed through the religious systems.[5]

What is also clear is that from early times we have differentiated between that which is good and that which is evil.[6] In addition to this, as history attests,[7] we have struggled to incorporate this recognition into codes of conduct in order to help us either control or neutralize the moral evil that we can identify. In other words, historically, we have created order through laws which have recognized a dichotomy within our nature; we have identified a world of light which has been set against a world of darkness which resides all around us and within us.[8]

As our species cognitively perceives and explains reality through oral and written communication, as well as through the arts, sciences, philosophy, and religion, we are the ones who control and transmit the record of interpretation. As a result of this, moral evil can be interpreted through whatever lenses of definition we choose. It is at this point where moral evil and human culpability can be identified. Consequently, we can exonerate a psychopathic leader, accept the unrelenting destruction of the environment for profit, and/or exploit the vulnerable while trapping them into virtual or economic literal slavery. We do this by creating such a desensitized gloss over our actions that we either not care about or comprehend the ramifications of our deeds and the suffering caused to others.

Consider, in the context of exploitation, the following brief account of *coal harrier* Patience Kershaw, age 17, who lived in Victorian England, and was cited in the Lord Ashley's Mines Commission Report of 1842:

> I go to pit at five o'clock in the morning and come out at five in the evening; I get my breakfast of porridge and milk first; I take my dinner with me, a cake, and eat it as I go; I do not stop or rest any time for the purpose; I get nothing else until I get home, and then have potatoes and meat, not every day meat. I hurry in the clothes I have now got on, trousers and ragged jacket; the bald place upon my head is made by thrusting the corves [coal wagons]….I hurry the corves a mile and more underground and back; they weigh 300 cwt.; I hurry 11 a-day; I wear a belt and chain at the workings, to get the corves out …[9]

Reviewing the above example it becomes clear that the owners of the mines did not see anything untoward about this brutal exploitation as there was profit to be made at the expense of the vulnerable. What this illustrates is that we can create myths of validation or excuses for our conduct based on the concept of virtuous exploitation and affluence. Those who were rich simply abused (and

still do) the vulnerable due to perceived moral and social superiority. Arising out of this, a fantasy was created about the right of the affluent to mistreat the poor and the Commission's Report laid bare the horrendous abuse of the vulnerable poor in such a way that it could not be dismissed. What is striking to note, however, is that the majority of the ruling class were so desensitized to the widespread abuse of the poor, that although in positions of privilege through which they could have changed conditions many years prior to the Commission, they did not. In this context, it is easy to understand how moral evil occurs so "naturally" and as a logical progression arising out of cruelty, greed, arrogance, and self-indulgence. Thus to envisage the countless permutations of suffering that arise from the consequences of our species' embedded actions does not require any major stretch of the creative imagination.

Carrying this argument further, consider the following relatively extensive but not exhaustive list of

actions and outcomes attributed to moral evil. What emerges is a shocking profile as to the far reaching impact of human nature. Note also that this list falls well within the 90th percentile as previously discussed, and reads as follows:

> violence, aggression, abuse, exploitation, fanaticism, murder, war, genocide, atrocities, racism, social injustice, slavery, starvation, rape, displacement of people, domination, misuse of power, theft of land, civilian casualties of war, refugees, threats and weaponry, torture, unethical medical experiments on humans and animals, child abuse, elder abuse, female abuse, cruelty to animals, sexual exploitation, environmental destruction—terrestrial, oceanic and atmospheric, objectification, greed, apathy, self-centredness, deceit, hedonism, vanity, arrogance, cruelty, disdain, contempt, greed, theft, assault, fraud, extortion, anger, manipulation—both through threat and psychological suggestion, ruthlessness, pleasure in engineering suffering, transmitted diseases, and finally unmitigated selfishness.

Also of note is that for every example given there are inestimable permutations that are generated as outcomes within the lives of victims and perpetrators alike. Thus, it can be safely concluded that as the consequences expand so do the opportunities through which to create a fertile breeding ground for more moral evil to arise.

THE LABYRINTH OF COMPLEXITY

The disquieting reality is, however, that even when these various forms of evil are somewhat identified, a major problem arises as to discerning the foundational causes of the initial event. The interesting consequence of many evils, or the suffering that is realized through these experiences, is that they create both a metaphorical and physical domino effect which nurtures a broader evil. In times of relative security human nature will generate a powerful but less overtly identifiable dynamic of personal will, domination, cruelty and opportunism that is disbursed throughout the world. It is, however, difficult to dismiss or control the power of aggression or ruthlessness generated in times of threat, upheaval, chaos, or unrestrained violence. In the words of Connie Zweig and Jeremiah Abrams, "We sometimes see these evils in the world with frightening clarity, though sometimes we do not see them at all."[10]

Part of the reason for this faulty discernment is that our perspectives or values often become blurred within the context of the struggle to live, or the will to survive. At times of stress or opportunistic advantage, our species will adopt strategies of emotional distancing through degrees of denial or acquiescence and/or violent participation to remain safe or comfortable. As a consequence of these actions, we will accept dominant group strategies and conduct, often predatory, which under normal circumstances we might be reluctant to live by. This will be adopted in exchange for relative protection and gain as members of a particular community.

Another interesting development is that due to the fact that in general the human psyche and character provide rich breeding grounds for multifaceted malevolent actions we often become the

victims of our own actions.   These negative actions take on an almost irresistible power and can prove to be overwhelming with the consequences of our "evil" actions scarring us emotionally. Yet, there are many who have the "strength" to stand against this emotional derailment. The reason for this is the potential within the human being to reject the negative and debased and to respond to adverse situations in positive and genuinely ethical ways. Fortunately, the reality is that there are many examples of tremendous human nobility and compassion in the face of overwhelming evil.[11] Sadly, however, at the same time, there is a massive corpus of evidence to demonstrate the more common tendency towards baser instincts and to run with the dominant and destructive crowd mentality. The fact is, the majority of human beings possess the potential for compassion, love, and various forms of positive action, whilst on the other hand, it also clear that all human beings possess the potential for aspects of evil to manifest. We seem to vacillate in challenging situations and respond to various predatory opportunities according to how we judge the moment; in other words, the majority of us lack consistency in our conduct and ethical value systems Indeed, the great Russian writer, Alexander Solzhenitsyn, discussed this murky complexity in his work, *The Gulag Archipelago,* and wrote concerning evil:

> If only it were all so simple! If only there were evil people somewhere insidi-
> ously committing evil deeds, and it were necessary only to separate them from
> the rest of us and destroy them. But the line dividing good and evil cuts through
> the heart of every human being. And who is willing to destroy a piece of his own
> heart? [12]

Arising out of this mystery regarding the germination of evil as it lives within human nature, any endeavour to unravel the complexity of evil and its resulting manifestations of suffering presents as somewhat of a daunting task. How can one explain the inexplicable origins and urges towards destructive conduct? How can one address the fact that, despite our good intentions and ideals, we are often incapable of controlling our baser inclinations?

Set against these realities, and despite our limited abilities, however, we do valiantly strive to make limited sense of evil's seemingly limitless capacity to morph and manifest into every aspect of life. Within the continuity of human history, and to the credit of our thinkers and researchers, there have been truly impressive explanations and discoveries pertaining to human consciousness and physical laws governing all life on the planet. Unfortunately, for the researcher, what arises out of these enquiries is the frustrating realization that each group, whilst providing a descriptive analysis for the mechanics of suffering, including human dysfunction, fails to satisfactorily identify the cause or origin of the very energy itself. What is it that drives this self-destructive implosion within all forms of life? What is this life force that drives us and then kills us? From a purely subjective human perspective, one could be prompted to enquire as to what constitutes the dynamic energy or force that fuels this seemingly irresistible juggernaut called "evil" and which creates the insanity of our own speciel conduct. One might conclude from a logical, analytical standpoint, that human beings are the most overtly, self-destructive, insane form of life on the planet. According to social philosopher Jacob Needleman, "Evil exists not only within [one]self, but in the whole of mankind." He also observes that "everywhere and in everything there is the struggle between good and evil."

Arising out of these realities, the question can be raised as to how this energy or reality sustains itself, or if indeed it is a field of outside conscious energy that takes on "personality" through physical expression. Does it exist in some supernatural realm feeding on the misery of sentient beings, or is it merely a relentless and arbitrary part of life itself as in laws of consequence that continue to destroy because it is simply the nature of the energy force? Some thinkers, without any belief in God or the devil, will say it is a product and expression of human nature, which is a very logical explanation. There is a problem with this explanation, however, insofar as the majority of our species possess an awareness of a reality which we define as "goodness" against which we can often judge our negative conduct as being evil, destructive, predatory, or unloving. Referring back to Joseph Needleman, the scholar poses the question: "What activity of the mind leads us towards the power to be good?"[14] So, if we are aware of the quality of goodness and have a desire to live within its domain, what impedes us from doing so? Are we merely prisoners of social conditioning who ascribe the designations of right or wrong as a means of societal control, or are we prisoners of emotional impulses that spark and bend unpredictably, fuelled merely by emotional constructs? Are we really that self-seeking or deluded that we prefer to do that which is negative while at the same time justifying our actions by believing ourselves to be "good" or "nice" or "just" or even "rational"?

In this context, consider the words of psychoanalyst Carl Jung,

> The change of character brought about by the uprush of collective forces is
> amazing. A gentle and reasonable being can be transformed into a maniac or a
> savage beast. One is always inclined to lay the blame on external circumstances,

but nothing could explode in us if it had not been there. As a matter of fact, we are constantly living on the edge of a volcano, and there is, so far as we know, no way of protecting ourselves from a possible outburst that will destroy everybody within reach.[15]

Jung's brilliant and insightful observation raises the gnawing question as to what really constitutes our intrinsic nature. Does our species live in a state of constant delusion as to its basic identity and do we deliberately cultivate a façade of "decency"?

IS THERE MORE TO EVIL AND SUFFERING?

© Yarygin, 2013. Under license from Shutterstock, Inc.

Owning our own culpability within this complex system of evil and suffering is sensible and realistic, but how does this explanation really address the suffering found among all life forms—events such as injury, sickness, fear, or death and mourning within animals?[16] Biologically speaking, our own species comes under the classification of "animal," so are we simply bound by the complex laws of nature? Would this mean that there is no necessity for personal and corporate accountability and no need to carry the cumbersome burden of guilt or shame? Are we merely purposeless life forms that create fantasies arising out of purely biological urges? Are the concepts of evil and suffering merely terms we use to explain our conscious pain, angst, aggression, and even murderous impulses? Is our experience of consciousness and sadness just a set of cruel psychological responses brought about by our higher awareness as self-conscious beings? Why are we plagued by sad or traumatic memories regarding suffering, often for which we feel somehow responsible or at least involved? Would this not be simply a clear example of suffering brought about by experiencing strong emotions of psychological pain? Would this not be a useful example of evil as a negative and corrosive return and review of that which causes us pain? Why can't we walk away from trauma, sad memories, enduring grief, or feelings of cowardice and/or shame because of our cruel actions?

The reality is that whatever approach or option one adopts, one is made keenly aware that there exists a dark side to our nature. Whether this awareness encompasses ideas about a personal deity to whom we will someday give account, or the function of karmic laws, or simply physical and psychological realities of consciousness, the fact is that suffering is endemic within all sentient life forms and we often feel its scorching heat. What makes it even more keenly defined for humankind is the fact that we comprehend a broader realm to suffering, one that is global and often compounded by our own actions.

From the historical record taken from art, poetry, religion, religious text, philosophy, history, and warfare, it is strikingly evident that our ancestors recognized and accepted evil and suffering. The evidence that we have attests to the fact that there is a continuity of recognition and an almost fatalistic acceptance pertaining to something disjointed or aberrant within life and within our patterns of conduct as a species. It is also clear from our historical records that our ancestors also turned to ideas of the metaphysical in order to address the root causes pertaining to the troubling experiences of lives touched by suffering, cruelty, and evil.

Religions have from recorded history, endeavored to adopt an immediate, spiritual, emotional, and even psychological apparatus for problem solving. It is to the core, unanswerable mystery of evil and resulting suffering that our global systems of religions have turned in order to construct explanations that are not merely intellectual, but comfortingly human and positive in emotional relevance. The reality of religious enquiry is that it will delve into the innermost origin of evil and suffering from a metaphysical perspective. This process of enquiry is conducted to equip the devotee with a tangible, if somewhat confusing array of answers and problem-solving skills in order to meet the individual and corporate answers within the mystery.

In the context of how religions grapple with cause and effect, suffering and various interpretations regarding evil, one thing becomes evident to the researcher: all religions acknowledge there is a definite problem pertaining to living, surviving, and finally dying. As a result of this, all religions will endeavour to provide explanations pertaining to the intricacies and sometimes unfathomable realities within these issues. To put it succinctly, religions give explanations for the causes of evil and for the origins of suffering. In addition to this, the majority of religions will also accept that there are evil forces outside of the individual that attempt to negatively influence conduct and distort compassion, thereby often creating greater suffering for the wider community of living beings.

PROVIDING EMPOWERMENT

How to stop the suffering is something that many devotees of all religions will aspire to through right conduct, prayer, repentance, and rituals evoking purity and/or protection.[17] It is believed that by adopting these protocols the benefits of comfort, courage, strength, and even safe passage through a particular occurrence will in some way be accessed. Following on from this, all religions will offer to their devotees the possibility of containment or eradication of evil, or at least some deliverance from it. Realistically speaking, however, and to the credit of most established religious cosmologies, the experience of combating this negative power will be described as one of intense emotional and often physical conflict, with no easy answers offered. What can also be identified through these teachings is that, despite various approaches to battle, control, or even gaining victory over this negative force, the religions will engage in their own particular explanation of the origin and function of good and evil in which all life is embedded. Applying a broad interpretation, this may be referred to as theodicy.[18]

INTERPRETATIONS OF THEODICY

Upon analyzing the characteristic similarities identified within the world religions the term *theodicy* has been adopted and expanded in recent times by scholars within the fields of Religious Studies and Sociology, to describe a wide range of theodic explanations contained within various religions. From this comprehensive perspective, identifiable theodic themes address the legitimizations of the chaotic and evil experiences faced by both individuals and societies. Theodicy is also used when discussing religions, to describe explanations for evil and suffering which do not necessarily hold monotheistic assumptions (belief in one god). In this context, therefore, an overview of theodicy within religions will now be discussed in order to comprehend the scope of this intrinsic human need that we express through making religious sense of evil and suffering.[19]

Theodicy is a Greek term derived from two words: *theos* meaning "God" and *dike* meaning "justice." Traditionally, this term was used by theists and monotheists to address the inherent problems encountered when considering the actions or non-actions of a just, loving, and omnipotent God in the face of evil and suffering. The basic quandary is: if God is the all powerful Creator, one who is just and loving, why does He permit evil and suffering within His creation? Why do all life forms suffer? Is God oblivious to the suffering in His world, or does He simply not care? This major contradiction between the love of God and the reality of suffering presents as an enormous challenge to the monotheistic traditions who have throughout the centuries presented many different explanations in answer to these perennial questions.

From the perspective of the Abrahamic monotheistic systems the problems posed concerning the existence of evil and the resultant explanations are somewhat more theologically complex when compared with other religious systems. This is due to the emphasis on the personal interaction of God within the created order, as a God who is kind and loving. The Abrahamics emphasize the reciprocity of God and creation, thus there is a divine relationship within existence and there is a plan for all life, in spite of the reality of the evil and futility that surrounds us. For the monotheist, life is placed within a greater plan or framework and in the fulfilling of God's purpose there is a hidden purpose and meaning. This belief imbues with significance and hope events that appear as crisis, chaos, hopelessness, and rampant evil.

It is, however, far too simplistic to generalize all three traditions in their appropriation of significance regarding suffering and evil as each cosmology has distinctive differences which cannot be ignored. For example, Judaism will interpret the root of evil and suffering as existing and originating in the choices made by Adam or man, who alienated himself/herself from God. This is in direct opposition to the belief that God made everything good and blessed it. Resulting from this rebellion on the part of the first man, evil and suffering made their entrance into the physical realm. As an outcome of these realities, death was "created" by God as a consequence of the rebellion and to also put limits on humankind which had corrupted itself. In addition to this, the choices made by humankind affected the whole created order which was then subjected to a similar futility or dysfunction. As such, a clearly defined concept of human accountability is presented with very little attention being given to an extraneous evil source as the instigator or perpetrator of chaos and misery; humans sin, humans rebel against God.

Central to the concept of sin and its resultant impact upon living beings, is the rabbinic teaching that there are two inclinations or tendencies within human beings. The *yetzer ha'tov* is the good inclination and *yetzer ha'ra* is the bad. The former "urges individuals to do that which is right, whereas the latter encourages sinful acts."[20] When the individual repents and returns to God, renewal and restitution can occur. In this way, hope and the opportunity to rectify corrosive, negative actions is offered to those who seek to live in the right path of covenant and Torah, thus following God and helping one's neighbour.

It is also evident within Judaism and Jewish history that there were other approaches and interpretations regarding the complexity and circumstances of evil and suffering. These evolved within the ancient Hebrew Bible (Old Testament) as religious leaders, thinkers, and prophets were faced with the intricacies and unpredictability of human experience. The legitimization of suffering, and the meaning it had within God's plan, became central to Jewish cosmology and became entrenched as pivotal interpretations in Jewish history. Based on the various interactions and experiences of God's covenant people, these resultant biblical theodicies can be identified as:

1) *Suffering as punishment for wickedness* which was a simple cause and effect explanation regarding lives lived in sinful rebellion for which the consequence was God's justifiable wrath.

2) *Suffering as a test of faith.* God was believed to try the faithful in order to prove their devotion to him. This would also include ideas concerning persecution through which they were encouraged to remain in covenant with God.

3) *Suffering as redemptive.* The atonement for sins either individual or representative of community repentance, through which one's suffering would contribute to the expiation of sin. One suffered under the hand of God in order to atone for one's sin.

4) *The eschatological/apocalyptic view.* At the fulfillment of God's purposes manifested with the coming of the Messiah, suffering, evil and death would all be abolished. God would recompense his people and all would be made well eventually. It is millenarian in form as it provides the prospect of postponed compensation that will be realized on this earth. It is for the Jewish faithful who believe that present sufferings can be endured because there is the expectation of a supernatural intervention making for a glorious future existence.

5) *The wicked would eventually be repaid under the judgment of God.* Thus justice would be meted out and the righteousness of God established on earth through His covenant people.

6) *There was a mystery* surrounding the injustice, cruelty, and suffering present in the world. Everyone—the faithful and those who rejected God—all suffered death. There was the mystery of why the just suffered more than the unjust. For the Jew who believes in an afterlife, there is the hope of recompense in an afterlife experience in Gan Edan (heaven) where only the righteous exist. Thus there is justice on the other side of existence where the righteous "live" in peace and joy, and the evil face their own personal reward, meted out by a just and righteous God.

7) *Suffering in the will of God could be viewed as redemptive.* Misery or travail could be legitimated and given reason when it resulted in a spiritual or physical victory. It could become the foundation of better things, collectively and individually.[21]

Christianity arose out of Judaism, and not surprisingly, includes these Jewish perspectives to vary-ing degrees. It does, however, develop distinctive explanations regarding evil and suffering and also offers the metaphysical means of overcoming what is perceived it be an intelligent, malevolent, personal force, known as *satan*, which seeks to destroy God's creation.

Central to Christianity's development of theodicy are the core beliefs that Jesus never promised im-munity from evil, suffering, and death to his followers. On the contrary, the gospels all present Jesus as a man who acknowledged the reality that "in this world you face persecution. But take courage; I have conquered the world!"[22] At the central point of reference for this tenet of faith is the event of the Crucifixion which at once identifies the meaning of suffering for the Christian and then leads the believer from the agony of evil to the assurance of final victory. The reason for this affirmation of victory over total defeat and agony is the core component of the Resurrection. For Christians, evil is an undeniable monster, but belief in the Resurrection leads the believer to look beyond the tragedy of injustice, cruelty, and grief to a time when all will finally come under the dominion of a good God.[23] Thus, the Crucifixion and the Resurrection provide hope for life and the courage to live it as those who fight against evil and suffering in this world.[24] Indeed, Jesus is considered to be the supreme example of how to face evil and provides the evidence of how God actively stayed by the sufferer even when the sufferer could not cope with the torment.[25] Thus, it can be stated that through Christ, "the Christian God has also been a fellow-participant in suffering, a sharer on the inside in the bitterness of the world, and not just a spectator on the outside."[26]

A further example of Jesus' practical and active engagement in the suffering world around him is to be found in the miracle stories of the gospels where he is often described as working to the point of collapse in healing people. Jesus was never dispassionate about suffering and the gospel narratives depict him as a man who was deeply affected by the suffering of others, and who was routinely characterized by deep empathy for the afflicted as a man of sorrows, acquainted with grief. But Jesus also had a practical approach to many of the causes of evil and he recognized that our own corrupt actions—moral evil—led inevitably to sorrow. Thus, although we were victims, fragile and vulnerable, we also were frequently the oppressors or perpetrators of evil.

Arising out of the teachings of Jesus, another evidentiary circumstance arises—good people suf-fer "undeserved" tragedy, whereas often the evil flourish through their cruelty and greed. Thus, Christians, following a crucified and risen saviour, are also faced with the fact that great injustice happens on a daily basis in our world. How does one reconcile the passion of identification as per the example of the compassionate Jesus, with the outrageous triumph of evil in an uncaring world? Again, consider the words of Jesus in Matthew 5:45 when he is recorded to have said, "[God] makes his sun to rise on the evil and on the good, and sends rain on the righteous and on the unrighteous."[27] It is in explaining or even understanding how an omnibenevolent, omniscient, omnipresent, transcendent yet immanent, just God, could allow suffering, that Christianity of all the religions is particularly exercised in arriving at a comprehensive and logical explanation as to why this misery is permitted.[28] It is comforting to look forward to the glorious time when Christ returns and establishes justice and holiness and at the same time abolishes death and suffering, but the perennial questions still remain: Why did God allow or create it in the first place? Why does God permit this horror to continue? Is God powerless to stop evil? God, in Christ, assures the believer that he is with the devotee, but does God not feel his "child's" pain? Is God remote from that pain? Does God care at all?

Set against these very observations, the Christian religion has endeavored from its earliest writings within the New Testament to address this challenging issue. As such, Christianity has developed various theodical approaches to provide reasonable explanations and these can be broadly identified as follows:

1. *Pauline theodicy.* The theodicy of Apostle Paul (c.d. 64 c.e.), in his *Letter to the Romans*, is a massive theological treatise through which he presents a picture of a fallen/corrupt human race and a suffering creation, made so as an outcome of human rebellion. Acting as moral, conscious agents, many humans create misery for themselves and for others. They are slaves to evil and corruption, and bring suffering upon others. The obvious hope for the amelioration of much suffering comes through the individual turning to Christ as saviour. Christians will experience suffering but will grow spiritually, receive hope, and finally at the end of time reap the full rewards of redemption. The crowning conclusion is that all will be made well through Christ, and evil (Satan) will be crushed under their feet as children of God.

2. *Irenaean theodicy.* Developed by Irenaeus (c.130–200), bishop of Lyons,[29] his theodicy is more concerned with the development of humanity. According to central, predominant Christian theological doctrine, humanity's state of sin resulted from the Fall of humankind. Irenaeus perceived this as more of an immature act of weakness than an adult crime of intentional malice and disobedience.[30]

   Core arguments within Irenaean theodicy propose a two-stage creation process in which humans require (1) free will and (2) the experience of evil to fully develop into God's likeness; thus creation was intentionally formed incomplete as humans were not made in a complete state of spiritual holiness. Humans were/are not fully developed, and it is therefore necessary for them to experience evil and suffering in order to develop into full spirituality. This concept became known as the *Vale of Soul Making* as suffering was believed to be the crucible in and through which humans are given the opportunity to grow into spirituality, through Christ. Suffering was therefore a necessary part of God's created universe as it was through suffering that human souls were made noble. As a consequence, our world was the best possible place to develop towards the perfection that God wills for each person.

   Irenaeus distinguished a difference of being between the "image" and the "likeness" of God. Adam was made in the form of God, meaning possessing a nascent spiritual potential. It is in the likeness that Adam/humankind was/is deficient, and that this deficiency can only be overcome with spiritual growth that brought the person through to eventual salvation, into the "likeness" or "content" of God in Christ. According to Irenaeus, Adam and Eve were expelled from the Garden of Eden because they were immature and needed to develop—that is, they were to grow into the likeness (content) of God. They were the raw material for a further stage of God's creative work

3. *Origen theodicy:* Origen of Alexandria (184/185–253/254)[31] addressed the perennial problems regarding the origin of sin and suffering and produced the hypothesis of preexisting souls who fell away from God into materiality, and of their often tumultuous journey and assent back to their Creator after an extensive journey of purification and illumination.[32]

Origen also held out the possibility, though he did not assert so definitively, that in the end all beings, perhaps even Satan himself, would be reconciled to God in what is called the apokatastasis ("restitution").

Origen grappled with the realities of why God had created a world where evil and suffering, injustice and helplessness abounded. On the surface, this reality was utterly unjust and Origen proceeded with his hypothesis to present a Christian apologetic with which to cover what could be viewed as utter cosmic mismanagement. In order to defend divine justice against the charge of cosmic ineptitude, Origen developed a theological cosmology that explained the ontological status and origin of evil as well as its cosmic implications, and he placed humankind as sentient beings, as active participants in the evil and suffering around us.

Origen's theodicy hinges on the journey of the soul back to God. Its themes correlate with the soul's creation, fall and descent into materiality, gradual purification, and eventual divinization. The world, for Origen, therefore functions as a training ground, a central zone of spiritual treatment for the journeying soul as it undergoes the necessary education and purgation. In this context, Origen presents God as a compassionate and judicious teacher, physician, and father who employs suffering for our amelioration.

Origen's teachings relating to the Fall of humankind bring his ideas concerning the origin of evil and suffering into a logical focus. He believed that God's first creation was a collectivity of rational beings which he defined as *logika* or pure mind, essence. The logika were created beings but were not created in time. These were entities existing in pure mind state and were originally created in close proximity to God, with the intention that they should explore the divine mysteries in a state of endless contemplation. These *logika* grew weary of this intense contemplation, and fell away from God into an existence fashioned by their own preferences, and separate from the divine presence and the wisdom to be found within him. This fall was not the result of inherent imperfection but was the result of a misuse of God greatest gift to His creation which was freedom. As a result of this, the logika became cold as they moved away from the divine warmth of God. Departing from God, they came to be clothed in bodies, at first as souls of a fine ethereal and invisible nature, but as the souls fell further away from God, their bodies changed into bodies of a coarser and more solid state. Origen believed that the bodies of redeemed souls were spiritual bodies, made of the purest fire, whilst still existing in physical form during their earth journey and were those who were the redeemed in Christ.

4. *Augustinian theodicy.* Augustine (354–430), bishop of Hippo, developed the *soul deciding argument*, which was based on judgment and salvation from sin through Christ. His argument is also referred to as the *Free Will Argument* and is based on two main assumptions: (1) God alone is supremely and immutably good, thus God could not create anything evil. Evil was not from God as God's creation had initially been created in a faultless and perfect state. Evil is a privation or lack in created things, it results in spiritual blindness that creates suffering; but God did not create this privation.[34] In this context, there had been the complete absence of evil and suffering initially in his created order. (2) Evil came from and was generated from within the world. All suffering is therefore a consequence of this abuse of free will. Natural evil is caused by the imbalance in nature brought about by the Fall. Moral evil is caused because the world has become estranged from God, and immorality has been able to thrive.

In addressing the systemic problem of evil and suffering in the face of the argument for a loving and compassionate God, Augustine proposed a solution to the problem by blaming the misery that surrounds us on the Fall of humanity after the disobedience in the Garden of Eden. From this view, man is responsible for evil by reason of being led astray by Satan. This argument not only absolved God of creating evil but also allowed Him to show the world His love by bringing Christ into the world.

Augustine's submission of the Free-Will Argument perceived that:

1. Evil is the result of human error.
2. Human error results from free will (the ability to do wrong).
3. If we did not have free will we would be merely created and unthinking entities.
4. God prefers a world of free agents to a world inhabited by those who serve with no choice.
5. Evil is therefore the unfortunate, although not unavoidable outcome, of free will.
6. For God to intervene would be to take away our free will.
7. Therefore, God is neither responsible for evil nor guilty of neglect for not intervening.
8. Reconciliation and redemption: God did not, however, relinquish responsibility for this world. God's grace brought about the possibility of reconciliation through Jesus Christ, whose crucifixion saved a certain number (the elect) from eternal punishment.

Although the above theodicies provide the foundational themes of debate, enquiry, and often disagreement, it should be noted that there are many other theodic interpretations within Christianity. As this religion addresses evil and suffering in great detail it is impossible to present a further overview of the many insights or arguments that have followed over the centuries. Suffice it to say, for example, that a history of theodicy in the Christian tradition would have to deal—in addition to the previous four theodicies—with the following thinkers to name a few: Lactantius, Pseudo-Dionysius, Anselm, Thomas Aquinas, The Mystics, Luis de Molina, Luther, Calvin, Malebranche, Pierre Bayle, Leibniz, Hume, Kant, Schleiermacher, Karl Barth, Simone Weil, Alfred North Whitehead, Charles Hartshorne, Dorothee Soelle, Teilhard de Chardin, Jacques Maritain, Austin Farrer, and John Hick.

According to Islam, the third monotheistic religion, when the Prophet Muhammad received his revelations from God via Archangel Gabriel, which later became the Qur'an, he received a corpus of material which would become the foundation for the faith. As the words of the Qur'an are regarded as having absolute and timeless importance, the straightforward theodic revelation that it contains remains the fundamental framework for interpreting the root of evil and suffering. The origin of evil is not an issue, and the belief that there is an evil force, known as Satan or Iblis who is allowed to act as a tool to provoke and punish humankind, are basic facts of cosmology. Thus evil and suffering are not treated as theoretical problems but are simply considered to be paradoxes which exist under the will of Allah. Islamic theodicy regards this reality to be a timeless, unchanging issue based on the struggle between good and evil within human nature, consisting of submission and rebellion, and repentance and purgation of sin, all under the hand of Allah.

Islamic theodicy sees all suffering as part of what it means to be alive and to be involved in the battle to be obedient to the will of the omnipotent Allah. In Islamic thought, life is a period of testing and temptations and people have to find their own solutions to these problems.[35] Allah said that he would forgive anyone who sincerely repented, but this could only occur if one turned to Islam and submitted to Allah.

Although the Qur'an emphasizes that Allah is all loving and compassionate, there is the underlying doctrine that Allah is all powerful.[36] As the omnipotent God, Allah can do whatever he likes without being held accountable to anyone. He is never to be questioned as to his purposes or the life occurrences people will encounter. One is called to submit under the hand of God, and in that way, there is a certain safety and assurance in that one is complying with the perhaps unknown intentions of the supreme Creator. Circumstances might often cause confusion regarding whether an event was evil under Allah's will, based on the fact that one experienced suffering within it, but it might be Allah's way of alleviating greater suffering in this world and the next. In this way, the ultimate meaning has to do with perspective because what may appear as evil may well be the kindness of Allah that one does not comprehend. The reason for this is that Allah does not will evil[37] and to doubt Allah is a sin.

Arising out of these basic concepts, there arose great theological debates concerning the intent and purpose of Allah. The earliest theological position argued that as Allah knew all things, and held all things in his will, he had thus also foreordained all things. It was asserted that the Muslim must accept these concepts without question and should be reconciled to whatever fate may bestow due to preordainment. Yet, set against this was the Qur'anic teaching that there would be judgment for all souls. The question was, if one was preordained to do certain things—both sinful and obedient—why would one be judged or held responsible?[38] Nevertheless, both evil acts and good deeds were all created under the will of Allah, because suggesting another source as the instigator of these things would be to rival Allah's creative power. The answer to this was that Allah was the source of all acts, but evil acts only arose out of human beings' rebellion against Allah.[39] This argument, one that exempts Allah from all evil, was first presented by the reformist Mu'tazilites of the eighth to tenth centuries C.E.

Suffering is perceived to be entwined within the very fabric of existence for the reason that Allah can use it to test the character of the Muslim.[40] The experience of suffering can also be construed as deserved punishment from Allah when a Muslim turns away from Allah's laws. Thus conscious disobedience, committed in life, will incur the punishment of Allah through suffering, which is viewed as a corrective measure in order to bring the believer back to the right perspective. It was, therefore, logical to interpret evil as wrong conduct and suffering as the resulting consequence meted out by Allah, either through fate or at the hand of religious leaders.

In the context of the suffering of the innocent, Islamic theodicy stressed/stresses that this suffering must in some sense be purposeful in the hands of Allah and although perhaps not understood by the sufferer, it has merit because it is interpreted as a trial of faith. The problems of pain and suffering are therefore viewed as positive experiences insofar as they act also as an earthly purgation of sins. Those who suffer in this life are believed to look forward to a path of ease and comfort in the world to come[41] which starts immediately after death with the Judgement of the Grave and is completed on the Day of Doom at the end of time.

The Muslim was/is considered to be engaged in a battle or struggle to follow Allah. This struggle began with birth and found completion at death, so one's temporary existence on earth was placed within the realm of meaning pertaining to jihad. Jihad means to be engaged in battle and the Qur'an recognized two types of battle: the Greater Jihad and the Lesser Jihad. According to which interpretive route or type of emphasis the believer took, the Greater Jihad referred to the lifelong battle to submit to the will of Allah, and the Lesser Jihad was to take up weapons/arms in defence of Islam. The Qur'an itself is ambiguous as to which constitutes the greater and the lesser, so the Greater may in reverse be to take up arms in defence of Islam and the Lesser to wage war against one's own sin. Considering, however, that life is viewed as a battle to follow God, with emphasis on the expunging of sin, the Greater Jihad in this context constitutes a broader scope for Muslims experiencing suffering throughout their lives. No matter the interpretative approach one adopts, it is clear that, in Islam, one would be expected to suffer due to the inevitability of life's vicissitudes.

Whatever the misery of injustice encountered in life it was to be accepted with hope because at the end of one's life and certainly on the Day of Doom (Day of Judgment, with the resurrection of the dead), there would be great recompense at the hand of Allah. It is this emphasis on the final reward dispensed by Allah to his faithful Muslims that functions to weave all aspects of Islamic theodicy into an intricate explanation pertaining to evil and suffering in this short and often tumultuous existence. At the end of time, there is the promise of paradise for the believer.

On the other end of the spectrum of religious theodicy, exist the religions of Hinduism, Buddhism, Sikhism, and Jainism, with their *karma-samsara theodicies*.[42] Once again, each tradition will contain variations regarding theodicy but will all accept that one's karma dictates the events of one's life and that evil and suffering in this context are deserved experiences brought about by previous lives of noncompliance with moral and religious codes of conduct. As an outcome of these negative actions and the accrual of karma, the soul/consciousness is trapped into the pattern of samsaric rebirth.

Hinduism will not only emphasize karma and samsara, but also one's fate or fortune often being at the whim or intention of a particular god or goddess if correct puja is not performed or, on the other hand, when devotion to a particular deity has led to the neglect of dharma relating to caste duty.[43] Thus Hindu theodicy incorporates the rule of the gods into the unrelenting adjudication of karma with its outcomes in life and the experience of suffering. At the root of the ancient system is the endeavour to provide explanations for suffering and to place it within a logical framework for all devotees in the context of adharma or inappropriate action.[44]

Another major theodic explanation is to be found in the concepts surrounding the caste system and its reason for existence. As taught within the Vedic system, one's station of birth, physical condition, and gender will be attributed to karma. In turn, this theodic system of interpretation explains how evil and suffering are viewed within the Hindu context of deserved pleasant life compared to a life of sorrow.[45] As a Hindu, born into the ancient and entrenched caste system, the person will find oneself, if fortunate, as a member of one of the three "twice-born" castes: the Brahmins—priests and teachers, the Kshatriyas—rulers and soldiers, or the Vaishyas—traders, farmers, and artisans. This in turn will present various interpretations of theodicy which are far more auspicious than if one is born into the lowest caste grouping. As a member of the lowest caste grouping known as the

Shudras, whose duty is considered to be that of serving the three upper castes; or as a member of the subgrouping of Shudras known as the Chandalas or untouchables, who work mostly in the grave-yards and cremation grounds, or as hunters, butchers, and cleaners of human waste, theodicy takes on another hue. The reason for this is that, despite all actions to achieve good karma and hopefully achieve a subsequent more favourable rebirth, there is no way out of one's caste for the Shudra.

The reason for this engrained approach to caste inequality is to be found with Vedic scripture. All men are created unequal and this is explained through the Rig Veda myth of the giant primordial being named Purusha from whose head the Brahmins were created, nobles and warriors from his arms, farmers and merchants from his stomach, and servants from his feet.[46] Further, from each caste grouping, there are in turn hundreds of hereditary castes and subcastes with their own strata within society, each with their own dharma which will affect the outworking of karma. Thus theodicy explains the reality of the caste system, and of deserved suffering arising out of the actions of a god or mythical figure, or the attributed total corruption that leads to continuous rebirth into conditions of extreme humiliation and subservience of the lower caste, but does not seek to explain the reasons for the perverse action of this mythic figure. It is simply the way it is.

Another aspect of Hindu theodicy is that it does not seek to explain away evil and suffering but simply identifies it as part of the inevitable samsaric cycle that individuals are trapped into until they gain moksha (enlightenment and liberation) and end the cycle of reincarnation[47] for a kalpa. One's actions, both negative and positive, create karma and one lives to experience the outcome. The Hindu is taught that it is in the negation of the ego and by concentrating on the divine that one can change the outcome of the next life, or even have an influence on existence in this life by concentrating on dharma and also devotion to a particular god through the practice of Bhakti (devotional love for a deity). Whatever the devotional or caste practice the Hindu observes, it is believed that one will rise or fall in subsequent existences according to the integrity with which one has lived previously.[48] Nevertheless, evil and suffering will come to all through one's own karma and the karma of others as they live their lives and affect the people around them. It is all part of the samsaric cycle from which there is only brief respite.

Buddhism, as noted in previous studies within this textbook, has many variations and interpreta-tions. Some traditions will be basically atheistic in outlook, while others will accept the role of enlightened beings known as Buddhas and Bodhisattvas. In addition to this, some traditions, such as the Thai and Balinese Buddhist traditions, will accept the role of godlike beings or spirits who inhabit the god realm,[49] and devotees will dedicate prayers and meditations to them. Nevertheless, despite the many variances in soteriological beliefs and worship rituals, the central theodicy in Bud-dhism pertaining to the definition of evil and the manifestation of suffering can be identified as:

1. The three selfish emotions which are desire, hate, and delusion.
2. The ten nonvirtuous actions: Their physical expression in physical and verbal actions as de-scribed by: killing, stealing, sexual misconduct, lying, divisive speech/slander, insulting words/harsh speech, idle gossip, covetousness, harmful intent/malice/ill-will, and wrong view.[50]

Arising out of these realities, evil manifests through suffering of all kinds. According to Buddhist teaching, the explanation for the cause of these emotions and actions can be found within the Four Noble Truths that teach:

1. The noble truth of suffering (dukkha): birth is suffering; aging is suffering; sickness is suffering; death is suffering; sorrow and lamentation, pain, grief, and despair are suffering; association with the unpleasant is suffering; dissociation from the pleasant is suffering; not to get what one wants is suffering—in brief, the five aggregates of attachment are suffering.
2. The noble truth of the origin of suffering is this: it is this thirst (craving), called tanha, which produces re-existence and re-becoming, bound up with passionate greed. It finds fresh delight now here and now there, namely thirst for sense-pleasures; thirst for existence and becoming; and thirst for nonexistence (self-annihilation).
3. The noble truth of the cessation of suffering is this: it is the complete cessation of that very thirst, giving it up, renouncing it, emancipating oneself from it, detaching oneself from it.
4. The noble truth of the path leading to the cessation of suffering is this: it is simply the Noble Eightfold Path, namely right view, right thought, right speech, right action, right livelihood, right effort, right mindfulness, right concentration.[51]

Applying these concepts, Buddhism addresses the problem of moral evil and the consequences of nonvirtuous actions which contribute to the wheel of samsara and the fueling of karmic outcomes through reincarnation. How it provides a theodic interpretation of natural evil is to apply the doctrines of *pratitya-samutpada* or dependent origination, where everything is interrelated but always in a state of impermanence (anicca), and thus always in flux. Thus when the biotic systems cause catastrophes it is regarded as part of the stream of becoming within that state of impermanence and when sentient beings suffer in the wake of these events it simply speaks to karma. The karmic fate of that life form, in a particular state of reincarnated existence at that time has merely led it to suffer an adverse situation caused by the event. Thus there is no problem presented regarding injustice, tragedy, or death as it is part of the karmic cycle.

Sikhism, a singularly monotheistic tradition, and Jainism, an atheistic religion, hold similar beliefs surrounding karma and samsara. However, it is in the appropriation of theodicy that both diverge.

Sikhism will make sense of evil and suffering in the context of a theistic concept that God sends both good and evil upon all. There is suffering throughout existence and this is acknowledged as "Poison and nectar, the Creator has created both,"[52] due to the fact that the Creator is both the doer and the cause. In this way, Sikhism acknowledges the root cause and mystery of the misery that human beings encounter.

The suffering of the innocent and the faithful is also addressed through the explanation that one may suffer for that which is right as life is a test of obedience, which in turn can cause the devotee to draw nearer to God, thus making one stronger. There is also punishment for sin whereby suffering through the experience can act remedially by burning off negative karma and allowing for a more favourable judgement after death, perhaps even warranting admittance into heaven which would result in the cessation of reincarnation. God sends all things and one can only submit to his wishes with courage, dedication, and trust.

Moral evil, according to Sikh teaching, is easy to identify. There are five evils through which much suffering is experienced and manifested in life and present a clear theodic explanation. The five evils are lust, anger, greed, pride, and attachment.[53] Suffering reaches us through illusion and attachment because we place other things before union with God and consequently the five evils manifest in the realities around us. So, therefore, humans create evil and suffering, and God allows the negative karma to manifest as the outcome of actions, but also provides through his grace a diagnosis and a cure in order to remit or expunge this force.[54]

As Jainism is a religion that perceives reality without any influence attributed to any one omnipotent, divine being, theodicy is used to explain evil and suffering as part of the karmic dynamic. Jainism teaches that everything in the universe has a soul or a jiva, which is enmeshed in matter. In order for the soul to be released it must be released from this embodiment in whatever form it manifests.[55] Karma is perceived as a flow of matter which imprisons the jiva itself and is believed to be subtle matter that surrounds the consciousness of the soul. As it weighs down upon the consciousness through the dulling of sensitivity, it is considered to be a parasite that saps the energy of the soul and is considered to be the root of all suffering. Its presence can be identified through acts of cruelty and selfishness. The only way to liberate the jiva from this karmic coating is to voluntarily practice austerities and these apply in varying degrees to both ascetic and householder alike. The requirement of nonattachment (aparigraph) calls the individual to avoid any deep emotional attachment that would entrap the jiva; and the most extreme form of nonattachment is that of *sallekhana*, a holy death caused by fasting,[56] which would be the goal of the committed ascetic.

Theodicies arising out of the South East Asian typology will also have a thematic consistency in so far as they will teach that suffering comes to all sentient life forms whether this misery is deserved or not. It may be interpreted as a consequence of failure to adhere to a moral code of conduct, negligence towards the ancestors, disharmony through specific actions, or as an opportunity to learn and grow morally by cultivating benevolence, goodness, and humanity.[57] As many of these traditions retain some of their earliest developmental concepts insofar as a belief in evil spirits or even angry demi-gods who have been offended by the conduct of a member of society, misfortune or bad luck is something that can occur at the whim of a spirit entity. In addition to this, evil can also come through the conduit of an evil spirit, a curse, or even spirit possession. Whatever the explanation, evil and suffering are acknowledged to be events that occur to everyone but to a certain extent are experiences which can be ameliorated through right practice.

For the complex and diverse indigenous traditions, theodicy encompasses acknowledgment of evil and suffering which come through the conduits of spirit beings or humans. If moral tribal codes are not observed, suffering can occur through a multitude of different events and consequences. In addition to this, ideas surrounding natural evil, especially those of sickness, famine, draught, or environmental displacement, can be interpreted as punishment for sin in the context of lack of respect for animals, or the land. In order to establish the most advantageous settings for survival, the various tribal systems have developed codes of conduct which are believed to have evolved over millennia surrounding ritual purity, hunting rituals, and correct protocols regarding taboos which have been established by shamanistic practices.[58]

As these systems also developed out of ancient religious cosmologies, it is common to find theodic concepts pertaining to evil spirits sent through curses, angered ancestors who have not been ritually respected, or angry ghosts who in human life were the victims of murder and/or abuse.[59]

CONCLUSION

According to the historical, anthropological, and religious evidence we have at hand, evil and suffering are realities that all religions address in their varied ways. Sometimes the explanations we discover offer very sophisticated philosophical explanations for natural and moral evil. What is fascinating to observe is the fact that historically what we have is a corpus of religious traditions that have never skirted around the reality of our vulnerability, brokenness, perversity, and at the same time have offered the possibility of overcoming adversity. Whatever the form of evil that has been identified, it is clear that our ancestors comprehended the harshness of our physical, emotional, and even psychological suffering and sought to provide answers in order to create understanding and hope out of our chaos. Speaking to the many and varied theodicies that this chapter has discussed, whatever the tradition, there is a clear motivation to understand our vulnerability by means of defining and sometimes avoiding that which we often cannot control and that which would harm us. The motivation behind the theodicies is to provide our species with explanations or legitimizations for the reality of evil and suffering through whichever definition the sufferer might find useful. The religious reality is that theodic explanations can offer empowerment to the lonely sufferer, the family unit, and the wider society. The basic reality stands, as always, on the facts. What we do know is that if we are able to identify that ominous reality which lives in the shadows of our consciousness, or even reaches out to burn us with its tangible presence, we can sometimes find comfort in perceiving its root of origin. If we can name it, we can sometimes overcome it or even cope with it more effectively.

GLOSSARY

Adharma: Hindu concept referring to inappropriate actions.

Coalhurrier: Term used to describe a specific task done in the Victorian coalmines. The work was carried out by older children and women who were harnessed to the tubs of coal underground. The hurriers would push the tubs of coal (often weighing over 600 kg each) from behind with their hands and the tops of their heads. The underground tunnels or roadways which were used to transport the coal to the surface were often only 60 to 120 cm high.

Creatureliness: The awareness that we are creatures within the biotic web; acknowledging that we are vulnerable and exist at the mercy of nature.

Free Will: Christian concept presented by St. Augustine. Humankind was given free will by God and chose to disobey Him. As a consequence, evil, suffering, and death came into the world. God did not create an evil world, but the created order was brought into dysfunction and futility as a result of human disobedience.

Jihad: Qur'anic concept. Refers to spiritual battle or combat; to wage war. Can be identified by the Greater Jihad (to wage war against sin) and the Lesser Jihad (to wage war in defence of Islam). There is ambiguity within the Qur'an as to which Jihad is the greater or the lesser.

Karma-samsara Theodicies: Evil and suffering are deserved experiences in life brought about by the accumulation of negative karma created in previous lives.

Letter to the Romans: One of the letters written by Paul to the Roman Christians (c 51–53 C.E.).

Logika: Christian concept developed by Origen of Alexandria referring to created spirits or minds that gradually drifted away from God and through a progressive downward spiral became souls who lived in human bodies. The saved Christian is one of these redeemed logika.

Sallekhana: Jainist belief in a holy belief by fasting.

Satan: Malevolent spirit that creates temptation, suffering, and all forms of evil.

The Five Evils: Sikh concept referring to lust, anger, greed, pride, and attachment.

The Noble Eightfold Path: Buddhist concept of right view, right thought, right speech, right action, right livelihood, right effort, right mindfulness, and right concentration

Theodicy: Traditional theistic and monotheistic argument for the justification of God's goodness, love, compassion, and justice in the face of evil and suffering in the world. Arguments presented through polytheism attribute evil to a conflict of wills between deities. In all karmic/samsaric cosmologies, all misfortune and death arise from karmic outcomes, thus one can only really blame oneself.

The Ten Non-Virtuous Actions: Buddhist concepts of killing, stealing, sexual misconduct, lying, divisive speech/slander, insulting words/harsh speech, idle gossip, covetousness, harmful intent/malice/ill will, and wrong view.

Vale of Soul Making: Christian concept presented by Irenaeus, bishop of Lyons. God did not create a perfect world as it was necessary for humankind to suffer and battle evil in themselves and through outside circumstances, in order to grow into spiritual maturity. The imperfect world provided the best possible place for humans to develop fully into God's likeness.

ENDNOTES

1. David Stewart, *Exploring the Philosophy of Religion* (4th ed.), (Upper Saddle River, NJ: Prentice-Hall, Inc., 1998), p 212.

2. Ibid., p 212.

3. Chris Hedges, *What Every Person Should Know About War*, (New York: Free Press, 2003), p 1.

4. David Stewart, *Exploring the Philosophy of Religion*, p 212.

5. Connie Zweig, Jeremiah Abrams, "Introduction," *Meeting the Shadow: The Hidden Power of the Dark Side of Human Nature*, (New York: Jeremy P. Tarcher/Penguin, 1991), p 129.

6. Ibid., p 165.

7. Ibid., p 167.

8. Ibid., p 129.

9. Parliamentary Papers, 1842, vols. XV-XVII, Appendix I, pp. 252, 258, 439, 461; Appendix II, pp. 107, 122, 205. The second of the three great reports embodies the results of the investigation into the conditions of labor in the mines made by Lord Ashley's Mines Commission of 1842. The Mines Act of 1842 that resulted prohibited the employment in the mines of all girls, women and of boys under thirteen. http://www.victorianweb.org/history/workers1.html

10. Connie Zweig, Jeremiah Abrams, "Introduction," *Meeting the Shadow*, p 166.

11. An example of this noble spirit can be seen in the conduct and work of Senator Romeo Delaire, who as commander of the UN Observer Mission in Uganda and Rwanda was instrumental against all odds, in protecting thousands of Tutsis during the program of genocide conducted by the Hutus in Rwanda. He is now an advocate for the world's victims of genocide. See: *The Canadian Encyclopedia*, http://www.thecanadianencyclopedia.com/articles/romeo-dallaire

12. Aleksandr I. Solzhenitsyn, *The Gulag Archipelago, 1918–1956: An Experiment in Literary Investigation*, vol. 2, trans. Thomas P. Whitney, (New York: Harper & Row, 1974), p 615.

13. Jacob Needleman, *Why Can't We Be Good?* (London: Penguin Books, 2007), pp 21-22.

14. Ibid., p 22.

15. Carl Jung, "Psychology and Religion" (1938). In CW 11: *Psychology and Religion: West and East*, (New York: Yale University Press, Inc., 1966), p 25.

16. Paul Waldau and Kimberley Patton, eds., *A Communion of Subjects: Animals in Religion, Science and Ethics* (New York: Columbia University Press, 2006), pp 472-473, 512-513.

17. Peter Berger, *The Sacred Canopy*, (New York: Anchor Books, 1967) p 54.

18. James C. Livingston, *Anatomy of the Sacred*, (Upper Saddle River, NJ: Prentice-Hall, Inc., 2001), pp 277-300.

19. Ibid., p 276.

20. Dan Cohn-Sherbok, *Judaism: History, Belief and Practice*, (London: Routledge, 2003), p 420.

21. James C. Livingston, *Anatomy of the Sacred*, pp 116-117, 277-290.

22. John's Gospel, *The New Oxford Annotated Bible* (3rd ed.), (Oxford: Oxford University Press, 2001), chap 16:33.

23. John Bowker, *Problems of Suffering in the Religions of the World*, (Cambridge: Cambridge University Press, 1970), pp 63-64.

24. Ibid., p 73.

25. Ibid., pp 63-64.

26. John Polkinhorne, "Christianity and Science," *The Oxford Handbook of Religion and Science*, (Oxford: Oxford University Press, 2006), Philip Playton, Zachary Simpson, eds., p 61.

27. Matthew's Gospel, *The New Oxford Annotated Bible* (3rd ed.), chap 5:45.

28. John Bowker, *Problems of Suffering in the Religions of the World*, p 81.

29. Is considered to be first great Catholic theologian, who through his writings helped establish the Canon of Scripture. His major work 'Adversus omnes Haereses' was a detailed attack on Gnosticism.

30. John Bowker, *Problems of Suffering in the Religions of the World*, p 85.

31. Origen lived through a turbulent period of the Christian Church, when persecution was widespread and little or no doctrinal consensus existed among the various regional churches. In this environment, Gnosticism flourished, and Origen was the first truly philosophical thinker to turn his hand not only to a refutation of Gnosticism, but to offer an alternative Christian system that was more rigorous and philosophically respectable than the mythological speculations of the various Gnostic sects.

32. Mark S. M. Scott, *Journey Back to God: Origen on the Problem of Evil*, (New York: Oxford University Press, 2012), ix.

33. Ibid., p 8.

34. Michael Peterson et al., "Evil Is Privation of Good," *Philosophy of Religion: Selected Readings* (2nd ed.), (New York: Oxford University Press, Inc., 2001), p 249.

35. http://www.bbc.co.uk/schools/gcsebitesize/rs/god/isgoodandevilrev2.shtml

36. Jonathon Brockopp, "Islam," *Evil and Suffering* (Cleveland: The Pilgrim Press, 1998) ed. Jacob Nuesner, p 123.

37. Ibid., p 122.

38. Mu'tazalism, http://www.muslimphilosophy.com/hmp/13.htm

39. Jonathon Brockopp, "Islam," *Evil and Suffering*, pp 124-125.

40. http://www.patheos.com/Library/Islam/Beliefs/Suffering-and-the-Problem-of-Evil.html

41. Ibid., p 127.

42. James C. Livingston, *Anatomy of the Sacred*, p 287.

43. Ibid., p 287.

44. John Bowker, *Problems of Suffering in the Religions of the World*, p 196.

45. http://ngm.nationalgeographic.com/ngm/0306/feature1/

46. http://larryavisbrown.homestead.com/files/xeno.mahabcomm.htm

47. John Bowker, *Problems of Suffering in the Religions of the World*, p 195.

48. Ibid.

49. Many of the other gods in the [Buddhist] Pali Canon find a common mythological role in Hindu literature. Some common gods and goddesses are Indra, Aapo (Varuna), Vayo (Vayu), Tejo (Agni), Surya, Pajapati (Prajapati), Soma, Yasa, Venhu (Vi u), Mahadeva (Siva), Vijja (Saraswati), Usha, Pathavi (Prithvi), Sri (Lakshmi), Kuvera (Kubera), several yakkhas (Yakshas), gandhabbas (Gandhar-vas), N gas, garula (Garuda), sons of Bali, Veroca, etc.[28] While in Hindu texts some of these gods and goddesses are considered embodiments of the Supreme Being, the Buddhist view is that all gods and goddesses were bound to samsara. The world of gods according to the Buddha presents a being with too many pleasures and distractions. https://en.wikipedia.org/wiki/God_in_Buddhism#Other_common_gods_referred_to_in_the_Canon

50. www.abuddhistlibrary.com/ Buddhism/ A%20 -%20Tibetan%20Buddhism/ Authors/ Sangye%20 Khadro/ The% 20Ten%20non-virtues%20and%20 their%20results/ The%20Ten%20Non-Virtues.rtf

51. Patrick S. Bresnan, *Awakening: An Introduction to the History of Eastern Thought*, (Upper Saddle River, NJ: Prentice Hall, 2003), p 224.

52. W. Owen Cole and Piara Singh Sambhi, *The Sikhs: Their Religious Beliefs and Practices*, (Brighton, UK., Sussex Academic Press, 1998), p 84. This is a quote taken directly from the Sikh scripture, the Adi Granth, (AG 921).

53. Ibid., pp 83, 94.

54. Ibid., p 84.

55. John Bowker, *Problems of Suffering in the Religions of the World*, p 278.

56. Warren Matthews, *World Religions* (7th ed.), p 160.

57. Ibid., p 444.

58. Ibid., pp 29-32.

59. Daniel L. Pals, *Seven Theories of Religion*, (New York: Oxford University Press, 1996), pp 24-28.

CHAPTER 9

Religion and Women

OVERVIEW

The role of women in religion is a highly controversial topic eliciting responses from people within the traditions and from others who view the cosmologies from the position of the outside secular observer. For those who are strong devotees to a particular religion scrutiny of their customs will often cause responses bordering on discomfort, defence, and sometimes open hostility or rejection. Set against a background of critical analysis the issue is, how can an objective presentation of facts fully speak to the spiritual nuances appreciated by the believer functioning within the inner sanctum of the religious tradition? Also to be considered is the fact that no study of religion with its particular signature and cosmology can ever be value free on the part of the researcher.[1] The devout within a system will stress the positive and deny the negative ramifications of various religious beliefs. They will stress that their tradition bears the marks of ancient authority and will take personal affront at any criticism no matter how factual it is. This is often problematic from the researcher's viewpoint because in the context of women within religions, there will be existing beliefs endemic in the traditions which speak to the subjugation, dismissal, and cultural inferiority of the female. These tensions have been noted to exist throughout history with some of the surviving works of religious women speaking to the depth and richness of transcendence within female spirituality and to the opposition they faced. Yet confusingly enough, at the same time, these texts often quietly acquiesce to the power of male authority which acts as the paradigm for proper conduct from a female perspective.[2]

CHAPTER 9

THE PATHS OF FEMALE CHRISITIANITY

From the viewpoint of a clear female religious voice in the Western cultural context long before the advent of official feminist methodologies and theologies, there are records of Christian women's writings dating from the first century C.E.[3] The content of the works indicate a clear sense of self, despite oppressive religious and cultural milieus.[4] During the course of history from that time on, recommencing in the fifth century and continuing through sixth, seventh, ninth, twelfth, thirteenth, fourteenth, fifteenth, sixteenth, seventeenth, and eighteen centuries, there are written works which stand as testimony to the strength and wisdom of women within Christian cultures who strove for change.[5] What is also evident is that from the nineteenth century onwards, just speaking to Western cultures alone, there arose a plethora of clearly focused specific writings pertaining to spirituality, leadership, equality, autonomy, physicality, intelligence, and the necessary right for female education.[6] These works were those which clearly critiqued and challenged patriarchal society and initiated campaigns to change the system. It is to their efforts and credit—as also to the men who believed in the same freedoms for women—that so much was done to achieve the modicum of security and equality for women in Western societies which is experienced today.

The role that Christian women have played historically in female emancipation in the Western world, however, faced enormous opposition, scorn, and rejection. At the inception of Christianity, or what is called the *Jesus Movement*, there appears to have been, as feminist scholar Rosemary Radford Ruether observes, a move towards "gender dissolution … [as] a general meaning of the new life in Christ effected through baptism."[7] In the words of Saint Paul (c 5–67 C.E.) in his letter to the Church in Galatia, written in the late forties to early fifties of the Common Era,

> … in Christ Jesus you are all children of God through faith. As many of you as
> were baptized into Christ have clothed yourselves with Christ. there is no longer
> Jew or Greek, There is no longer slave or free, there is no longer male and female;
> for all of you are one in Christ.[8]

Sadly, these great, inspirational concepts were way before their time, in the context of a living human reality. Unfortunately, the genesis for egalitarianism, especially pertaining to female spirituality and equality of thought did not flourish into a continuous, established tradition within the developing and then established Church. For example, consider yet another New Testament interpretation taken from Paul's letter to Timothy[9] where he says:

> Let woman learn in silence with full submission. I permit no woman to teach or
> to have authority over a man; she is to keep silent. For as Adam was formed first,
> then Eve' and Adam was not deceived, but the woman was deceived and became
> a transgressor. Yet she will be saved through childbearing, provided they continue
> in faith and love and holiness, with modesty.[10]

Obviously, there are some great glaring theological problems with this male-oriented sentiment. Indeed, the misogyny in the 1 Timothy reading has been identified by many women over the centuries. Nevertheless, for many conservative Christian groups these verses remain a mainstay in the

Woman in the Orante prayer stance

subjugation of women. In the fundamentalist Christian groups, together with the Roman Catholic and Orthodox Traditions, this keeps women in place as biological entities. The 1 Timothy text states clearly that the first woman ever created was responsible for bringing every single potential for sin into creation. As daughters of that first transgressor, Eve, the only way a woman can be saved is through reproduction, which is often extremely painful and frequently life threatening (especially for women in the third world), but it is required that a woman must suffer. Another problem with the salvation through reproduction idea is that in reality there are women who are infertile, and sadly, if a woman is married to an infertile male, she is damned in two ways. Sadly she cannot reproduce ergo she cannot be "saved" due to her own bodily dysfunction and further, she cannot be saved also because her husband is infertile. Of course, the husband can be saved because he did not bring sin into the world. The problem with this malicious and very uneducated perspective is that it speaks much to the latent contempt that can exist in this religious interpretation but not to a sound theological explanation for the Atonement of Christ. Paul taught that salvation was given only through faith in Christ and was not contingent on gender, race, or social standing.

Another reality in the Christian religion is that women have a long and undeniable history of teaching, preaching, leadership, healing, scholarship, scientific discovery, and also governance within various Christian traditions. Oddly enough, on the part of the detractors, there is an almost palpable discomfort in acknowledging these realities as it would speak to the definite display of God-given talents and equality. From this perspective, no acknowledgement of the equality of female spirituality and intellectual ability is addressed, and in the words of the Southern Baptist Church's 1998 statement on matters of female submission, a wife should "submit herself graciously to the servant leadership of her husband."[11] What this says about the validity of the unmarried, infertile, or nonreproductive woman who might have deep spirituality and great intelligence, is left swinging in the metaphorical breeze.

From these two basic interpretations of varying degrees of equality in Christ, the divided camps have evolved during the centuries as to the role and intellectual standing of women. One interpretation is to view the role of woman as being one of submission, always deferring to male authority. The other interpretation accepts the claims of women to full spiritual equality, autonomy, possessing the right to lead, preach, and teach men as well as women.[12] In this stream of acceptance, there are traditions which will ordain women in ministry and recognize their many spiritual talents. These religious communities will ordain women, without requiring celibacy as a condition of ordination, only requiring a deep and practical faith, commitment in leadership, well-rounded scholarship, grounded morality, stability, and, of course, good teaching skills. Other Christian traditions will acknowledge limited forms of ecclesiastical leadership, such as nuns or female deacons. In the case of ecclesiastical leadership, such as nuns who function as teachers and doctors in medical missions, it is stipulated that they must be celibate—and preferably virginal. In the Roman Catholic or Eastern Orthodox traditions, women cannot, however, consider for a fleeting moment, being called to the office of pope or patriarch, nor even to the more humble but dedicated role of priest because this is solely the domain of men.[13] The reasoning behind this is that Christ was a man and a woman cannot represent the personal maleness of Jesus Christ, the Second Aspect or Person of the Trinity. Of course, there is no problem with this line of reasoning as it pertains to men, who can represent the divine Second "Person" of the Trinity because of their maleness, physiology, and hormones! Thus spiritual divinity, once again, is reflected and represented only by the masculine projection of divine wisdom. This is made even more confusing and ironic as within Judaeo-Christian thought, the divine is represented by the feminine—which is wisdom, and known as Sophia!

Having regard to these historical and very current issues, it can be observed that it has taken around twenty centuries for these profoundly serious issues to be honestly addressed between men and women in the traditions. Realistically, however, there are many who still view this propagation of injustice as per female inequality as a triviality, with no relevancy or real bearing on the outside world. Unfortunately, this is a glaring denial of global reality and a dismissal of the very real need to raise the status of women in the global community.

THE PATHS AND PERCEPTIONS OF FEMALE JUDAISM

Speaking to the widespread existing historical literature and mythologies that note the presence of the feminine and the roles prescribed for Jewish women, there is an abundance of literature describing their influence and required conduct. The exemplary roles of Jewish women throughout Jewish tradition is presented as indispensible in the continuance of Jewish identity. Of note, however, is the fact that what is now considered to be the norm in Jewish practice and held out to originate in ancient Israel through the first five books of Moses[14] was probably revised and developed around early sixth century B.C.E. after the destruction of Solomonic Temple in 586 B.C.E., and the resulting deportation into the Babylonian Empire.[15] By the fifth century B.C.E. the tradition of the *rabbis* had become a major influential force within late Second Temple Judaism, and the interpretations they set down as laws changed the pre-exilic traditions, mythologies, and customs into post-exilic rules. According to religious tradition, it was customary to speak of the dignity and bravery of individual Jewish women, but what the rabbinic tradition changed was the perception of the female presence. As Serenity Young writes,

> While non-Jews and the Jewish tradition itself spoke of the dignity and bravery
> of individual Jewish women, in general the rabbinic tradition perceives women,
> going back to Eve, as wholly other than men. This notion is most vividly ex-
> pressed in the daily prayer of Jewish men who thank God for not making them a
> gentile, a slave, or a woman.[16]

After the massive cultural upheaval following the Roman destruction of Jerusalem in 70 C.E. and the systematic removal of the Jews from their homeland over approximately the next hundred years, the Jewish community relocated to other parts of the Mediterranean world. What we know is that during this cultural upheaval women were essentially excluded or at least limited in their access to two major aspects of Jewish spiritual life: the study of Torah (law) and the public rituals within the synagogue. In addition to this, the realm of domestic rituals was emphasized and the ritual of lighting the Sabbath lights by the women became a central affirmation of family solidarity and of keeping the Sabbath commandment. In traditional interpretations relating to the Sabbath lights, the conventional explanation of the role of the woman is that: "It is the task of women to light candles to make amends for the fact that Eve, the first women, brought the darkness of sin into the world."[17] So much store is set in the female transmission of family ritual observation, dietary laws, family traditions, and female purification rituals, that these things in themselves almost mark female identification as a Jewess. An example of this is the *mikvah,* or ritual purification bath that women take after completing their menstrual cycle or a short time after childbirth. This obser-vance reinforces female identification and cleansing through which they create their own form of religious expression. This aspect of female exclusion through perceived physical pollution and her ritual return to the community through purification, have become central identification marks of the women's community, which is bound by purification and pollution, inclusion and exclusion.[18]

In Judaism, the religious writings abound with detailed rabbinic guidelines and pronouncements on the role of women, their rights and their impurity.[19] Further, there are other horrific, cautionary tales provided depicting the folkloric account of Adam's disobedient first wife, Lilith, which appear to have been reinforced in Jewish communities during the Middle Ages. This evil wife basically did not conform to the role of the acceptable servant to her husband and ran away from her God-given mate simply because she really did not like him. The evil reputation ascribed to this rebellious wife is that she was transformed into the demonic killer of small children. This story was a very popular part of Jewish medieval culture and was taught to young children, especially girls, wherein Lilith was por-trayed as murderous in that she stole the breath of newborns. There are also contrasting stories within the cannon of Torah of great and noble female leaders, with one such story concerning the courageous

Queen Esther who saved her people from slaughter.[20] Other writings come to us from women such as of sixteenth-century Sara Copia Sullam of Venice, who demonstrates her devotion to Judaism and her scholarly knowledge.[21] There is also the story of Gluckel of Hemeln who offers advice in both secular and religious matters, establishing herself as a wise religious women.[22] What we do know from the historical material is that there are many texts written by literate Jewish women on all manners of issues and subjects. Some are accepting of the dominance of patriarchy but there are others who existed within the traditions, especially in the cultures of first and second century B.C.E. who functioned as leaders, patronesses, and wise women who rose in prominence as scriptural interpreters for other women. These historical and later ethnic profiles suggest that women were not as excluded as traditionally perceived[23] and this reality can be seen in the ways that American Jewish women, based on existing Jewish social mechanisms, organized communities such as the Ladies of the Sisterhood during the period between 1900 and 1930. These Sisterhoods were attached to the synagogues and created cultures that changed the expectations of their "proper" religious roles. Through this raising of cultural acceptance and visible involvement, they gradually became more accepted within the religious sphere, thus enabling the Sisterhood to expand Jewish women's public religious roles.[24] The role and influence of women, particularly in the North American Jewish context, later contributed to opening up the rabbinate for females, and although this was a major cultural battle, by 1982 some fifty female rabbis had already graduated from the Hebrew Union College and also the Reconstructional Rabbinical College.[25]

Nevertheless, for the female Jewish reformer there remains the ever present reality of control, consensus, and major tensions within traditional Jewish culture. While there is the potential for expanding female religious participation in worship, the wearing of traditional male prayer attire (*talith* and *yamulke*) especially at sacred sites such as the Wailing Wall in Jerusalem, is a contentious and sometimes volatile issue.

ISLAMIC CULTURE AND THE ROLE OF OBSERVANT WOMEN

There are four major sources of Islamic authority which govern the *Ummah* (religious community). These are the Qur'an, Hadith, Sunnah, and Shariah. As is dramatically and rigorously taught, the Qur'an is the verbatim word of God, without error and defying any criticism regarding textual authenticity. In addition to this, there are the Hadith which are held to be the documented collections of Muhammad's words and stories about his life. There is also the Sunnah of the Prophet—the teachings—spiritual and legal. The fourth of these central authorities is that of Shariah, which is Islamic law. All these sources deal with women, their conduct, rights, responsibilities, and under whose direction their lives are to be controlled.[26] It is also customary in Islamic cultures for females to be under the guardianship or custody of a male custodian, whether it is a father, a husband, an uncle, a brother, or even a son.

What can be gleaned from early Islamic society is that female Muslims had the opportunity to establish themselves in varying, although limited forms of leadership. There were women like Khadija, the Prophet's first wife and first convert to Islam. Aisha, the Prophet's child bride of between eight and nine years of age upon marriage, who was another influential woman in Islam and who lived until the age of sixty-five.[27] Aisha rose to become an established authority in Hadith and tradition in later life. Along with Aisha there was another of the Prophet's many wives named Umm Salamah, who was also acknowledged as a great source of Hadith. Another portrait of an ideal Muslim female image is that of Fatima, the only surviving daughter of Prophet Muhammad, who is depicted as a tragic, loyal, long suffering, noble figure. Fatima, due to her depth of spirit and courage, coupled with her self-denial, poverty, charity, and deep devotion, later became the ideal Shi'ia female saint.[28] The Prophet's granddaughter, Zaynab, daughter of Fatima and the sister of Husayn, is also presented as a model for Shi'ite Muslim women. In 680 she was present during the battle of Karbala in Iraq in which her esteemed brother Husayn was martyred. The legend portrays her as a valiant fighter who was later captured and taken to Damascus.[29]

The Islamic material, outside of the Qur'an, such as Hadith, Sunnah and historiographies, present a picture of women who where female poets and several who were recorded Sufi mystics. These women directed their energies towards spirituality, love for God, and to helping the poor. For the Sufi mystics both male and female were considered equal in standing with Allah [30]

There is, however, a recognized problem pertaining to female spirituality found entrenched within Islamic theology. In the revered Qur'an itself, in Sura IV entitled *Women,* and in Sura II entitled *The Cow,* the role and standing of women is uncomfortably disconcerting. In Sura IV there is reference to the secondary status of women as the female was created from the soul of man, so her soul comes from the male or Adam. Not surprisingly for an ancient text, women are the property of men and even their legal personal dowries may be in "consumed with wholesome appetite," should the wife hand over her property to her spouse. There are also full instructions as to how women are to be treated by men, which may seem encouraging, but in Sura IV: 35, it also reads:

> Men are guardians over women because Allah has made some of them excel others, and because they [men] spend of their wealth. So virtuous women are those who are obedient, and guard the secrets of their husbands with Allah's protection. And as for those [wives, concubines] on whose part you fear disobedience, admonish them and leave them alone in their beds and chastise them. Then if they obey you, seek not a way against them. Surely, Allah is High, Great.[31]

In Sura II: 106, *The Cow,* although most definitely presented as a guide for correct sexual practice, conduct, purity, and codes of honour presents some interesting perspectives of female sexuality.

There is the following authoritative pronouncement from
the lips of Allah, which reads
as follows: "Your women are a
tillage for you; so come unto
your tillage as you wish."[32]

Another very serious consideration pertaining to female
equality and worth in Islam
is the noted Hadith of the
Prophet in which he stated, "I
was shown the Hell-fire and
that the majority of its dwell-
ers are women."[33] Suffice it to
say, this is a contentious statement with a series of explanations offered.

In spite of these issues, male and female Muslims will claim that their religion offers the greatest
amount of freedom and nobility to women because it teaches people to control their passions and
be moderate in all things. Further, arising out of the issues of women's social standing, there are
a growing number of female Muslims who are now working to change the dominant cultural and
religious perspectives regarding the status of women and to create a climate of respect in the more
conservative sections of the ummah.[34]

HINDUISM, THE FEMININE, AND SPIRITUALITY

Within the Hindu cultures there abounds a diversity of scripture and mythology which describe
the feminine as a powerful force, known as the *Shakti*. This force is also referred to as Devi or
mahadevi, and is believed to assume different roles as goddesses such as Sati, Parvati, Durga, and
Kali. This divine force is perceived to be the feminine creative power which is sometimes referred
to as "The Divine Mother" and as such embodies the active feminine energy known as *Prakriti*.
This force represents material nature or matter, which is a constituent cosmic factor in life and is
characterized in all nature.[35] In addition to being a fertile force which creates and recreates, the
Shakti is also the bringer of death and destruction and can often be interpreted as dominating the
male gods.[36] Given these strong representations of the feminine in positions of power and leadership, there is a striking gap between myth and reality. Even the great writings of female saints and
poets do not appear to make a cultural impact on ordinary society. What is surprising is that the
writings and examples that exist on the part of females have until present times been mostly related
to achieving moksha (liberation) but do not speak to the physical realities endured by ordinary
women. The great saints like Mirabai (c. 1498–1557), or the fourteenth century Lalla, or Bahinabai
(1628–1700) and Ananda MoyiMa (1896–1982) are representational of a large number of the
Hindu female voices over the centuries but do not form part of a cultural memory that changes the

actual importance of female spirituality in the everyday lives of ordinary women.

In reality, the sobering fact is that despite this reverential and awe-inspiring approach to this creative force and the respect for motherhood and the feminine, these concepts are still not translated into cultural empowerment. The fact is that existing alongside the power of the feminine in divinity and the importance of female ritual to protect the family and home, there is the ever present influence of the *Manusmrirti,* or *Laws of Manu,* which originated around 100 B.C.E.[37] This body of legal code exists as a reality in Hindu cultures, and the sentiments and prohibitions it embodies still carry enormous influence in modern daily life.

Before the Manusmirti was compiled and became widely entrenched in Hindu society, the position of women in early Vedic India appears to have been relatively positive. The Laws of Manu,[38] however, demonstrate the efforts of the Brahmin or priestly elite to restrict women's legal inde-

pendence in the later period between 200 to 400 C.E.[39] by enforcing control over women as never before. Consider the following estimation of female competency:

> Nothing must be done independently by a girl, by a young woman, or by an old woman, even in her own house. In childhood a female must be subject to her father, in youth to her husband, and when her husband is dead to her sons. A woman must never be independent. She must not seek to separate herself from her father, husband, or sons. By leaving them she would make both her own and her husband's families contemptible.[40]

Thus what the lofty goddesses, or the great saint/poetess may represent is in reality out of reach for the ordinary Hindu woman, based on this ancient Brahmin law code. Female Hindu reformers are very cognizant of this on going religious and societal discrimination and are among some of the most articulate, resourceful, and successful catalysts for change. In reality, however, the path to raising social consciousness is surrounded by thousands of years of entrenched religious and cultural patterns.

THE PATH OF THE FEMALE BUDDHIST

On the surface, Buddhism presents as a religion that offers the path of transcendence to both men and women. This is, in theory, correct, but there are obstacles that are acknowledged to stand in the path of female Buddhists seeking enlightenment and liberation that are not presented to their male counterparts.

Siddhartha Gautama's teachings, originating in northern India, created a strong following of both male and female devotees. For the males it was a simple social evolution to form a distinctive religious grouping because the Indian/Hindu culture allowed for men to pursue paths of celibacy and renunciation. This transformed into the order of monks or the Bhiksu. For the women, however, it

was a different scenario. Women were traditionally bound to family, home, and community and so for them, the path led them into relatively uncharted areas of spiritual exploration.

Canonical Buddhist texts record that there was a desire on the part of a number of female devotees to form a celibate order, devoted to meditation, renunciation, and the achievement of liberation and enlightenment. Giving heed to this female religious movement, Shakyamuni (Buddha) grudgingly gave permission for the creation of the Bhikkuni sangha of female renunciants after several requests made by Pajapati his stepmother, who was also his aunt, and the one who had functioned as his mother figure, raising him from a baby.[41] Pajapati was also in the company of 500 other women who were also seeking ordination and she acted as their leader and spokesperson. Eventually, Buddha gave permission, based on his own teachings that females could also reach enlightenment, but predicted that admitting females into the order of renunciants would lead to the decline of his teachings.[42]

For the Buddhist community under Shakyamuni's direction, it was a generally held tenet of the movement that women could achieve enlightenment, but that it would be a much more difficult path for them. Another general belief held by the male renunciants was that women posed various threats to the male Sangha. This belief can be identified in a pivotal text recording the establishment of the Bhikkuni sangha wherein they are burdened with much harsher rules compared to their male counterparts. The rules are interesting given that Buddah compounded the difficulties of the path before them. Siddhartha pronounced a series of eight *Garudhammas,* or grave rules, not required of men. These were and still are the enforcing codes of conduct for the nun:

- A Bhikkuni must reside within six hours of traveling distance from the monastery where Bhikkhus reside for advice.
- On observance days a Bhikkhuni should consult the Bhikkhus.
- A Bhikkhuni must spend rainy season retreats under the orders of both Bhikhus and Bhikkhunis.
- A Bhikkhuni must live her life by both the orders.
- A Bhikkhuni must in two years obtain the higher ordination (Upasampatha) by both orders.
- A Bhikkhuni cannot scold a Bhikkhu.
- A Bhikkhuni cannot advise a Bhikkhu.
- A Bhikkhuni who has been ordained even for a hundred years must greet respectfully, rise up from her seat, salute with joined palms, do proper homage to a monk ordained but that day.

Of further note, is that in a canonical text entitled the *Vinaya-pitaka* there is a list of 250 rules for monks and 348 rules for nuns.[43]

From the historical data that is available, and as can be seen from the above material, it is clear that Buddhism has from its inception acknowledged the path of the ordained person as a member of the spiritual elite, which is called the *Sangha*, or ordained religious community. There was and is, however, broad recognition and reliance upon the other Buddhists who form the second and foundational component of Buddhism, namely the laity. So closely related is the relationship between ordained and layperson that the religious community as a whole is also referred to as the sangha. What this means, therefore, is that the term *sangha* can apply to (1) the whole religious community of Buddhists, (2) the laity, and (3) the ordained members who are set apart within the community to fulfill religious rituals, provide spiritual guidance, and act as role models on the path to enlightenment. The importance of laity to this day, however, is to provide vital economic support for the ordained sangha.[44] Indeed, the practice of generous donations of the laity fulfils two goals for the whole community. First, it means that monastics can devote all their time to religious duties because they are freed from work to support themselves. Second, it means that by giving to monasteries and monastics, the layperson earns great merit out of their self-sacrifice and generosity to the greater cause of spiritual enlightenment.

Problems arise regarding Buddhism's claims at spiritual egalitarianism when one considers the realities of religio-cultural settings. From the very earliest period of Buddhism and even into modern times, it is evident that women were and are by far its greatest supporters. At the same time, it is evident that there is great disparity in that they were and still are overshadowed by the male hierarchy in a male-dominated tradition.[45] As Tessa Bartholomeusz observes in *Women and World Religions*

> … women are the main participants at almsgiving ceremonies and in temple life and are also the majority of participants at the lay insight meditations centres that have emerged in recent decades in Thailand, Burma, and Sri Lanka.[46]

Yet this support is not gratefully accepted by the Buddhist institutions in S. E. Asia. In fact, it is the prevailing belief that "women fulfill their spiritual obligations through their domestic duties as wives and mothers, and are not required to make additional efforts."[47]

What does emerge from an overall perspective pertaining to traditional Buddhist cultures and mainstream Buddhism is that the best path towards enlightenment for women is through renunciation. This means choosing the convent system as a nun, or as a member of a semi-monastic vegetarian society.[48] In the context of both female societies this enables the woman to avoid marriage and all family ties. The problem with these institutions is the fact that financially, according traditional belief, it is more meritorious to make donations to monks rather than to nuns. This kind of reasoning presents financial problems for religious houses that exist to offer spiritual training to girls and women. These problems will vary according to the country and culture in which Buddhism exists, with some communities such as Napal, with its strong Theravadan tradition, providing equal support for female renunciants who are not allowed ordination, alongside ordained male monks.[49] In other Buddhist monastic communities there is strong opposition directed towards the Bhikkhunis' teaching of the Dhama and their endeavours to help women in poverty and to stop prostitution.[50]

JAINISM AND ITS CONTRADICTIONS

The Jain tradition is marked with ambivalence towards women. One the one hand, the role of the woman is identified in her nurturing, motherly, and protector functions and on the other, she is considered subordinate whether living as a celibate nun or functioning as a wife and mother.

The ancient mythic mothers, such as the figure of Marudevi, who is considered to be the mother of the first Jina (or first emancipated soul of this current era of being) are highly revered in Jainism. It is also believed that all mothers of the emancipated successive male Jinas function as role models for today's Jain laywomen. These great mothers are considered to be the embodiment of the continuity of the Jain tradition and demonstrate the "attainment of the goal [that] comes from perfect

fulfillment of their role as mothers."[51] Strangely enough, although Jainism does not acknowledge the role of supreme deities of any kind, there are several groups of powerful goddesses who are connected with Jain doctrine.[52] The real inconsistency of the female role, however, is brought into focus with the realities pertaining to the Jain nuns, where the concept of the lesser soul is most definitely identified among both the Digambara and Svetambara orders. The Svetambara monks believe that women are capable of the same spiritual achievement as men, and that the nineteenth Tirthankara was a woman. In reality, however, all Jain nuns are of lower status than monks[53] and yet of today's religious orders within Jainism it is the nuns who form the highest percentage in both groups.[54]

Most of these women in both orders will be widows of varying ages. Sadly, it is also the monks' position that nuns are "empty, given to haughtiness, sensual, inconstant and cannot be relied upon."[55]

SIKHISM AND FEMALE RELIGIOUS IDENTITY

Sikhism presents a challenge to those researching the role of women within the tradition. If one consults websites the image presented is of true equality, although differing in specific duties regarding gender. The material also indicates that women are highly revered and quotes from the sacred text of the *Guru Granth Sahib* in which Guru Nanak writes:

> ...from the woman is our birth, in the woman's womb are we shaped; To the
> woman we are engaged, to the woman we are wedded; The woman is our friend
> and from woman is the family; Through the woman are the bonds of the world;
> Why call woman evil who gives birth to the leaders of the World? From the
> woman is the woman, without woman there is none.[56]

From the perspective of scholarly analysis, however, regarding various sources of Sikh history, religion, culture, and literature, a contrasting societal picture emerges. The materials indicate a strong androcentric bias and an ambivalent attitude towards women. This cultural sketch is also rendered

more difficult to understand due to the fact that there is little known of the ordinary Sikh woman. There are lists of great and virtuous women who existed in the mists of history during the formation of the religion. These great female figures were renowned for their guidance, wisdom, bravery, and missionary achievements and these role models appear to provide inspiration for wom-

en to mobilize behind any social or political movement. The movement itself, however, is usually initiated by young men and the role of the female is made into that of an auxiliary support group with little clout.[57]

In spite of the websites which assure the researcher that all is well within Sikhism and that the role and treatment of women within the tradition is egalitarian, other facts emerge from scholarship. From this outside research material it becomes clear that there are extremely misogynist views expressed in Sikh society.[58] This is further enforced by the utterances or *gurbani* of the founding gurus themselves. Although the sacred *Guru Granth Sahib* might express views of egalitarianism and reverence for females, over time, the culturally narrowed views of the gurus themselves surfaced as voices of authority. The gurus, whilst refusing all intimations of divinity, were still held by their followers to be closely aligned with the divine and their pronouncements carried great influence. It was simply a male cultural progression to invest *gurban*i texts with the aura of infallibility and holiness. In this way, the male voice established itself as dominant within Sikh scriptural cosmology.[59] Thus male authority was assured and assumed as the natural order of all things Sikh.

Arising out of established cultural patterns dating back before the arrival of Sikhism, and even flying in the face sometimes of what the *Guru Granth Sahib* teaches, the age-old Indian perceptions of the feminine endure within the tradition. These attitudes relegate the feminine to the sensual realm as opposed to the spiritual. Those ever present evil and seductive powers and limited intellectual ability that women were perceived to embody, went unchallenged in succeeding generations of Sikhs. In accordance with these views, ideas concerning pollution and contamination and volatility are still prevalent in the cosmology. On the one hand the woman is respected in her role as wife, mother, and integral member of the family unit, yet on the other hand, she was and is also clearly identified with suffering through childbirth, attachment to this world through children, and vulnerability and dependency through the loving bonds of family. Women were and often still are very dependent upon males within the family unit and rely on them for support and protection. From the religious perspective of transcendence, it was and can still prove to be, in fact, those very traditional qualities and characteristics that might hold the male back from his quest for true spirituality.

The gurus imposed limitations on women recognizing and emphasizing female weakness, sexuality, seductive powers, and impulsive influences. Thus the female was even more constrained to live within the confines of domesticity in order for her to receive protection and guidance. It was feared that if a woman pursued her spiritual or intellectual goals too ardently it might lead to the dissolution of the family unit. It was therefore culturally emphasized that "happily wedded wives were capable of respecting the *gurumat,*" or religious and social rules, within the home and within a closely constructed social environment. Functioning within this traditional, cultural mileu, Sikh women were and are supposedly treated for the most part with respect in public but in the family context, are regarded as inferior to men.[60] In the words of Rajkumari Shanker in her essay on *Women in Sikkism,*

> Certain texts go on to suggest that the female sex was weaker both physically and
> mentally, more vulnerable to ignorance, and perhaps even somewhat defective,
> in terms of spiritual weakness and physical handicaps. ... The idea that woman
> is evil, unclean, or an impediment is not rejected as often made to think, but
> endorsed in the Guru Granth.[61]

THE WORTH OF FEMALE CHINESE SPIRITUALITY

The participation of women in Chinese religious traditions has a long and varied past and the presence of goddesses in ancient Chinese society can be identified dating back into the second millennia B.C.E. There was a goddess named Xi Wang Mu, the Queen Mother of the West, who was believed to hold the secrets of immortality. In order to access this goddess, the forces of nature, and many of the other divinities in the early Chinese pantheon there were shaman, most of whom were female.[62] The shamans functioned as healers, guides, and mediums; they also dealt with problematic ghosts, assisted in arranging marriages, and acted as consultants offering political guidance. Their power was considerable, but as respective Chinese societies developed, the power of these shamans declined and among the other various transformations that occurred, women were banned from court entertainments. In addition to all this, as indicated in various texts dating from 692 and 509 B.C.E. women now began to be characterized as dangerous and the source of moral and political decline.[63]

By the time of Confucius (551-479 B.C.E.), women were virtually overlooked and their status had declined so drastically that they were dismissed as having any intelligent or important part to play in public ritual.[64] This was a major act of rejection as prior to that, in ancient society, women had been integral to community ritual performance and social morality. Confucius dismissed all this and emphasized the role of male moral virtues, through loyalty, sincerity, respect for one's superiors—fathers and grandfathers (filial piety), moral courage, and through humanity which meant dignified conduct and fair treatment of others.

In addition to this, ritual was only valid if it was conducted by moral beings who were trained to reflect upon their actions and consciences. This process could only be conducted by the junzi, or gentlemen as females lacked the ability to do this. It was the role of the gentleman to lead in government, offer political advice, make wise judgments, and establish a code of Confucian ethics. Not surprisingly, in Confucian philosophy and culture, there was little or no room for the participation of women, due to the fact that they were intrinsically flawed and were a major impediment to the implementation of an ordered, civilized, rational society.[65] Women were inferior by nature, capricious, emotional, narrow minded, suspicious, indiscrete, and full of gossip. Filial piety addressed male action towards fathers, grandfather, and even the ancestral spirits, through whom patriarchal lineage was the only valid source of supernatural authority. Confucius also believed that the destabilization and downfall of states was often attributed to the influence of meddling women[66] possessing limited comprehension of their own misguided actions.

Another Confucian scholar who followed in this philosophy was named Mencius (371-289 B.C.E.). Mencius pursued Confucian thought to even more divisive degrees, increasing regulations on how one should eat and live. He developed a set of rules which included separate living quarters for husbands and wives, males and females, and rigorously designated separate spheres of activity. In addition to this, he even laid out a code of reserved conduct by which men and women should act towards each other even within the family unit.[67]

This social code of conduct emphasized proper and balanced relationships because it was believed that when the earth and the cosmos functioned in harmony, through right action, order was maintained. Human relationships reflected the hierarchal harmony established within the heavens as it was reasoned that the heavens were the active force, holding sway over the earth, which was the passive force. In human relationships the most important persons held authority over the least important, therefore political leaders expected respect and obedience from their followers. In turn, families also followed this chain of hierarchy with the grandfather, father, and sons all holding dominion over their wives, daughters, and sisters. The reasoning behind this was that if each person in decreasing social clout deferred to their superiors, there would be a stable and happy environment. It was when mutual obligations were not fulfilled and there was disharmony within the perfectly balanced system that the family suffered.[68] Suffice it to say, there was tremendous pressure and control through coercion, placed upon all people to comply with Confucian ideals.

In the context of the female reality within this system, consider the internalized inferior, almost masochistic position, reflected in the writings of a first century C.E. female scholar named Pan Chao in her work entitled *Lessons for Women:*

Chinese shamaness

> On the third day after the birth of a girl the ancients observed three customs: (first) to place the baby below the bed; (second) to give her a potsherd with which to play; and (third) to announce her birth to her ancestors by an offering.[69]

Pan Chao went on to explain that placing the little girl below the bed plainly indicated teaching the little female from an early age, that she was lowly and weak. Under that conditioning she would take it for granted that it was her primary duty to humble herself, or be subservient before others. The second point emphasized to the little girl that this was all she could really expect! Useful household implements were to be her toys, which would in turn train her to be industrious and not given to flights of fancy in play! The third step was to introduce the ancestors to the girl and the girl to the (male) ancestors within her biological family and later to her husband's family to whom for the rest of her life, she was required to offer reverence and worship within her husband's home.

The ideas within the Confucian perspective, together with its enduring influence on politics and home, held sway from the sixth century B.C.E. until the Chinese Communist Revolution.[70] Not surprisingly, however, the family-oriented ideas and the perception of women endures in Chinese society today despite the impact of Communism. Although there are still female shamans who function in scattered areas of remote China to this day, there are no recorded female spiritual leaders within the traditional communities.

These ideas also continued in Daoism, where even though the Dao is perceived as feminine it did or does little to elevate the position of women or to provide a genuine argument for the equality of men and women. Unfortunately, even though yin (female) and yang (masculine) must be in balance and harmony, it is always the yang that presents as the strong, dry, and and stable force. On the other hand, the yin is presented as dark, moist, malleable, and the weaker of the two because it is the yin that usually bends to the yang.

There was also a secret religion called Nushu or "Women's Hidden Writings," which was developed by women in rural areas. There is no clear date that can be used to clearly identify its formation but the rare, existing texts indicate that it developed around 900 c.e., and lasted in secret until the Chinese cultural revolution. At the very core of its belief system was the solidarity of women standing together with a secret code language through which they could record their pain, write out their prayers and supplications, offer solace to other women, and display their insight. As Lee Rainey observes:

> There are very few references to the Buddha, Confucius or other common religious figures. The women write about the Buddhist concepts of karma and samsara; they boast that they have 'done their duty' to their husband's family, according to the Confucian traditions. They know the teachings, but there is remarkably little awe felt towards the 'great' traditions. The local, mostly female, deities were central to these women, as were festivals and pilgrimages in these deities' honour.[71]

What has emerged from further research regarding Nushu is that it was a woman's religion which incorporated into its cosmology the voice of personal identity. It was, therefore, not overshadowed by male religious interpretations and spoke to women's needs and expressed women's beliefs.[72]

From the perspective of female religious emancipation, the role of the traditional Chinese woman remains entrapped within the residue of Confucian philosophy and practical reality.

JAPANESE WOMEN AND ANCIENT TRADITION

All forms of Japanese indigenous religions will incorporate forms of spirit possession or invoke the guidance of spirit forces known as kami. Customarily, the kami identified as a deity, or perhaps a ghost or ancestor, will channel through the medium, or sometimes, in the case of particularly esteemed kami, through a shinto priest. In the context of females in these possession cults, the role of the female *Miko and the Itako* figured strongly as central actors/officiants in the early religious structures.[73] As such they are evidence of a female shamanistic tradition that existed before the composition of the influential and far reaching *Kojiki* text.[74]

Japan reflects the influence of various religions including the indigenous religion of Shinto (*Way of the Gods),* and other various forms of shamanism, from which two clearly identifiable female traditions developed. These traditions still exist in Japan today, each having changed over centuries, but still retaining their original functions to varying degrees of cultural acceptance.

The Miko, or shrine maiden, lived within a specific shrine or temple precinct, and would assist with ritual worship devoted to the kami or spirit forces. The Itako medium was and is usually a female shaman from northern Japan. The Itako are believed to have the ability to communicate with the dead and even to evil spirits, consequently making them prized as exorcists.

As far as can be historically established these early accepted female traditions continued without interference until the composition of the sacred text entitled the *Kojiki*[75] which was composed in the eighth century at the command of the Empress Gemmei. The intent of this text was to record the ancient Japanese myths in such a fashion as to clarify and sanctify one single line of imperial descent that began with the birth of the Great Goddess Amaterasu in heaven and continued, generation after generation in imperial succession through the Emperor, down to the present reign.[76] As a consequence of this text and its emphasis on particular religious traditions and interpretations later known as Shinto, the participation of females was gradually associated with pollution. The Kojiki emphasized the significance of ritual purity and the dangers of impurity and this gradually led to the identification of pollution within women and to the specific requirements for purity in order to please the ancestral kami. As the kami were believed to be disgusted by bodily pollution, menstruation became an issue of some significance. Through the rules and ritual exclusion of females as pollutants women's roles were greatly diminished. The purity requirements within Shinto as the broad-based expression of Japanese religion required that the central officiant be a pure male priest. Surprisingly, it is the influence of this ancient text which still subtly exerts its definitions and perceptions regarding the participation of Japanese women in religion today. As Heather Kobayashi writes concerning Japanese women's religious and physical perspectives, "women have historically been pushed out of the public eye and out of public religious spaces because of their supposed impurity and to this day women are haunted by the belief in their inherent pollution."[77]

Despite the traditional discomfort regarding female pollution, the revised role of the Miko was and is still, however, a prestigious one as in the case of the sacred royal shrine at *Ise* where they participate in sacred dance ceremonies and the preparation of sacred offerings for the kami. In earlier historical times, a virginal girl, preferably a child around the age of five, was chosen to live in seclusion as representative of the emperor at the sacred shrine.[78] The shrine itself was and is still believed to be inhabited by the great kami Amaterasu Omikami, the sun goddess and ruler of the Plain of Heaven. Amaterasu is the legendary ancestress of the emperors and as a consequence, only members of the royal family and specific guests, together with the Shinto priests and special Miko, may attend the site.

The ancient roles of the Miko at Ise and the Miko at other shrines included the function to act as mediums between the kami and the physical realm. In addition to this, the roles included possession trances, assisting in state Shinto worship ceremonies, conducting exorcisms, and acting as mediums in healing practices. As the tradition has adapted to the demands on modern Japanese society the Miko are not so generally associated with shamanistic practices, although these still do occur. In general in modern Japan, they now function at specific shrines and temples, participating in festivals, weddings, and other ritual observances.[79]

In the case of the Itako female shaman, she remains an itinerant religious figure who traditionally and into modern times, can be based at one particular shrine or may travel around with others of the cult. These women are still consulted on healings, exorcisms, and séances. The traditional and mandatory requirement for an Itako is still that she be blind or at least severely visually impaired. As part of her training she will also undergo an initiation ritual through which a kami or god is believed to supposedly possess her and she then becomes its bride or wife. [80]

During and after WWII due to the major social changes that occurred in Japan, there was a dearth of male Shinto priests and the official organization of Jinja Joncho which represents the Shinto shrines, allowed women into the ranks of the Shinto priesthood. In order to accomplish this the Jinia Joncho lifted the tradi-

Miko shrine attendants

tional ban on female pollution.[81] Despite conflicting arguments regarding pollution, female power, and purity, many of these women work alongside their Shinto priest husbands and officiate at the smaller shrines in rural areas. Overall, despite the opening of the priesthood to women, females function in the minority, in spite of the more progressive perspectives of the younger generations.[82] Nevertheless, as part of their cultural conditioning, female Shinto priestesses will still interpret menstruation and even recent childbirth as polluting forces. As anything connected to blood is offensive to kami sensibilities and might cause the spirits to anger, many women will take precautions against this by carrying salt, matches, and a sacred plant with them should they encounter an enraged divine force.[83]

In addition to these indigenous religions, there were other religions that were introduced into the Japanese archipelago, beginning with Daoism (early Common Era),[84] Buddhism in the sixth century C.E., Roman Catholicism (sixteenth century), and Protestant Christianity and Eastern Orthodoxy arriving in the mid to late nineteenth century. In the context of these outside religions and their contact with females in accordance with each of the other religion's biases towards women, the role of the female is still very restricted.

In the context of reform or women's participation in shamaness religions there are several new religions emerging under what is known as *Sectarian Shinto*. These new movements have their roots in a movement which began in the mid-nineteenth century and were tied strongly to various aspects of nationalism. From the mid to late twentieth century, however, there has been an increase in new religious traditions inspired in some part by female interpretations and these have become a popular trend. Not surprisingly, however, due to conventional Japanese Shinto perspectives they are not considered part of mainstream Japanese belief systems.

INDIGENOUS TRADITIONS AND THE POWER OF FEMALE BIOLOGY

The world of the woman in indigenous traditions is not easily or briefly explained. Each tradition will have its own concepts and protocols pertaining to gods, spirits, ancestors, altered states, spells, healings, birth, death, marriage, and power. Due to the complexity of each system it is impossible to identify specifically one voice of consensus, apart from the fact that women interact with life and spirit. There will be women who function as priestesses, shamanesses, mediums, healers, and fortune tellers. Indigenous culture and perspectives can also be carried on by ordained women within larger global religious traditions, who at the same time retain some of their tribal or indigenous perspectives.

As Sylvia Marcos observes,

© Urosr, 2013. Used under license from Shutterstock, Inc.

> Not all religions function in the same way. Indigenous religions are indeed quite complex, vary from society to society, and have been affected considerably by change. Since naming, defining, and conceptualizing these traditions is and will remain problematic, it is better to regard any definition as a working definition.[85]

Considering, therefore, that there are so many myths, stories, and rituals, how can one possibly understand the female perspective in such complex individual systems? One of the best ways to come to a rudimentary comprehension of the various cosmologies is to approach through the stories told by and about women.

INDIGENOUS JAPAN

In the context of possession, mediumship, and guidance, there is the story of the Empress Jingu who also functioned as a shamaness or seer in indigenous Japanese religion. Jingu lived during the second century C.E. and represents what some scholars interpret to be a matriarchal society that existed in western Japan during this period. From existing Chinese and Korean material reference is made to the Japanese country of Wa, which was known as the Queen Country and was in close contact with China and Korea.[86]

Jingu became possessed by a divinity who revealed to her that her emperor husband could conquer Korea. Her husband ignored her revelation and died as a consequence. Jingu then proceeded to conquer Korea and reigned as empress regent for her infant son.

FROM THE OGLALA SIOUX

Another interesting perspective comes from the Oglala Sioux of South Dakota. This is the story of the appearance of a beautiful sacred woman who appears to the Lakota Sioux. After due ceremony, the woman presents the chief and the people with a sacred bundle which contains a divine means by which to communicate with the Great Spirit, or Wakan Tanka, who is their Father and Grandfather. The gift is the sacred pipe and she instructs the people on its use. She tells them to hold it in great respect and love and ensure that no man who is impure ever be allowed to see it. The explanation for the pipe and its function is one of the most beautiful descriptions of environment consciousness and ethical values to be found anywhere in native legends. Holding the stem of pipe facing towards heaven, the wakan (holy) woman's words are

> With this sacred pipe you will walk upon the Earth; for the Earth is your Grandmother and Mother, and She is sacred. Every step that is taken upon Her should be as a prayer. The bowl of this pipe is of red stone; it is the Earth. Carved in the stone and facing the centre is the buffalo calf who represents all four-leggeds who live upon your Mother. The stem of the pipe is of wood, and this represents all that grows upon the Earth. These twelve feathers which hang here where the stem fits the bowl are from the Spotted Eagle, and they represent the Eagle and all the wingeds of the air. All these peoples, and all the things of the universe, are joined to you who smoke the pipe – all send their voices to *Wakan-Tanka*,…. When you pray with this pipe, you pray for and with everything.[87]

AMAZON DISEMPOWERMENT

There were also stories explaining how women lost their power and became subservient to men. In an Amazon myth, this designation of lowly status is not one that is offensive to women but nevertheless one they are forced to endure.

The myth describes how women invented sacred pipes or hollow trumpets. The women became so engrossed in playing music that they neglected their husbands and housework. There ensued a coup whereby the men became enraged, and took over control of the women through force, trickery, and theft, prohibiting their further access to the beautiful musical instruments permanently.[88]

!KUNG (LOCATED IN BOTSWANA, ANGOLA, AND NAMIBIA)

Nisa's experiences with *n/um*, or the power to heal, explain this female healer's perspective on trance and healing powers. This traditional healer explains how the power to heal "is a very good thing." It is a very strong force that is accessed in and through trance like states and is a very painful experience for the healer, who sometimes becomes ill after healing others. The trance is usually brought on by drinking the extract from a sacred plant and hearing drum-medicine songs. In this state the healer—whether male or female—can cure the sick person. When n/um takes over the healer lays hands upon the sick and works in a state of altered consciousness. When the power abates the healer collapses.

Insight into Nisa's perceptions of God are interesting as she says,

> I know how to trick God from wanting to kill someone and how to have God give the person back to me. But I, myself have never spoken directly to God, nor have I seen or gone to where he lives. [89]

EVOLVING NEW AGE CONCEPTS

As in the previous case of female indigenous traditions, the evolving Neo-Pagan, Wiccan, and goddess movements display an enormous variety of beliefs and rituals. Once again, it presents as a problem for the researcher to provide an overall creedal belief system because there are many differing views. Suffice it to say that it can be reasonably assumed that worship of the feminine is central to all the belief systems.

Neo-Paganism is an umbrella term for various and diverse beliefs with many elements incorporated from a plethora of world religions. As such it represents a wide and often unconnected group of beliefs and practices within New Age religions. The New Age community of religious beliefs combine ancient Pagan and magical traditions pertaining to the feminine, fertility, and power and demonstrate the modern views that incorporate Wicca, Goddess worship, Druidism, Asatru, Shamanism, and neo-Native American traditions including nature worship. Some Neo-Pagans also find no conflict in practicing their Neo-Paganism while adhering to another faith, such as Christianity or Judaism. [90]

The central beliefs that can be identified in these systems are as follows:

- Belief in Deity: Some believe in a Supreme Being.
- Belief in a supreme Mother Goddess

- Others believe in a God and a Goddess duality.
- Others believe there are countless spirit beings, gods and goddesses, in the cosmos and within all of nature.
- Most believe that God is all and within all; all are one God.
- There is a central belief in the Great Mother Earth, or Mother Nature.
- Divinity is imminent and may become manifest within anyone at any time through various methods.

These religions are presented as being developed by women for women and although possessing aspects of ancient religions that were in themselves not particularly egalitarian, they are considered to create a female-friendly perspective on faith. In addition to this diverse religious perspective, or perhaps as a consequence to this, there is no official theology and leadership is held to be more of a cooperative association.

Whatever the religious philosophy or particular female New Age religion espoused, there is at the root of its belief system some form of egalitarian partnership which creates rituals, symbols, and imagery.[91] There is no hierarchal structure presented and inclusive participation rather than exclusive doctrines are encouraged. Nevertheless there is leadership, no matter how relaxed it might appear to be, and the seriousness of worship requires an expert or acknowledged leader or teacher to guide the ritual. As a result of this, the role of priestess is highly esteemed and in some traditions, leadership can be held by a couple as in priest and priestess.

The one major problem with the traditions that favour and stress the feminine within the New Age movement is that there can be a notable exclusion of males from either full participation or even from within their groups. In many ways, this is a natural outcome of women choosing to explore female spirituality without being impeded by male interference or perspectives. On the other hand, however, this can present as a serious concern, as this only reflects partial representation of spirituality. This can cause imbalance within a community of faith because it might be construed as projecting bias and exclusion of the masculine as unwelcome or irrelevant. The irony in this instance would be that just as females have experienced gender prejudice directed towards them over the centuries, they then in turn exercise that same bias towards members of the opposite sex.

SOCIAL AND CULTURAL REALITY—DO WOMEN MATTER AT ALL?

From a scholarly perspective there have been advancements in the study of women within religious traditions which incorporate the "feminine voice," or validity of presence. The reason for this is that throughout history, scripture and religion have been for the most part dominated by male perspectives. These perspectives are the norm when one reads central texts and studies the major religious rituals in the world religions. Women are present and seen but they not identified with strong leadership capacities in mixed congregations of men and women. In addition to this, they do not figure as clear and decisive policy makers—they simply fade into the background of a religious community.

Objectively, when one views the religious, cultural, political, and social discrimination that women face to varying degrees, the reality of subjugation is hard to dismiss. Frequently, this overall religio-cultural portrait will cause a devotee to become very defensive concerning the obvious discrimination that is endemic within their particular religious tradition. Their responses will vary but routinely range between denial or an endeavour to explain the various ways and concepts that lead to these often insulting and demeaning classifications or exclusions. Whatever the explanations, the reality is that within all of the major faith traditions, and the majority of indigenous traditions, the role of the female is customarily excluded from the inner sanctum of the faith and religious policymaking in the community, whilst relegating them to the periphery. So deeply embedded is the exclusion of women, due to the various culturally perceived social concepts and entrenched social conditions, that the majority of women within a religious system will accept it as the correct spiritual path. This breeds a reality of dependence which follows the female from cradle to grave, from small child, to marriage and the socially required reproductive role, to the dependent woman after menopause. She may also be a widow who is dependent upon her family for survival and therefore is not willing to cause problems within the existing family unit. Further, due to constraints of ill health or limited mobility, or the very natural love of family, or also loyalty towards their religion, the normal role for the traditional woman will be as a dependent, or supporter, not as a spokesperson for women's rights. Whatever the situation, the reality is that females within the religious context will have their expected functions mapped out for them and for many, it is very difficult to stand against these socio-religious constructs. The fact is in many of our societies, that men rule and women have to obey them due to their social circumstances.

Suffice it to say, that when the role of the female is actually analyzed from an informed secular perspective, the reasons given for this discrimination are shocking, demeaning, and full of prejudice. These explanations will range from diminished spiritual capacity due to spiritual inferiority—even the total lack of a soul[92]—through to intellectual "difference," emotional vulnerability, and resultant instability, or even to the designation of scapegoat where she is to blame for all sorts of physical and social evils. In addition to this, religious prejudices and social mores will definitely address in much depth the biological functions specific to females. This myopic reasoning process will lead to complex rituals and taboos regarding their physical impurity or vulnerability relating to body, mind, and spirit which can cause all kinds of problems for "pure" men. Whatever the culture, and whatever the typology, these wild female irregularities will be presented as justification for the exclusion of the feminine from major roles and authority within religious leadership. Women can participate in rituals officiated by and through men but due to their reproductive cycle and their "special" emotional construction they cannot participate as frequently, or share equal spiritual footing with men. Confusingly, within many religions, the feminine may be celebrated as lifegiving and often beautiful, but in reality the woman herself is rendered impure or insignificant and her role is as a background member of a male-dominated system. Bluntly put, patriarchy is an ancient system of societal control that is still a fully functioning aspect of society which often excludes women from full spiritual and physical dignity. Even more irrational is the claim that God (who is spirit) is male and therefore must be represented in all forms of earthly leadership by men, albeit that these men can be flawed and corrupt in various aspects of their own lives. What this means from the perspective of Religious Studies is that the female continues to be excluded in many cultures from full and equal participation in the sacred rituals and equal respect within society.

From the perspective of factual investigation, the female role in many religions still relegates her duties to the profane sphere. Even though she may be a devoutly spiritual person, her endeavours will customarily be considered as not equal in "quality," content, and importance to that of her male counterpart. Suffice it to say that even access to the divine in prayer, or through pure meditative states, will present as a greater challenge for women due to the fact that pure thought, balanced reasoning, or even access to the divine is impeded by their female biology. This in itself presents to the educated secular observer as clearly incongruent because if the divine is the source of all life, and thus created the female as part of that life force, with the ability to produce life and give birth to life, why then is the female considered polluted and weak? Or why is enlightenment through meditation impeded by women's biology? What has physicality to do with the quest for spiritual transcendence? What caliber of divinity would impede access to it due to mere physiological difference? If the great spiritual force of enlightenment, or the force others term God or the Creator, exists and is free from limited vision and bias, why does this force show definite discrimination against the female? Does this not present flawed perspectives or punitive characteristics within the perfect realm? Does this not merely reflect biased human projections of what is superior and what is inferior?

ENFORCING PREJUDICE

There will be those within the religious traditions who will acknowledge that prejudice and hier-archal domination exists, but they will accept the status quo as "it was ever thus." In this context, their acquiescence to the existing inferior place of females in the majority of religious systems adds to the inference that women are most definitively spiritually second class. Proponents of the "don't rock the boat" approach will argue that it is something women just have to accept as their desig-nated place, despite the harsh realities regarding their spiritual status and social standing. Reversely, and to their credit, there will be others who actively campaign to change the systems from within. These campaigners will acknowledge, however, that this is often a very difficult task as it will en-counter hierarchal entrenchment and "authorized" discrimination.

Laying all the various excuses and reasons aside, the reality is that there is massive discrimination—both subtle and obvert—directed towards women. Perhaps if one is an individual who exists in a world of cosseted privilege, or is one who exercises domination as a right of gender, these realities could be dismissed as no more than social trivialities or even heretical disobedience. However, from the position of the educated outside observer, the facts are evident. The denial of women's spiritual and intellectual equality and resultant cultural prohibitions against the exercise of spiritual and community leadership is a grave denial of human rights. The socio-religious reality is that this process of discrimination and societal control to enforce the status quo is exercised through what-ever means is available from a "religious" perspective. This will further be culturally emphasized through community, family, and scriptural authority. Further, the means of delivery to emphasize spiritual and physical inequality can be benignly or brutally reinforced and may be experienced through demonstrations of family sanction, broader community displeasure, or even outrage at the very thought of true equality and autonomy. Sadly, these forms of societal control are still prevalent, resulting to keep women in the religious background as they fulfill their designated sexual, biologi-cal, and reproductive roles.

ADDRESSING THE MYTH

It is often difficult for the scholar to critically analyze the role of women in religion because there exists a strong tension between simply conveying the entrenched social realities whilst at the same time appreciating the contribution of women within the systems. Historically, what becomes evi-dent from the study of women within many religious structures is that they have contributed tre-mendously to its function, maintenance, and outreach. The question is why have they not assumed major leadership roles and through these established a greater spiritual feminine profile in general society? The simple answer to this is that of power entrenchment and that in most religions men would rancor at women in positions of widespread spiritual authority.

One of the reasons for the reluctance to give full credence to the female perspective is that it could challenge the officially sanctioned male interpretation within a religious system as it is male lead-ership that speaks in nearly every religious society. At the root of these male-oriented religious systems is the faith position that the relevant traditional scriptures place masculine representation as the standard guideline for religious normalcy. What also becomes very clear is that, as Serenity Young observes in her work *An Anthology of Sacred Texts By and About Women,* the "vast majority of religious texts have been written by men, for other men and are considered the normative texts of the traditions."[93] Revelations encoded within the sacred texts were and are acknowledged to have been sent to male leaders such as priests or prophets, seers, and mystics. This in itself presents a problem because what we now know from scriptural and devotional records is that many of the seers and mystics were women.

This fact, however, is not something that is generally addressed in a serious consideration of authority within patriarchal religious systems. There will be religious traditions that acknowledge and even laud the fact that there were revelations or inspired perspectives given through exceptional women. These women were usually noted to be ascetic hermits, or nuns and/or virgins, but these are not officially recognized as falling within the same authoritative criteria set for bona fide scriptural authority received by men. The official widespread interpretation is that the great sacred texts, embodying the depths of spiritual reality and bearing the seal of eternal insight and authority, were delivered to the male religious. Only men could discern the mind of the eternal because men, especially those set apart as particularly spiritual, were the most logical and the most rational. They were also, in some inexplicable way, possessed of a spiritual quality far superior to that of any woman religious. As such they represented the best examples of the "holy." It was their writings that formed the basis for scriptural authority and routinely reflect the author's culture, civilization, historical time frame, and embodiment of cultural perceptions.[94]

To the believer, this argument or faith position is in no way compromised by the fact that the writing of scripture was historically the domain of literate men. Writing was a gift from the gods and those who recorded the revelations functioned as scribes, priests, kings, and lawgivers. Thus the role of women and how society viewed women, was interpreted through the perspectives of men and this was seen as quite logical because God, or the most dominant deities, were male. Thus when the observation is made that the generally accepted scriptures were all written from the male perspective and do not necessarily reflect the observations made by the female experience, it will not present an interpretive problem. The underlying reason for this is the cultural acceptance that the male voice is the one of inspiration and strength. This is not to deny the validity of the source of origin through inspiration which can be that of the ancestors, or even God "Himself" but what it also functions as is an enduring stream of male continuity and authority. Consequently, the transmission of the knowledge and description of the most powerful force that humans can envision, is most likely to be interpreted as male as it represents the greatest line of continuity and stability. Sadly, women are simply an addendum, with a social role to follow.

The commonly held belief regarding the spiritual superiority of the male is identifiable in all religions that are controlled through doctrine and ritual within the male hierarchal systems. The earliest systems of society were ruled for the most part by men and their concepts shaped religious society. If one then refers back to Robert Bellah's hypothesis of the developmental stages, and aligns these ideas with other archaeological and anthropological data, it is quite clear that all religions evolved from out of other more ancient tribal customs and systems. From an archaeological, anthropological, and sociological perspective this is quite easily identifiable. Surprisingly, however, if the scholar from a Religious Studies perspective speaks of such identifying characteristics and then discusses their origins as the foundation for women's designation as spiritually inferior, there is often a strong element of defensiveness registered on the part of the devotee.

Arising out of ancient antecedents of tribal superstitions and ignorance, interpreting the female as impure or simply dangerous, our societies merely adapted and incorporated these concepts into holy law or the will of the gods. It did not matter that some of these mythic divinities were female, it was still believed that the goddess was the most capricious, the more merciless, and often the most dangerous of the gendered supernatural entities. However, in order for the cosmos to be in balance and function in an orderly fashion, the male gods were presented as ruling for the most part with the upper hand. In many instances of the mythic figures the goddess was controlled or vanquished by a victorious male deity who kept her in her place; thus the blueprint for human society reflects these antiquated beliefs.

THE FEMININE REALITY

For many women, functioning in situations of religious, family, social, and political inequality, to challenge the male authority figure is tantamount to deviancy. The consequences for the independent voice of reform can often lead to shunning, or even severe punishment resulting in death, arising from the authorities or within their own families and communities. Within many cultures, the voice and the contribution of the female challenging repressive systems is controversial and fraught with repression or downright denial concerning any bias regarding the abilities of women. There can be official lip service given to the "special" role of women in their various societies, but these will all, if critically analyzed, emphatically reinforce the concept that women should support, look after, and assist, but never be instrumental in effecting positive change through female authority and leadership.

Women will also routinely acquiesce concerning their perceived roles because they are uncomfortable with challenging the systemic prejudice towards them. Given limited freedom, autonomy, education, cultural oppression, and religious indoctrination, women are vulnerable to physical, sexual, mental, and emotional abuse both within their families, religious institutions, and definitely within the broader cultural setting. Sociologically, women are commodified to such an extent that serious study of the feminine profile in societies often leaves the researcher amazed as to the pernicious nature of this accepted part of social values. No religion is exempt, despite the denials on the part of the male leaders and also women within the systems, who genuinely believe that their ascribed roles are right and acceptable. For the researcher, it is often the more sobering when women within the systems validate some of the outrageous religious concepts regarding their inabilities and even their physicality. The taboo of the unclean is one that is routinely accepted and enforced often by women themselves through to their daughters and sons, which makes it even the more tragic. In addition to this, why should the ever recurring, hackneyed debates regarding menstruation and childbirth, or even female sexuality, still be considered as a spiritual blight? Why should women's conduct be so regulated and scrutinized while the conduct of men is given so much more leeway?

Set against this background, the researcher has every right to ask: What is the role of women in religion? Just exactly what do they do? Are they of any real importance at all from a spiritual perspective? Do religions perpetuate abuse directed towards women? How do women view themselves within a religious context? Why do women in many traditions accept the designation of inferior? Why can't women be at the forefront of religious teaching and reform? Why is it that women are not allowed to teach with authority in the context of male and female assemblies? Why do women always have to defer to the male ruling? Why are many women and men so uncomfortable with this whole scenario? Is there such a thing as a religious "Old Boys Club" that excludes women because religions dismiss them in contempt or fear them? What are the reasons for the entrenched dismissal of women?

What is even more uncomfortable is that when one considers any of the above questions, legitimately based on facts as evidenced in religions themselves, one encounters varying degrees of admonition from religious authorities. Why is it wrong to seek full disclosure on these matters? The reasons are many and varied and carry within them all sorts of cultural, doctrinal baggage that appears like a giant wall in front of those wishing to bring dignity and freedom to many women who face extreme oppression within their traditions.

CONCLUSION

Having regard to all of the above material, the observer might be driven to ask, "Why do women care about spirituality?" The answer to this is based on an age-old reality—women are spiritual beings—they too are *Homo religiosus!* Throughout the ages, despite oppression, dismissal, and often contempt, the religious woman has proceeded on her religious path because she has desired and needed to reach for transcendence. She has also needed to find meaning in her life, inspiration to live by, courage to face the vicissitudes of life, and the comfort of fellow believers, both female and male.

Religions, despite their many faults, have provided women with access to an interior path; one which has often been heightened and affirmed due to marginalization of the feminine. Women have created their own traditions within the larger patriarchal systems and developed significant rituals for themselves despite cultural and psychological conditioning that would dismiss their innermost perspectives. Through their personal struggles with identification, societal demands, love for family and the broader community, and personal spiritual longings, they have contributed to the matrix of society. For the most part, it is the role of the spiritual woman who is the unsung heroine behind the reality and history of true religious experience.

GLOSSARY

Ecclesiastical ordination: In Christian churches, a rite for the dedication and commissioning of ministers. The person is publicly and spiritually set apart by the laying on of hands upon the head of the candidate being ordained. This is done by the ordaining minister or bishop. There are prayers offered that the person will receive the gifts of the Holy Spirit and the grace required in order to carry out of the ministry.

Garudhammas: Buddhist monastic rules known as grave rules, eight in total, which the Bhikkuni (nuns) are required to observe at all times. These rules are not required of the Bhiksu (monks).

Gurmat: In Sikhism, is a theological term which incorporates both faith and practice into the social structure of Sikhism.

Hadith: Collections of anecdotal material regarding the life of Muhammad. This material serves as a guide for Muslim practices and law, and functions as an addendum to the material found within the Qur'an. The Hadith cover material that is not covered either directly or fully within the Scripture itself.

Itako: Japanese female medium who was thought to be married to a deity. It was specified that the female should be blind before initiation and service.

Manu: In various Hindu texts, Manu is presented as the progenitor of humankind. He is also believed to have been the first king to rule the earth. In early Hindu scriptures Manu is recorded as being the one who saved mankind from the great flood—after being warned by an avatar of Vishnu to build a giant boat so that people and animals could survive.

Manusmrirti, or **Laws of Manu:** Earliest body of law codes found within Hinduism. These relate to the definition of the dharma (caste and family duty), initiation, the study of the Vedas, marriage, hospitality, dietary restrictions, pollution, and purification; the conduct of women and wives; the control of females, and the law of kings. There are judicial laws, religious topics such as donations, rites of reparation, the doctrine of karma, the soul, and hell. The text makes no categorical distinction between religious law/practices and secular law. Its influence has been monumental upon the lives of women, and it has provided the Hindu with a system of practical morality.

Miko: Japanese shrine maiden, dedicated to the service of the kami and located at shrines and temples.

Misogyny: Hatred, disdain, dislike, mistrust towards women. Women are considered inferior and reduced to merely biological entities. Dismissal of female intellect due to this contempt.

Prakriti: Hindu term denoting matter.

Rabbis: Jewish religious scholars who function in community and academic leadership.

Sangha: Buddhist term denoting the religious community. Can be used to describe (1) the whole community as social groupings; (2) the laity; (3) the ordained monks and nuns.

Sectarian Shinto: Generally refers to a set of thirteen New Religions that were founded in Japan prior to World War II. Sectarian Shinto is not a denomination but rather a categorization applying to a number of individual religious systems.

Shakti: Hindu term for the divine, creative feminine force of the universe.

Talith: Traditional Jewish prayer shawl.

The Jesus Movement: Description of the nascent church shortly after the death of Jesus Christ. This was an evangelizing, mission-based movement which was represented by men and women brought together in the common faith that Jesus was the Christ and that he had commanded them to go make disciples of all nations. Women appear to have held far more esteem and showed initiative in evangelizing the pagan Mediterranean world.

Ummah: Islamic term denoting the religious community. This can refer to a localized context or applying to the global Pan-Islamic community.

Yamulke: Skull cap, also known as a prayer cap. Usually worn by Jewish men but also worn by females in the Conservative and Reform traditions during prayer.

ENDNOTES

1. Rita M. Gross, *Feminism and Religion: An Introduction*, (Boston: Beacon Press, 1996), pp 12-13.

2. Serenity Young, ed., *An Anthology of Sacred Texts By and About Women*, (New York: Crossroad Publishing Company, 1993), p xii.

3. Amy Oden, ed., *In Her Words: Women's Writings in the History of Christian Thought*, (Nashville: Abingdon Press, 1994).

4. Mary Kinnear, *Daughters of Time: Women in the Western Tradition*, (Michigan: The University of Michigan Press, 1990), pp 1-2.

5. Amy Oden, ed., *In Her Words: Women's Writings in the History of Christian Thought*, pp 7-8.

6. Ibid., p 8.

7. Rosemary Radford Ruether, *Women and Redemption: A Theological History*, (Minneapolis: Augsburg Fortress Press, 1998), p 14.

8. Paul's Letter to the Galatians, New Testament. *New Revised Standard Version, The New Oxford Annotated Bible* (3rd ed), (Oxford: Oxford University Press, 2001), chap 3:36-39.

9. This sentiment would appear to negate the egalitarian views of Paul in Galatians. There are many N.T. scholars who view the Timothy passage as an interpolation. This means that it was added by another writer or even scribe who acted on behalf of Paul. If it is not an interpolation it would appear that Paul was undergoing some theological challenges and was doing an about-face. This is a contentious body of teaching.

10. Paul's Letter to Timothy, *New Revised Standard Version*, 1 Timothy 2:11-15.

11. Religious Tolerance: Ontario Consultants on Religious Tolerance, *The ordination of women by conservative Protestant denominations*, http://www.religioustolerance.org/femclrg4.htm. Retrieved May 12, 2012.

12. Susan Hill Lindley, *You Have Stept Out of Your Place, A History of Women and Religion in America*, (Louisville: Westminster John Knox Press, 1996). This book documents the intellectual, social, and religious input of a variety of women in various traditions dating from the seventeenth to twenty-first centuries.

13. Why Can't Women Be Priests? About.Catholicism.com http://catholicism.about.com/od/beliefsteachings/f/Women_Priests.htm

14. Genesis, Exodus, Leviticus, Numbers, and Deuteronomy.

15. IGanzfried: Code of Jewish Law, vol 2, chap 75, #5.

16. Ibid.

17. Ibid.

18. Serenity Young, ed., *An Anthology of Sacred Texts By and About Women*, p 94.

19. Marianne Ferguson, *Women and Religion*, pp 102-103.

20. Serenity Young, ed., *An Anthology of Sacred Texts By and About Women*, pp 12-15.

21. Ibid., pp 32-24.

22. Ibid., pp 34-35.

23. Lucinda Joy Peach, *Women and World Religions*, (Upper Saddle River, NJ: Prentice Hall, 2002), p 164.

24. Ibid., p 177.

25. My Jewish Learning: http://www.myjewishlearning.com/history/Modern_History/1948-1980/America/Liberal_Politics/Feminism/Female_Ordination.shtml Retrieved May 13, 2013.

26. Serenity Young, ed., *An Anthology of Sacred Texts By and About Women*, 95

27. Leona M. Anderson, Pamela Dickey Young, eds., *Woman and Religious Traditions*, (Toronto: Oxford University Press, 2010), p 201.

28. Ibid., p 201.

29. Ibid., p 202.

30. Serenity Young, ed., *An Anthology of Sacred Texts By and About Women*, pp 272-273.

31. Holy Qur'an, http://www.alislam.org/quran/search2/showChapter.php?ch=4&verse=31

32. Ibid.

33. SaHeeH Bukhari: 29, 304, 1052, 1462, 3241, 5197, 5198, 6449, 6546 (FatH Al-Bari's numbering system)

34. Margot Badran, *Feminism in Islam: Secular and Religious Convergences*, (Oxford: Oneworld Publications, 2009), pp 280-282.

35. Warren Matthews, *World Religions* (7th ed.), (Belmont, CA: Wadsworth, 2013), p 79.

36. Arvind Sharma, ed., *Women in Indian Religions*, (New Delhi: Oxford University Press, 2002), p 14.

37. There are other dates that contradict the 100 B.C.E. date. Some estimations take the code back to around 500 B.C.E.

38. Manu appears as the progenitor of humankind in many Hindu traditions.

39. Nirmukta: The Status of Women as Depicted by Manu in the Manusmrirti: http://nirmukta.com/2011/08/27/the-status-of-women-as-depicted-by-manu-in-the-manusmriti/

40. Robert E. Van Voorst, *Anthology of World Scriptures*, (Belmont, CA: Wadsworth Publishing Company, 2000), p 44. Quoting the Manusmriti, 5:147-149.

41. Serenity Young, "The Ordination of the First Nuns," *An Anthology of Sacred Texts By and About Women*, p 313.

42. Ibid.
43. About.com.Buddhism, http://buddhism.about.com/od/buddhisthistory/a/buddhistwomen.htm. Retrieved May 12, 2012.
44. Arvind Sharma, ed., *Women in Indian Religions*, p 64, note 22.
45. Linda Joy Peach, *Women and World Religions*, pp 65-66.
46. Ibid.
47. Ibid., p 66.
48. Ibid., p 66.
49. Ibid., pp 66-67.
50. Ibid., pp 88-89.
51. Arvind Sharma, ed., *Women in Indian Religions*, p 80.
52. Ibid.
53. Ibid., p 86.
54. Ibid., pp 88-89.
55. Ibid., p 87
56. Sri Guru Granth Sahib Ji, 473
57. Arvind Sharma, ed., *Women in Indian Religions*, p 128.
58. Ibid., p 129.
59. Leona M. Anderson, Pamelo Dickey Young, *Women and Religious Traditions*, p 229.
60. Arvind Sharma, ed., *Women in Indian Religions*, pp 130-131.
61. Rahkumari Shanker,"Women in Sikhism," Arvind Sharma, ed., *Women in Indian Religion*, p 130.
62. Lee D. Rainey, "Woman in the Chinese Traditions," *Woman and Religious Traditions*, p 110.
63. Ibid.
64. Ibid.
65. Ibid., pp 110-111.
66. Ibid., p 111.
67. Ibid., p 111.
68. Marianne Ferguson, *Women and Religion*, (Upper Saddle River, NJ: Prentice Hall, Inc., 1995), pp 80-81.
69. Serenity Young, ed., *An Anthology of Sacred Texts By and About Women*, p 358.
70. Marianne Ferguson, *Women and Religion*, p 80.
71. Leona M. Anderson, Pamela Dickey Young, eds., *Woman and Religious Traditions*, p 125.
72. Nüshu: A Curriculum of Women's Identity - UBC Library ojs.library.ubc.ca/index.php/tci/article/download/67/279. Retrieved May 14, 2013.
73. Lucinda Joy Peach, *Women and World Religions*, pp 121-122.
74. Japanese sacred text.
75. Japanese Historical Text Institute, University of California at Berkley. Kojiki http://sunsite.berkeley.edu/jhti/Kojiki.html
76. Ibid.
77. Linda Joy Peach, *Women and World Religions*, p 120.
78. Ibid., p 4.
79. Miko, http://inuyasha.wikia.com/wiki/Miko. Retrieved May 15, 2012.
80. Heather Kobayashi, *The Miko and the Itako: The Role of the Women in Contemporary Shinto Ritual*, http://digitalwindow.vassar.edu/cgi/viewcontent.cgi?article=1159&context=senior_capstone, p 42.
81. Lucinda Joy Peach, *Women and World Religions*, pp 122-123.
82. Heather Kobayashi, *The Miko and the Itako: The Role of the Women in Contemporary Shinto Ritual*, p 28.
83. Lucinda Joy Peach, *Women and World Religions*, pp 122-123.
84. A Short History of Daoism, http://www.daoiststudies.org/dao/daoism-a-short-history. Retrieved May 15, 2013
85. Sylvia Marcos, *Woman and Indigenous Religions*, (Santa Barbara, CA: Prager, 2010), pp vii-viii.
86. Jing , http://www.britannica.com/EBchecked/topic/303999/Jingu. Retrieved May 16, 2013.
87. Serenity Young, ed., *An Anthology of Sacred Texts By and About Women*, pp 228-229.
88. Ibid., pp 242-243.
89. Ibid., pp 248-249.
90. Lucinda Joy Peach, *Women and World Religions*, pp 349-350.
91. Ibid., p 351.
92. Emile Durkheim, *The Elementary Forms of Religious Life*, (New York: The Free Press, 1995), trans. Karen S. Fields, pp 242-243.
93. Serenity Young, ed., *An Anthology of Sacred Texts By and About Women*, p. xvii.
94. Theodor H. Gaster, ed., *The New Golden Bough: A New Abridgment of the Class Work by Sir James Frazer* (New York: Criterion Books, Inc., 1959), p xxvi. See Frazer's study on culture and interpretation of religious structures.

CHAPTER 10

Religion and the Environment

BASIC FACTS—AN ECOTHEOLOGICAL[1] OVERVIEW

We are living in the Sixth Great Dying of the Planet but the stark reality of this statement loses some of its impact when we are not clear about what that statement means. For many of us, living in urban environments, surrounded by technology and information snippets that are often only twenty-five to thirty seconds in duration, the reality of a catastrophic juggernaut-type event happening around us is perhaps hard to focus upon, let alone comprehend. The reality is, however, from an environmental perspective, that there is a rapid dying of species, affecting terrestrial, marine, and avian species, not encountered on a global scale since approximately 65 million years ago with the extinction of the dinosaurs, in the Cretaceous-Tertiary event.

The five previous mass extinctions or *Dyings* are relatively easy to identify according to geological and fossil records. They are:

First Extinction: The Ordovician-Silurian which brought about the death of 85 percent of all marine species over a period of 10 million years. Records indicate that this was caused by a devastatingly long ice age.

Second Extinction: Late Devonian. More than 75 percent of both marine and terrestrial species disappeared. Extinction was caused by a lack of environmental oxygen (anoxia). This mass extinction lasted over 25 million years.

Third Extinction: The Permian-Triassic, which is roughly estimated to have eliminated 95 percent of species. Extinction was caused as a result of a combination of anoxia (total depletion in the oxygen levels), volcanic activity, and one or more asteroid impacts. This extinction, which lasted only 100,000 years, is often referred to as the Great Dying.

Fourth Extinction: Triassic-Jurassic Extinction which lasted 10,000 years. During this time 90 percent of all species died within this relatively short period. The Fourth Extinction was also caused by severe climate change due to massive volcanic activity and asteroid impacts.

Fifth Extinction: The Cretaceous-Tertiary occurred approximately 65 million years ago. This is the most well-known of the mass extinctions and is believed to have ended the reign of the dinosaurs. It caused the death of 85 percent of all species existing at that time. This mass extinction is widely accepted to have been caused by major asteroid impacts.[2]

Bearing these earth changing events in mind, scientists from various disciplines identify that we are living through a period of mass extinction with the outcome shrouded in pessimism and sometimes resignation. Acknowledging the twenty-first-century data, taken from credible, independent, and balanced scientific sources, drives home the reality that climate change will impact the majority of life forms presently supported by the biosphere. Bleak and alarming data is now before us through reputable institutions such as the Worldwatch Institute and the David Suzuki Foundation which reinforces the reality of our situation. In addition to this, the planet's human population is rapidly increasing, there is rapid biotic decline due to our population impact, and the demands made by our own species upon the planet are now reaching overload capacity.[3] As a consequence to this, the depressing fact is that many in our scientific community agree that our planet is now entering into the Sixth Great Dying within its history. The Worldwatch Institute states that,

> The world lives amid the greatest mass extinction since the dinosaurs perished 65 million years ago, and most of this loss is caused by human activities. Habitat loss, the introduction of exotic species through trade and travel, and climate change all contribute to biodiversity decline.[4]

Pitched against this loud background extinction noise, it is somewhat inconclusive as to whether our species will successfully maintain some sort of comfortable level of existence of be forced to live at a much more confined level of survival, or perhaps even survive at all in some areas of the world. This may sound strangely apocalyptic and exaggerated but consider the scientific facts. The reality is that with rapid climate decline and escalating disastrous weather patterns it would appear that our environment is definitely sending out warning signals. If we then factor in water and food shortages, degradation of soil and water, together with destabilization and violence, it is debatable as to whether our standard of living in the Western world can be maintained. Indeed, environmental scarcities are now factored into projections for future existence. It is also a reality that environmental depletion causes major social and political problems throughout the world. Despite what world commerce would have an affluent public think, the global reality is that there is a substantial rise in poverty and shortages of food, together with major water shortages in various parts of the world. In addition to this, there is escalating competition for resources, rocketing financial costs of nonrenewable energy, over 25 million environmental refu-

gees[5]: displacement of people forced from their homes due to climate catastrophes, a serious rise in sea levels, rapidly increasing desertification, global warming, growing political unrest and war.[6]

What is clearly evidenced within human interaction through these social, political, and environmental events is that where there is environmental scarcity and competition for existing supplies, there is always escalating violence; it is a battle for survival.[7] Expert Thomas Homer-Dixon[8] addresses the devastating ramifications of human instability when he writes that

> We will see a decline in the total area of high-quality cropland, along with widespread loss of remaining virgin forest. We will also see continued degradation and depletion of rivers, aquifers, and other water resources, and the further decline of wild fisheries.[9]

What is also observed about the severe imbalances that occur due to shortages and privation is that they are generally caused by the unequal distribution of wealth, power, supplies, and intense pollution, all of which destabilize social and natural systems. In other words, there are many complex stress factors which contribute to the environmental crises we are now experiencing.

There are also major economic stresses experienced through debt-led economic development, trade debt, global industries, subsides for global industries and monopolies which make it virtually impossible for third-world countries to compete. This causes the "developing" countries to provide only partial care through education, health care, and social support systems like social services. There are also pressures, influences, and incentives for various governments to relax, ignore, or even not implement efficient environmental protection laws.[10] All these factors are clearly identifiable in resource-based countries with the trade their nonrenewable assets and in countries seeking to rapidly industrialize to do business within a global economy. Broadly speaking, it is the more affluent or powerful industrial countries that manipulate trade and economic and political systems in order to gain access to existing supplies within the third world, without much concern for the destruction and havoc that is wreaked.[11] This unequal distribution of power and unchecked deleterious environmental impact leads to friction and destabilization which in turn engenders unrest and outrage both locally and globally as those adversely affected respond to the abuse. As a consequence a ripple effect is created which contributes to added pressure on the most vulnerable and disenfranchised as they try to live within a growing economically unbalanced world of the haves and have-nots. This also means that there are tremendous stresses exerted among nations or communities who might wish to access the resources of their adjacent neighbouring groups. These factors may create greater tension within a specific area which in turn can lead to resource wars.

THE BIGGER PICTURE

These simple facts of human interaction and survival mechanisms seem, however, to elude us in envisioning the greater scheme of things. Through our scientific cultures, technology, and commercial hype we have been indoctrinated to believe that things are not all that bad. Also through our cultures of consumerism and Gross National Product indexes, we are encouraged to consume for the sake of the economy, with the same rapacity or even increased consumption of the earth's resources without any heed to consequences. In our cultures of consumerism it is believed that more of everything material will make us happy and emotionally fulfilled. If we do experience unease regarding our wasteful squandering of the earth's resources, resulting pollution, and rising greenhouse gas emissions, we are cautioned not to overreact as it is merely alarmist conjecture. We are further indoctrinated to believe that humans can overcome every challenge that nature and economics may assault them with. This is a somewhat dangerous misinterpretation of environmental reality and denial of the biological, climatic, and biospheric facts that surround us. Living in a technological age, often far removed from agrarian reality, we are somewhat blunted to the fact that we still vulnerable puny beings who are vitally dependent upon the planet. Historically, we know that our species is gifted with enormous powers of imagination and at times alarming powers of denial bordering on dangerously uninformed reasoning. This has led to disturbing historical accounts of uninformed decisions based on cultivated stupidity[12] which have in turn led to catastrophic outcomes. We believe that all will be well as nature will sort it out beneficially for us, or that our scientists and technicians can save the day. These critically flawed beliefs mirror what Frederic L. Bender, professor at the University of Colorado, styles, "The Cornucopian Argument," in his book *The Culture of Extinction*.[13] Bender argues that we have been taught as an unchallenged fact that the "Earth is a horn of plenty" and one that will provide unlimited resources for human consumption, without any adverse effects. Bender notes that this philosophy of consumption has five main points:

1. Progress (ever-increasing material production and consumption) increases human happiness without limit.
2. Earth provides all the resources humans may need and absorbs all the ecospheric impact humans may create; or, if limits do exist, human ingenuity can overcome them, therefore
3. There are no natural limits to progress, i.e., unlimited exponential growth is ecologically unproblematic, therefore
4. Unrestricted human use of nature is morally justified (human chauvinism principle, therefore
5. Dominate nature![14]

The reality is, the biosphere does not work according to our philosophies and plans; she works on her own time and through her own systems. Realistically, when we ignore the basic facts, we open a Pandora's box of untold suffering. The facts are, plain and simple, we are quite literally gutting the planet and severely hampering its ability to maintain an orderly system of self-regulation which is the basis of existence for all life forms within and upon her.

In our headlong rush to dominate nature we seem to vacuously skip by the problems of global degradation which are overwhelming in scope and undeniable to any person of reason. Based on strong scientific and sociological data, the reality of a coming crisis seems inevitable.[15] Greed, mismanagement, destruction, and poverty are conditions that humans generate, often without heeding the full ramifications of their actions. In 1987, Dr. Gro Harlen Brundtland, as chairman of the UN Commission on Environment and Development stated,

> . . . poverty itself pollutes the environment, creating environmental stress in a different way. Those who are poor and hungry will often destroy their own environment in order to survive.[16]

THE DEATH OF BIRTH SCENARIO

For whatever reason, be it abject poverty or the superabundance of goods and possessions, we seem as a species to be hell-bound on killing our life support system. This defies logic but it is an event that can be clearly identified. Paul Hawken, the famous environmental and economic critic, analyzes our rapacious appetite and inability to fully comprehend the ramifications of our resource gluttony as follows:

> The ability to overexploit the earth's store-up supply of resources is what we call economic progress. One statistic makes clear the demand placed on the earth by our economic system: every day the worldwide economy burns an amount of energy the planet required 13,000 days to create. Or put another way, thirty-seven years' worth of stored solar energy is burned and released by utilities, cars, houses, factories, and farms every twenty-four hours.[17]

Hawken then goes on to quote Herman Daly once a World Bank economist, who stated very clearly that we are destroying the "capacity of the earth to support life and counting it as progress, or at best as the inevitable cost of progress." In Hawken's book, Daly is again quoted as saying, "'Progress' evidently means converting as much as possible of Creation into ourselves and our furniture." Daly then further explains what he means by "ourselves," which he defines as "the unjust combination of overpopulated slums and over-consuming suburbs."[18] Of note also is the fact that this material is taken from a chapter in Hawken's book entitled, "The Death of Birth." What this means in stark reality is that we are killing or consuming the biosphere which gives us life at such a rapid rate that we are almost parasitic in our actions. It is indeed as though we are waging war against life itself, without giving heed to the consequences of such brutal self-centredness.

WHY DO WE DO THESE THINGS?

To be fair, however, from an intellectual, philosophical, and moral perspective, there are many people who are seriously concerned with the problems of the environment, our culpability, and the tragedy of the Sixth Great Dying. Most informed, conscientious people will acknowledge the problems surrounding us but they ask quite reasonably, "How does one stop the juggernaut?" How does one metaphorically stand in front of the mighty machines of commerce, greed, exploitation, unwise policies, and shockingly unethical transactions, when we too have to survive within the systems? Is it possible to stand as some grand—but dismally doomed to failure—lone crusader? How can one change the system? These are not new questions, for deep down within many people's consciences is the realization that it is the responsibility of educated and involved citizens everywhere to implement protective environmental measures and to expose corrupt systems of exploitation. The problem is that despite the plethora of environmental data that proves the justification for these concerns, the material is routinely dismissed, discredited, or considered unimportant in the grand scale of commerce and politics. A rational, informed person might be tempted to ask why this is the case. Consider the facts regarding environmental degradation, climate change, the plight of environmental refugees, alarming speciel die off, and the massive risks posed to health by pollutions of all kinds. Why do our governments and trade leaders not respond for the common good? What are their reasons for lethargy? Our scientists have been thorough and our data clearly presented and so it provides a valid basis for immediate change. Alarmingly, however, and even to the point of total incredulity, when scientists, environmentalists, educators, religious leaders, writers, and reporters voice their concerns, they seem for the most part to go unheeded by policy makers. It is as if in the frenetic rush to make money the voice of reason goes unheard and is trampled underfoot.[19] To use the words of Socrates in *Plato's Republic*, "We are discussing no small matter, but how we ought to live."[20]

UNDERSTANDING BASIC PHILOSOPHIES

Our species has established a long history of interaction with, and mismanagement of, the planet. Archaeology bears witness to the fact that areas throughout ancient Europe, the Mediterranean, Mesopotamia, the American Southwest, and also South America, were radically altered by human occupation. With the opportunity through crop management to support growing villages and cities, it became necessary to specialize in intensive farming with the resultant need for complex water control and irrigation systems. As archaeology attests, these systems not only proved destructive to the environment and increasingly difficult to maintain but also financially costly to support.[21]

The question can also be raised at this juncture, as what are the reasons we choose to change the environment without regard for cost or consequences?[22] The answer to the question is twofold: (1) it is necessary to support human survival, and (2) because we just can! The problem is we never really learn from past mistakes either due to ignorance or arrogance. Blithely, we think that this time around, we will succeed and all will be well. Our species has the biological right to survive, but why do we always use such aggressive and destructive practices to do this? Why do we still, in our modern societies tolerate and also implement practices which cause harm to many forms of life, including our own? From the perspective of survival, it makes no sense, yet we still perpetuate short-sighted approaches in many of our dealings with the environment as a result of our myopic reasoning. Utilizing this unlimited strong arm or what some might call a "practical" approach to utilizing the environment, we construct businesses, power structures, and economies which are within their own infrastructures detrimental to the long-term survival of our species and that of countless other life forms on the planet. The reasons for our actions are varied but are based on the age-old premise that nature is property which can be used simply because we possess unalienable access rights to it as human beings. These given rights of ownership are based on perception, cognition, logical structures, evaluation, past routines, decision making, external constrains, feedback, prestige, security, religious doctrines, and philosophical concepts pertaining to the natural financial environment as we perceive it.[23] The problem is that this is a very narrow interpretation of the natural rights on domination and the Sixth Great Dying reflects our mistaken concept of ownership and value. In the words of the famous English philosopher John Locke (1632–1704) regarding the perception of value,

> An acre of land that bears twenty bushels of wheat, and another in America
> which, with the same husbandry, would do the like, are without doubt of the
> same natural, intrinsic value. But yet, the benefit mankind receives from one in a
> year is worth five pounds, and the other possibly not worth a penny.[24]

HUMAN-CENTRED INTERESTS VERSUS
BIOCENTRIC PERSPECTIVES

At the root of the majority of our value-laden ideas is the concept of anthropocentricism, which looks at the environment from a utilitarian, human-centered perspective. We feel that we are the centre of all things and that nature exists solely to be manipulated by us and for our use. This leads to enormous ethical and social dilemmas as we attribute the importance of the environment based on what we perceive it to be worth. The problem with this type of arbitrary evaluation is that we place ourselves as the sole interpreters of that worth and this can prove dangerous.

Victim of an oil spill

The danger behind ascribing value in this way is that it will depend on who is attributing the classifications of worth and whether it is based on an anthropocentric scale or on one that perceives the rights of nature.[25] If someone in a position of power is one who possesses very little environmental sensitivity, lacks an established code of moral, ethical behaviour, and only values life from a monetary perspective, worth is most definitely compromised. In the hands of someone lacking in environmental responsibility, many life forms are candidates for annihilation or extinction in the pursuit of monetary gain. If we are to solve, or at least contain, some of the environmental problems we are already encountering and will encounter in the Sixth Great Dying, we will have to face the truth about ourselves. The problems we have created and which have brought such crises on our biosphere demand that we truthfully confront our humanocentric ruthlessness and lack of spiritual accountability.

There is, however, a biocentric or holistic approach which can be adopted that will perceive the environment and our species' place within it in a more constructive and respectful manner. This approach factors into its philosophy and practice a more easily identifiable spiritual and reverential perspective which acknowledges nature and the biosphere as an expression of life's right to exist in and of itself with its own inherent worth and creativity. A biocentric approach will acknowledge the scientific fact that we are a species among many, and that in truth, our existence depends on respecting the planet and allowing her systems to work without decimating the natural infrastructure, or what is known as the biotic web.

SPIRITUAL PERSPECTIVES AND GROUPS

From a Religious Studies' perspective there are also a variety of biocentric approaches that will incorporate religious or reverential philosophies attached to the biotic web. These approaches will embody a variety of "truth milieus" or spiritual and philosophical constructs from which to gain "realistic" spiritual perspectives on these issues. These milieus will include an eco-theological approach as identified within new environmental philosophies such as (1) ecofeminism, (2) deep ecology, and (3) ecotheology which analyzes the teachings already established within the historical religious cosmologies, together with the religious approaches to caring for nature. These will now be considered.

ECOFEMINISM

Ecofeminism is a branch of feminist critique that locates the source of environmental degradation in the structure of dualist thinking—male/female, nature/culture, domination/nurture. It will interpret the environmental crisis as being the result of a male-oriented set of values termed patriarchy. This entrenched locus of power hierarchies and the established authoritarianism are interpreted through basic social structures that create suffering for the vulnerable. It will also identify the subordination of nature with that of the historical subjugation of women

One branch—cultural ecofeminism—interprets the feminine principle as being more in touch with nature and natural cycles and rhythms but there is a distinction made between sex and gender. The term *sex* applies to female and male, whereas the term *gender* applies to the masculine and feminine. The reason for this is that one may be male but still possess feminine qualities and vice versa.

Arising out of this classification feminine is perceived to function as the nurturing qualities within humankind which are life affirming and protective. On the other hand, patriarchal culture is interpreted to arise from a fear of death, so domination and strength are presented as the acceptable norm. This ultimately creates a culture of death.

These ecofeminists interpret history to indicate that there was a historical displacement, demotion, or elimination throughout the ancient world, of the nurturing goddess figures by powerful, dominating male deities. In turn, this has been interpreted as a massive war between the sexes, which women have lost. Women are traditionally associated with nature, so nature also bears the brunt of patriarchal domination.

There are other ecofeminists, styled "social ecofeminists," who point out that what is called for is not a war against men, or the replacement of patriarchy with matriarchy, but rather a rejection of patriarchal values such as hierarchies and ideologies of domination and submission. In this context, it is also noted that gender is routinely related to issues of class and that women and poor people bear a disproportionately large share of the costs of environmental degradation, with economically disenfranchised poor women bearing a double burden of exploitation and deprivation.[26]

Deep Ecology

Deep ecology is a term coined by the late Norwegian philosopher Arne Dekke Eide Næss (1912–2009). Naess was an important intellectual and an inspirational figure. His term refers to deep questioning about environmental ethics and the causes of environmental problems. It presents a methodological approach to environmental philosophy and policy. It also stresses that rather than simply adjusting existing policies or amending conventional values, there must be a critical reflection on the fundamental worldviews that underlie specific attitudes and environmental practices. The approach taken by Naess addresses these worldviews, and deep ecology itself inevitably is concerned with religious teachings and spiritual attitudes.

Deep ecology affirms the intrinsic value of nature, thus espousing the philosophy of *inherent worth*. It will also recognize the importance of biodiversity and call for the reduction of human impact on the natural world. It stresses a greater concern pertaining to the quality of life rather than material affluence. Deep ecology also commits itself to changing economic policies and the dominant materialist view of nature.

Naess articulated the eight central platform principles as follows:

1. All living beings have intrinsic value.
2. The richness and diversity of life has intrinsic value.
3. Except to satisfy vital needs, humans do not have the right to reduce this diversity and richness.
4. It would be better for humans if there were fewer of them, and much better for other living creatures.
5. Today the extent and nature of human interference in the various ecosystems is not sustainable, and the lack of sustainability is rising.
6. Decisive improvement requires considerable changes: social, economic, technological, and ideological.
7. An ideological change would essentially entertain seeking a better quality of life rather than a raised standard of living.
8. Those who accept the aforementioned points are responsible for trying to contribute directly or indirectly to the necessary changes.[27]

The main characteristics of deep ecology can be described as follows:

Deep ecology is usually characterized by the following qualities in that there will be:

- Emphasis on the intrinsic value of nature (biocentrism or ecocentrism);
- Value all things in nature equally (biocentric egalitarianism);
- Focus on wholes—ecosystems, species, or the earth itself, rather than simply individual organisms (holism);
- Affirmations that humans are not separate from nature (there is no "ontological gap" between humans and the natural world);
- Emphasizes interrelationships;

- Identification of the self with the natural world;
- Intuitive and sensuous communion with the earth;
- Spiritual orientation that sees nature as sacred;
- Tendency to look to other cultures (especially Asian and indigenous) as sources of insight;
- Humility toward nature, in regards to our place in the natural world; our knowledge of it, and our ability to manipulate nature in a responsible way ("nature knows best");
- A stance of "letting nature be," and a celebration of wilderness and hunter-gathered societies.[28]

ECOTHEOLOGY

Ecotheology arose out of an expressed need within various faith traditions to come together to find common ground in addressing nature in relation to their respective cosmologies. This was done in order to identify traditional teachings within the systems and to interpret these in modern terms and channels of interpretation and communication. It addresses the interrelationships that exist between religion and nature; focuses on environmental concerns; studies the connection between human religious/spiritual worldviews; and seeks to identify links to environmental degradation based on the lack of spiritual connection and the existence of anomic separation within their respective communities. Ecotheology also investigates the strong representations and associations in religious systems that combine ethical teachings to those of similarities within all religions. This is done in order to create positive potential solutions to environmental degradation based on spiritual paradigms as an alternative to the destructive and prevalent culture of materialistic consumption. Ecotheology endeavours to create new methods of interpretation within the religious systems and to forge bonds of emotional and intellectual association with the environment based on spirituality. It will argue that scientific solutions cannot address the spiritual malaise that our cultures are exhibiting. The answers to the solutions must come through a religio-spiritual appreciation of nature.

As an example of this interpretative ecotheological approach, consider a faith statement made in 1991, that was issued by the heads of many denominations and faith groups. This statement voiced "the growing consensus about the importance of environmental issues in North American religious life."[29] In addition to this there was a call made to people of faith in all traditions to "contribute their wisdom, courage, creativity, and hope" in a global effort to preserve and protect the planet.[30]

> One spring evening and the following day in New York City, we representatives of the religious community in the United States of America gathered to deliberate and plan action in response to the crisis of the Earth's environment. Deep impulses brought us together .... we note mounting evidence of environmental destruction and every increasing peril to life, whole species, whole ecosystems.... This is an inescapably religious challenge.... Global warming, generated mainly by the burning of fossil fuels and deforestation is widely predicted to increase temperatures worldwide, changing climate patterns, increasing drought in many areas, threatening agriculture, wildlife, the integrity of natural ecosystems and creating millions of environmental refugees.[31]

The group went on in the statement to issue an eight-point manifesto through which they committed themselves to raising public awareness in the religious community and work for environmental protection by lobbying politicians and religious leaders. They also declared that they would develop literature and curriculums that would address the environment and prepare environmental educational materials for congregations. The manifesto was sent to Protestant, Catholic, and Greek Orthodox branches of Christianity as well as to Jewish faith groups and educators.[32] In 1991 this was an early example of ecotheology as a movement, one which would later branch out the next year in 1992 to bring scientists and religious leaders together in a similar environmental affirmation regarding protection of the environment. As such it emphasized a deep sense of common purpose, respect for nature, and serious concern regarding health issues resulting from environmental pollution, depletion of the ozone layer, and the threats that these things posed to the health of animals, children, and obviously "the poorest among us."[33]

Arising out of this, and still within the context of ecotheology that we will now consider the ideas historically encoded within many of our religious systems as they contain evidence of the most enduring forms of environmental values and teachings. In the routine quest for spiritual understanding in all religions there will be emphasis laid upon the need for self-scrutiny, or an inner debriefing, based on the spiritual code contained within the respective cosmology. From the perspective of confronting our self-generated environmental nightmares, the ability to utilize the processes of spiritual self-scrutiny opens up for the sincere enquirer a process of growing awareness regarding the biosphere. For many people it is a revelatory experience, which is often referred to as an "environmental epiphany" as it causes the enquirer to understand the magnificence of nature and the teachings within the religions concerning that same thing and the need, as in any true religious experience, to address abuse or wrongful action, and change it. In the religious systems this will generally be understood to mean repentance and positive change.

Stating that religions contain environmental ethics is a sweeping assertion that, without corroboration will appear as an empty claim to the secular mind. It is therefore necessary at this juncture to consider the fact that most ethical behaviour takes place in the context of religions[34] and so it is worth examining what the religions actually do say.

Judaism bases its relationship with God on the premise of Covenant; the land was given to Abraham as an inheritance and the outcome of faith and obedience. As time evolved, there were complex and definitive laws established to govern conduct and usage of the Promised Land by the people of the Covenant. The cost of disobedience regarding following God and keeping his commandments would be experienced in physical exile and environmental degradation. Restoration and forgiveness meant also that the land would also be restored to them.

A major critique that is, however, leveled at this faith tradition is that is has often been dominated by a practical, self-interest approach to nature.[35] As is evident from the Pentateuch, there were laws concerning treatment of land, animals, and other resources, but it is emphasized that this meant that there was an awareness of the dependence of humans on the natural environment and the need to ensure its continuity. These sentiments, however, were based on the need to preserve the environment merely for posterity and that there was no loving connection with nature. Thus from the perspective of environmental anomie and anthropocentric reasoning, nature was and is valued mainly because of its usefulness to humans. As a result of this when the Jews lost their land after the Roman destruction of the Temple in 70 C.E., they gradually created a portable civilization that valued learning and scholarship over nature. This culture of separation can be identified in many aspects of Jewish life, but those who deal with the restoration of the land of Israel, value its worth from a covenantal perspective.

In this context, consider an ecotheologically Jewish perspective. This approach explains what it means to live in covenant and how Jews should conduct themselves with regard to environmental stewardship and these concepts are summed up in the words of Rabbi Arthur Waskow (1933):[36]

> Now that we live in the era of high-tech industrialism and are not shepherds
> or farmers or orchardists in the ordinary sense, we must learn to be shepherds,
> or farmers, or tree-keepers again in a difference sense. For [these people] know
> you must not exhaust the earth you live on.... What does it mean for us to renew
> that shepherd's wisdom ...

He continues by saying

> I want to imagine a new version of the Jewish people—a new way of understand-
> ing and shaping ourselves. Imagine that we were to decide to see ourselves as
> having a mission, a purpose on the earth....to heal the earth—one that is not
> brand new but is described in the Torah as one of the great purposes of the Jew-
> ish people.[37]

Christianity also possesses an anthropocentric perspective on nature. The religion, which was orig- inally a Jewish sect, "believed that nature had been created by God to provide for human needs."[38] There are also discussions and accusations concerning the abusive interpretation of Genesis, Chap- ter 1, verse 28 wherein God grants humankind dominion over all living things. Historically, this has proven to be the cause of major abuse and exploitation on the part of kings, rulers, and business- men, as they exercised exploitive dominion in the form of ruthless and unconscionable abuse upon creation. Notwithstanding that this was indeed the interpretation used by specific groups of human predators, it is the wrong cultural interpretation of the word "dominion," which should actually be described as "stewardship," and has totally different connotations.[39] Indeed acclaimed scholar Har- old Coward, associate fellow at the Centre for Studies in Religion and Culture at the University of Victoria, states that "there is no biblical or archaeological evidence to suggest that the Israelites or the early Christians believed that God commanded humans to use nature in such a way."[40]

Adopting an ecotheological approach, the ethical framework of Christianity views the environ- ment as the creation of God, to whom all things belong. Also, even though nature was created for human use, it is interpreted as having inherent worth and value because it is God's good and beautiful creation. Humans have a duty to care for the environment and must only use it in ways that respect God and all forms of life. The Christian function is that of stewardship and requires care for one's fellow men. The ethical teaching embodies duties to humans everywhere now and in the future, so the environment must not be abused and brought into collapse, as all life forms must have the right to share the earth. As theologian Ian Bradley writes in reference to Paul's teaching concerning the suffering of all creation in Romans 8:18-23,

> Of all the passages in the bible that refer to the world of nature none is surely so profound, so mysterious or so relevant to our present ecological crisis as this. It takes up and amplifies the two themes we have already found in the Old Testament: the interdependence and common destiny of the whole creation and the special role of humans in liberating and perfecting the non-human world. In particularly graphic and moving terms, Paul portrays us as standing side by side with the rest of creation in our groaning and travail, frustrated and impatient at our imperfections and shortcomings, but waiting expectantly and hopefully for liberty and fulfillment.[41]

Also of note in Christianity is the teaching on *The Divine Imperative*. In Genesis, Chapter 1, God blesses the animals and instructs them to be fruitful and multiply and fill the earth. Therefore when humans impede this directive by stealing habitat, killing the animals who inhabit the land, and placing enormous stresses upon the animals, humans are countermining God's direct order. They are therefore responsible for the suffering, defying God and having sinned.

Islam believes that nature was created and is owned by Allah's creation. Human are allowed to take from its resources for their benefit and survival but it is prohibited to be used by humans other than in respectful and mindful ways. Hence, creation is not to be exploited, over used, or abused for selfish, wasteful purposes. Nature is also to be respected and protected, as it is seen as fragile and innocent. There is a divine balance set by Allah but this can be easily upset by human misconduct, or as it is described, wickedness. When natural catastrophes occur they are attributed to the will and anger of Allah as manifestations of punishment. In the climate change upheaval now occurring, many Muslims interpret the events as signs of Allah's displeasure over human sin, including that of the mistreatment of nature.[42] Some conjecture that it is a sign that Allah is about to strike back.

Understanding Allah's injunctions against despoiling the environment, consider the words of a famous Islamic teacher named Abu A'la Maududi:

> Islam does not approve even of the useless cutting of trees and bushes. Man can use their fruit and other produce, but he has no right to destroy them. Vegetables, after all, possess life, but Islam does not allow the waste of even lifeless things; so much so that it disapproves of the wasteful flow of too much water. Its avowed purpose is to avoid waste in every conceivable form and to make the best use of all resources—living and lifeless.[43]

Much responsibility is placed upon the Muslim believer, who in ecotheology has adopted the ancient title of Caliph (m) or Calipha (f) which meant vice regent, one who was a successor or someone who functioned in place of an absent ruler. An environmental Caliph from an Islamic environmental perspective, now describes a believer who works to protect nature as part of the mandate of Allah.

Hinduism as one of the karmic/dharmic traditions, sees all nature as interconnected and "capable of progressing from matter into life to consciousness and ultimately to divine spirit."[44] Vedic scholars have presented various texts and rituals that extol the earth, the atmosphere, and sky, as well as the goddesses associated with the earth, and the gods associated with water, with fire and heat, and the wind. These same scholars have noted that the centrality of these gods and goddesses suggests an underlying ecological sensitivity within the Hindu tradition and it is believed that in later Indian thought, these Vedic concepts become formalized into the identity of the five great elements: earth, water, fire, air, and space.[45] It is also necessary in Hindu meditative and ritual processes to be conscious of and be respectful to these constituents of materiality, as in daily prayer and ritual (puja) these powers will be evoked and called upon in prayer.

In addition to this, Hinduism has long revered the tree and early seals from the Indus Valley cities (ca. 3000 B.C.E.) depict the tree as a powerful symbol of abundance with various depictions and imagery of the tree referenced in Hindu literature. As part of this respect for the tree, India has historically maintained a special protective relationship with forests. In the case of modern events, the modern Chipko movement, led initially by only a small group of women, protected ash trees near to their villages. In one case, the women staved off forest destruction, despite abuse and threats of physical violence, by forming a human chain around various trees, by holding on to and literally hugging them.[46]

Rivers have also been and continue to be an integral part of Hindu religious practice. More than fifty Vedic hymns praise the Sarasvati, a river (now dry) associated with the goddess of learning and culture. The Ganges River which flows through northern India likewise is referred to as a goddess originating from the top of Shiva's head in the Himalaya Mountains, giving sustenance to hundreds of millions of modern Indians. Traditionally, the rivers of India have always been considered pure. Modern industrial contaminants and human waste have fouled the water systems, though Ganges water still plays an important role in India's ritual life.[47]

From an ecotheological perspective the Hindu and Indian populations are now facing environmental degradation through decreasing air quality in its cities and degraded water in various regions, religious thinkers and activists are facing enormous challenges. Through their writings and social campaigns they endeavour to make relevant the broader ancient values of Hindu conservation tradition in order to foster greater care and respect for the earth. With appreciation and acknowledgment of the five great elements, together with a new interpretation of social duty *(dharma)* that includes the nature, the environmental community is seeking to reinvest in ancient wisdom in caring for the earth.

Jainism as an ancient Indian, non-Vedic religion represents a tradition where there is nonviolence towards all beings, whether animate or nonanimate. This dictates a particularly restrictive lifestyle with stringent purity and dietary restrictions. Its famous religious 'motto' is "Tread Lightly Upon the Earth," and this speaks to the necessity for Jains to be at peace and pose no threat to anyone or anything. Even the earth cannot be tilled, but only lightly disturbed in order to refrain from any suffering caused to other life forms within or upon earth.

The goal within Jainism is to ascend to the Siddha Loka, which is a world beyond heaven and earth, where all the liberated souls dwell eternally in a state of energy, consciousness, and bliss. Although this goal utterly removes one from all worldly entanglements, the path to reach this highest attainment entails great care in regard to how one lives in relationship to all the other living beings that surround one in the earthly realm. Hence, from the aspect of practice, Jainism holds some interesting potential for ecological thinking although its final goal transcends earthly concerns.

In Jainism there are life particles *(jiva)* in earth: water, fire, air, microorganisms, and plants each experience the world through the sense of touch. Worms add the sense of taste. Crawling bugs can feel, taste, and smell. Flying insects add seeing. Higher level animals, including fish and mammals, can feel, taste, smell, see, hear, and think. For observant Jainas, to hurt any being results in the thickening of one's karma, obstructing advancement toward liberation and the Siddha Loka. To reduce karma and prevent its further accrual, Jainas avoid activities associated with violence and follow a vegetarian diet. The advanced monks and nuns will sweep their path to avoid harming insects and also work at not harming even one sensed beings such as bacteria and water.[48]

In the context of ecotheology, Jainism's emphasis on non violence and respect for nature are core components of an environmental ethos. The Jain community is very conscious of the "ecological implications of their core teachings" and young Jain environmentalists are redefining some of their ancient traditions in order to make them relevant and applicable to environmentalism.[49]

Buddhism stands without the need for supervision from a deity to whom one is responsible and accountable; instead, an accounting process was developed through karma and samsara which ruled and influenced the lifespan of sentient life forms. Buddhism recognized and still does recognize the interconnectedness of all things and all elements and through their doctrine of praticca-samuppada they teach dependent origination. This means that "things do not exist in their own right, but only in interdependence," and that "Things in nature, including humans, are said to be empty of any essence or self-existence. Their existence arises from their relations of interdependence with the rest of the cosmos."[50] The implications behind this is that every single form of existence in physical and spirit form is deserving of respect for each is important in its journey of becoming. The general observation has also been made that although traditional Buddhism may privilege humans over animals, animals over hungry ghosts, male gender over the female, monk over laity, all forms of karmically conditioned life-human, animal, divine, demonic forms, are related within contingent, samsaric time.

There are, however, strongly negative concepts in Buddhism's earliest Indian phases as it was an essentially world denying religion. Essence was conceived as having the characteristics of suffering (dukkha), impermanence (anicca), and insubstantiality (anatta). The goal of the monk was to attain nirvana which was thought of as outside this world and in this way escape to the best of one's ability, the world of physicality, distractions, and suffering—mental and/or physical.

As there are many forms and traditions of Buddhism it is also difficult to present a consensus pertaining to Buddhism's approach to the environment. Further, scholars will also acknowledge that Buddhist sources are sparse with regard to positive depictions of the natural world. The reason for this avoidance of beauty and teaming life in the natural environment from the perspective of traditional Buddhist teachings is that Buddha himself taught a very dismal picture of nature. Buddha taught that the natural environment was subject to corruption, with suffering all around and within it. It was therefore intrinsically unsatisfactory. Buddha perceived that one could be instantaneously seized with pleasure on viewing something in nature but this was no more than a fleeting perception, with no value attached to it holding onto the memory of it.[51] It is this perception of nature that endures in many traditional Buddhist societies.

Western Buddhism, however, presents as a progressive environmentally conscious religion and this is no more evident than in the development of the *ecosattva,* or Buddhist environmentalist.[52] These environmental activists are very serious about their path. They take the bodhisattva vow to save or liberate all sentient forms of life, as a lifelong calling and commitment to create enlightened perspectives, disburse information, and engage in political campaigns to stop the destruction of the environment. For them, it is a personal call to save all endangered species, decimated forests, and polluted rivers.

Buddhist environmentalists see their worldview as a rejection of hierarchical dominance of one human over another or humans over nature. As a consequence, this perspective forms the basis of an ethic of emphathetic compassion that respects biodiversity.

Taoism, as one of the indigenous religions of China, is profoundly ecological in its theoretical disposition. Taoism emphasizes the Tao and the necessity to rest passively within its flow. There is emphasis on the primacy of unmediated closeness to nature through which to encourage simplicity and spontaneity in individuals and in human relations.[53] In this context great emphasis is placed on developing meditation techniques. In order to be open to the flow of the Tao or force, also known as The Mother, one must withdraw from active involvement in social and political affairs and learn to persevere and nourish nature and human life.

The reason for emphasizing this connection with the Tao is that it is believed in Taoist cosmology that this forms a metaphysical framework of transformation. This is done so that the individual will be able to eventually transform into that of a celestial being who is fully translucent within the cosmic environment. Such a perfected person is thus able to penetrate beyond the gross physicality of ordinary existence and, as a celestial immortal, be in attentive harmony with the subtle and mysterious transformations of the Tao (the ever changing flow of cosmic processes) at its core primordial level.

For the Taoist the universe is one, but infinitely diverse. The dimensions of existence from the budding of a flower to the orbit of the stars may be discerned in terms of the Qi (ch'i). The Qi is the fundamental energy-matter of the universe whose dynamic pattern is a cosmic heartbeat of expansion (yang) and contraction (yin). It is also a single, vital essence, not created according to some fixed principle but spontaneously regenerating itself.

Taoism believes that the Taoist universe is one great cosmic ecology, and that humans exist within it in their immediate lives. Only by paying attention to the minute details of one's local context is one able to penetrate to the deep roots of the Tao.

In the context of ecotheology for the Taoist, it will mean that one intuitively responds to the natural environment and seeks to function peacefully within its systems. There is a distinct emphasis in Taoist thought on valuing nature for its own sake, not for utilitarian ends.[54]

Confucianism, as another indigenous Chinese religion, accepts the Tao and perceives the world to be part of a changing, dynamic, and unfolding universe.[55] It also perceives the Tao within a cosmological context or worldview which promotes harmony amidst change. Further, all human relationships and the actions of each person are embedded in concentric circles of relationships and ethical responsibilities.[56] This means that orderly continuity is manifested in orderly systems of hierarchal control, and through the family including past, present, and future generations. In these ways, the social system stressed loyalty to rulers, elders, and teachers. This was also reinforced through education by which to cultivate the individual, enriching the society, and contributing to the political order. This form of worldview is described as *anthropocosmic* as it embraced heaven, earth, and human beings as an interactive whole. [57]

Confucianism in an early classical text entitled *The Book of History* refers to heaven and earth as the "Great Parents." It is these great parents who have provided life and sustenance. Just as human parents deserve respect, known as filial piety, so do heaven and earth. In the context of ecotheology, the concept of the "Great Parents" has an added dimension because within *The Book of History*, Confucians are instructed never to wantonly exploit heaven and earth.

Shinto, or *the Way of the Kami,* is an indigenous, animistic Japanese religion that perceives spirits to inhabit the planets, mountains, rivers, waterfalls, water, rocks, forests, trees, and the weather, through winds, rain, and snow. They can also be found in animals at certain times should they wish to either possess the animal itself or assume animal likeness. In addition to this, Shinto believes that the term and the form of kami also applies to ancestors.

In Shinto there are three basic classifications for these mighty spirits: Celestial—referring to the sun, moon, stars; Nature—referring to those who manifest in nature in its diversity; and Ancestral—referring to ancestors, both recent and long past. The kami are respected and honoured but are traditionally accepted as aloof unless angered or specifically requested to be present to aid in a wish or prayer. They are neither inherently malevolent or beneficent, but shrines honour their presence and much ritual is undertaken to approach and worship them.[58]

The world, in Shinto cosmology, comprises many different kinds of beings and apart from the kami, there are gods and spirits who also flow within the cosmos. These beings, including the kami, have no particular responsibilities over and above other kinds of beings. They simply exist within the cosmic flow and there is no theology or religious explanation for many of these entities.[59]

Shinto shrines are aesthetically beautiful and constructed to induce serenity within their precincts. It has long been recognized that shrines, together with traditional gardens, are a particular art form, and the cultivation of beauty within nature is an identifying characteristic of the religion. Art depicting nature, music, and poetry that speaks of nature are also traditional cultural characteristics still identifiable within Japanese culture today.

The religion also functions as a local cosmology and not a universal one. It is therefore a tradition that does not broaden its perspectives on global issues unless the implications would affect their local community. As such they have little sensitivity to environmental devastation unless it is accepted as belonging to and affecting the location community, which may often be more broadly construed as Japan or Japanese interests. In addition to this, they have little sensitivity to their own culpability regarding environmental devastation in other parts of the world should they have been the perpetrators of that event.

From an ecotheological perspective, unfortunately, Shinto does not set an ethos of environmental protection. Set against this appreciation for nature and a cultivated environment is the fact that there exists a tremendous disconnect. The fact is that air and water pollution are caused by Japanese companies both at home and abroad. There is widespread logging of the rainforests in South Asia, and the national parks are covered with litter.[60]

For these reasons, Shinto proves to be an anomaly within ecotheology. There are traditional values that can be emphasized to create an environmental sensitivity but attempting to do this presents as a daunting endeavour.

Indigenous traditions: Probably the most significant insight which draws together indigenous environmental knowledge and insight is the experience of interacting with the larger whole of reality. Their many and varied traditions incorporate an interrelationship of the microcosm of the body with the macrocosm of the larger world. This is mirrored most immediately for indigenous peoples in their local bioregion, with its particular myths, rituals, rites of passage, gods, deities, ancestors, or God.

What will be a common identifying factor in all traditional systems that still live close to the land and exist or survive at its good pleasure, is that they are keenly aware of this fact. Embedded within their myths are cautionary tales of catastrophes, angry gods, irresponsible humans who do not heed the taboos or cautions of their divine ancestors.

From an ecotheological perspective, there is much to build upon within these traditions as their awareness of the complexity of nature and its unforgiving laws, is something that is still impressed upon the minds of old and young alike. Unfortunately, however, due to the influences of urbanization, poverty, loss of land and dignity, much of the old wisdom has dwindled. Some groups, however, still maintain their myths, rituals and concepts. Whatever is still retrievable can be maintained and reworked to provide relevant, modern reinterpretations of ancient truths. One enduring fact remains in the tribal myths—show disrespect and abuse to the environment and one will pay dearly.

REALITY CHECK

From the material presented regarding each religion's environmental teachings, it is apparent that religions address these age-old issues of survival and conduct. In addition to this, there are clear prohibitions within most of the religions regarding environmental abuse. The reason for this is that religions are repositories of ancient, hard earned wisdom. Through our human cognitive systems we have sorted and arranged issues and passed down our wisdom to our descendents. Employing this process, we have established our religious teachings and the necessary codes of conduct and this has been done for the very practical reasons of both physical and spiritual survival. Having reviewed our religious data bank addressing these basic realities, and in light of their perspectives, it is reason-able to pose pertinent questions in order to focus upon understanding what we generally perceive to be our "right" to handle nature. Underlying this right is the reality that our collective, accumulated conduct has led us to this Sixth Great Dying. These questions are:

- What is the place of human beings in the natural world?
- Do human beings have a responsibility to other species?
- Is human destiny entwined with the destiny of other species?
- Are human beings primarily of nature or above or apart from it?
- Is human nature and destiny realized in shaping, perfecting, and developing the natural world?
- Is human nature and destiny primarily realized in attempting to accept the world as it is and conform to it?[61]
- Whose interests count?
- Whose interests must we consider?

By placing human beings firmly within the biotic systems, and incorporating a philosophical, intel-lectual, and sacred morality, thinking, caring human beings are faced with a level of accountability that takes them into the realm of serious ethical and spiritual values. This approach, as we have been reviewing the religions, is referred to as eco-theology and challenges the pervading material-istic and mechanistic perspectives that have evolved in secular society.

WELCOME TO SECULAR MATERIALISM

In order to gauge the far reaching influences of our secular environment versus the value of nature, consider the foundational precepts of materialistic perspectives. These are easily identifiable and widespread features of commerce and modern living:

1. Neglect of the environment amid emphasis on material progress;
2. Affirmation of self-interest over the interests of family and community;
3. Rejection of pre-modern agricultural traditions and rural values in its pursuit of material progress;
4. Privileging of scientific ways of knowing over aesthetic ways;
5. Reaffirmation of a single "rational" way of being in the world at the expense of cultural diver-sity, and identified within globalization;
6. Tendency to reduce all categories of value to economic value;
7. Its assumption that almost all social problems can be solved by means of economic growth; and
8. Tendency to assume that all models of human development must follow a Western paradigm.[62]

In considering these basic tenets of our global reality, it might be reasonable to consider whether this is an intellectually feasible or practical working model for the future of humankind. This

flawed perception of our own importance or authority in defining value and reality is described by Roger Gottlieb in his book *A Greener Faith,* as "a deep and frightening shift in our relations to both our physical selves and to nature."[63]

ENVIRONMENTALISM AND CONSERVATION

In facing the realities of environmental degradation it is sometimes difficult to face the challenges ahead. Is it possible to construct viable, "green" alternatives and in so doing help the planet heal? What we do know from cold, hard fact, is that our overconsumption is rapidly compromising the planet's biotic systems. It is, however, a simple reality that people do not want to face facts or change their lifestyles. It would certainly not be good for the global economy if large numbers of people found alternative energy sources, reduced emission, switched to more sustainable farming, and overall just generally cleaned up their environmental act. The reason why a drastic change in our lifestyle habits would wreak such havoc is because our economic systems are built on faulty economic paradigms and industries that are unwilling to change their modus operandi. People would lose jobs, profits would go down, and there would be political and financial instability. The strange thing is, this is already happening in many parts of the world and it has nothing to do with changing our environmental habits. Would it, therefore, be unreasonable to consider reshaping and revamping faulty systems in order to facilitate a move to a more environmentally friendly global reality?

Could we really run the world based on a more ethical approach to people, the environment, health, and respect for animals? Is this merely a wild fantasy? The fact is, we cannot continue along the path we are travelling and the environment is telling us that.

The major question that is routinely raised is: can there be an alternative system that we can implement—one that is built on practical realities but powered by ethical perspectives that actually change the realities around us? Can we effect efficient and viable environmental change? Where do we go to find these clues to a better world?

Historically, what we do know is that enlightened religious traditions and en-

lightened people of good will possess the vision of a better world, and they also possess the ability to change and adapt. Also, and contrary to the voices of their detractors, religious systems possess the power to call their people to action in positive, life affirming ways. Surprisingly, addressing the power of religious systems to create ethical environmental climates by educating their followers about environmental decline has never really been taken seriously. In the words of Gary T. Gardner, Senior Fellow at the Worldwatch Institute in Washington, D.C.:

> If the world's faiths choose to embrace these issues in a comprehensive, large-scale way, they could give a distinctive spiritual and ethical stamp to progress in the 20th century—a stamp that may be indispensable to building sustainable societies.[64]

It is now the twenty-first century, and the issues have escalated, yet still the religious systems do not organize. It is therefore necessary for the people within the traditions to encourage their religious leaders into action because we face serious environmental problems. If people become serious about environmental decline major positive steps can be taken to stop or at least retard some of the adverse consequences that we will undoubtedly face. This choice is most assuredly ours!

It is also recognized that religions possess five major assets that can be utilized in motivating and organizing their adherents in the task of creating and networking sustainable environmental ideas and campaigns. When analyzed these assets provide a substantial foundation for creating an environmental movement. These are

- **Provide people with a sense of meaning and purpose**. Emotional and physical support links people together in a common cause; provides people with a sense of backing from people in authority.

- **Moral capital**. Religious leaders can speak as the official voice of their community. This validates and lends credibility to the project; through networking with other religious leaders it can enhance the influence of the group.
- **Numbers of adherents**. The sheer number of followers can add clout to the movement, thus increasing public profile.
- **Land and other physical assets**. Religions often have substantial financial and real estate assets. Money can be funded to an authorized environmental campaign. The necessary office and campaign space can also be made available.
- **Social capital**. Religions have the capacity to generate bonds of trust between members. This is done through building strong and supportive communities.

FACING REALITY AND CREATING CHANGE

There is no magic wand solution to our environmental problems but the good news is change can occur because we make it happen and this is the whole dynamic behind any social movement. People make change happen. The key to change, and in our own particular instance ameliorate the Sixth Great Dying, is that we can use knowledge, information, and networking to create positive outcomes. The question is how can we possibly know or make all the right choices? The answer is that we cannot, but we can use logic in our actions for the common good and not for the vested interests of a few.

An example of a logical environmental approach is often referred to as the Precautionary Principle (of Least Harm) and is a term used to define a five-point approach to assessing environmental risk/harm. It is a risk assessment process and can apply to scientific protocols and environmental assessments equally well.

From an environmental perspective, the Precautionary Principle is a legal guiding framework in the United States for decision making that anticipates how our actions will affect the environment and health of future generations. It represents a major shift in the process of decision making because it mandates five key elements that must be fully addressed and resolved in any project in order to prevent irreversible damage to people and the environment. The Precautionary Principle consists of five points and lays emphasis on public participation and stakeholder collaboration in long-term environmental health and ecological policies and programs.[65]

The five points are:

1. *Anticipatory action*: There is a duty to take anticipatory action to prevent harm. Government, business, and community groups, as well as the general public, share this responsibility.
2. *Right to know*: The community has a right to know complete and accurate information on potential human health and environmental impacts associated with the selection of products, services, operations, or plans. The burden to supply this information lies with the proponent, not with the general public.

3. ***Alternatives assessment:*** An obligation exists to examine a full range of alternatives and select the alternative with the least potential impact on human health and the environment, including the alternative of doing nothing.

4. ***Full cost accounting:*** When evaluating potential alternatives, there is a duty to consider all the reasonably foreseeable costs, including raw materials, manufacturing, transportation, use, cleanup, eventual disposal, and health costs even if such costs are not reflected in the initial price. Short- and long-term benefits and time thresholds should be considered when making decisions.

5. ***Participatory decision process:*** Decisions applying the Precautionary Principle must be transparent, participatory, and informed by the best available science and other relevant information.

These points constitute a framework for environmental justice and can also act as a guide for our own decision making in matters of ethical environmental choices. It matters what we think and how we use our freedoms and intellect.

CONCLUSION

The environment is our home and the planet sustains us. The environmental challenges that face us are due in major ways to our mishandling and abuse of the biotic systems. These are realities that cannot be denied; nevertheless, from both an environmental conservation perspective and the perspectives gleaned from our religions, we know we must change our approaches and attitudes. From an ecotheological perspective, and as religions will always teach, it depends on us, our actions, and our commitment.

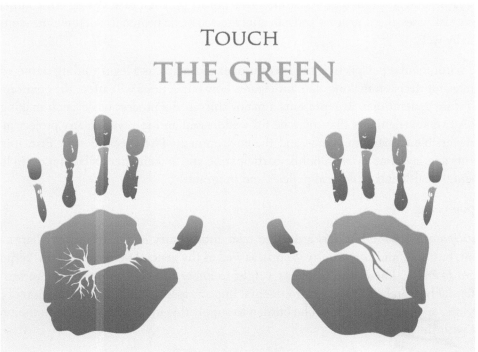

GLOSSARY

Anthropocosmic: Chinese religious worldview that perceives heaven, earth, and human beings as an interactive whole.

Biocentric: Considering the enivronment as a whole functioning system. Making it of major importance.

Divine Imperative: Christian perspective. In Genesis 1, God blesses the animals and tells them to be fruitful and multiply. When humans impede the animals from reproducing and by taking away their habitat people are going against the direct command of God. The animals have God's blessing to inhabit the earth.

Doctrine of Inherent Worth: The biosphere and all species have of themselves the right to be. By virtue of its existence each manifestation of biodiversity should be respected as a valid expression of life and should be treated with respect on that basis alone, irrespective of its perceived human use and importance.

Dyings: Also known as mass extinctions. Our plant has undergone five of these events.

Ecosattva: In the Western Buddhist context. Represents a Buddhist environmental activist, motivated by ecological concerns. They take the bodhisattva vow as a personal call to save all endangered species, decimated forests, and polluted rivers.

Ecotheology: Studies the interrelationships that exist between religion and nature. It focuses on environmental concerns and analyzes the connections between human religious/spiritual worldviews and the links to environmental degradation based on the lack of spiritual connection.

Environmental Caliph/Calipha: term used by Muslim environmentalist to describe the responsibility of humans to act as vice-regents for Allah in the protection of the environment.

Environmental Epiphany: Becoming aware of the biosphere as a sacred entity.

Environmental refugees: People who are displaced owing to environmental causes, notably land loss and degradation.

Environmental Stewardship: Earth keeper; protecting yet using the planet's resources in a sensible way.

The Precautionary Principle of Least Harm: Term used to define a five-point approach to assessing environmental harm. It is a risk assessment process and can apply to scientific protocols and environmental assessments.

The Sixth Great Dying: A global mass extinction that is underway. First one in which human beings have been present and are in large part responsible for.

ENDNOTES

1. Ecotheology addresses the interrelationships which exist between religion and nature. It focuses on environmental concerns and studies the connection between human religious/spiritual worldviews and the links to environmental degradation based on the lack of spiritual connection.

2. http://6thextinctiondoc.com/extinctions/the-first-5-2

3. Corinne Podger, BBC science correspondent Tuesday, 21 May 2002, 13:48 GMT 14:48 UK Quarter of mammals 'face extinction' http://news.bbc.co.uk/2/hi/science/nature/2000325.stm. Retrieved May 20, 2013.

4. *Biodiversity,* http://www.worldwatch.org/taxonomy/term/103. Retrieved May 20, 2013.

5. Data taken from the Canadian Standards Association: www.csa.com/discoveryguides/refugee/review.pdf. Retrieved May 21, 2013.

6. Environmental Refugees: http://rstb.royalsocietypublishing.org/content/357/1420/609.abstract. The Royal Society is a self-governing fellowship of many of the world's most distinguished scientists drawn from all areas of science, engineering, and medicine. Retrieved May 20, 2012.

7. Thomas Homer-Dixon, *Environment, Scarcity, and Violence,* (Princeton, NJ: Princeton University Press, 1999), pp 6-7.

8. Thomas Homer-Dixon holds the CIGI Chair of Global Systems at the Balsillie School of International Affairs in Waterloo, Canada. At the University of Waterloo, he is Director of the Waterloo Institute for Complexity and Innovation and Professor in the School of Environment, Enterprise, and Development in the Faculty of Environment, with a cross-appointment to the Political Science Department in the Faculty of Arts.

9. Thomas Homer-Dixon, *Environment, Scarcity, and Violence,* p 14.

10. Steven Hiatt, "Global Empire: The Web of Control," *A Game as Old as Empire: The Secret World of Economic Hit Men and the Web of Global Corruption,* ed. Steven Hiatt, (San Francisco: Bennett-Koehler Publications, Inc., 2007), pp 13-29.

11. Bruce Rich, "Exporting Destruction," *A Game as Old as Empire,* pp 197-218.

12. Examples of this denial syndrome would be when people place their faith in undeniably insane or sadistic leaders, dictators, and despotic regimes, believing that all will be well. This routinely leads to immense suffering.

13. Frederic L. Bender, *The Culture of Extinction: Towards a Philosophy of Deep Ecology,* (Amhurst, NY: Humanity Books, 2003), p 86.

14. Ibid.

15. *Our Common Future: World Commission on Environment and Development,* (Oxford: Oxford University Press, 1990), pp 27-42.

16. Ibid. p 28.

17. Paul Hawken, *The Ecology of Commerce: A Declaration of Sustainability,* (New York: Harper Business, 1993), pp 26-27.

18. Ibid., p 41.

19. Open Letter to the Prime Minister of Canada, on Climate Change Science, dated April 18, 2006. Ninety Canadian scientists were signatories to this communication. In addition to this, the Canadian Meteorological and Oceanographic Society has called for immediate government action on climate change.http://www.cbc.ca/news/background/harper_conservatives/pdf/lettertoharper2.pdf. Retrieved May 20, 2013.

20. Louis P. Pojman, Paul P. Pojman, as quoted in "What Is Ethics?" *Environmental Ethics: Readings in Theory and Application,* (Australia: Wadsworth Cengage Learning, 2008), p 4.

21. Emilio F. Moran, *People and Nature: An Introduction to Human Ecological Relations,* (Malden, MA: Blackwell Publishing, 2006), pp 64-65.

22. Ibid., p 93.

23. Ibid., pp 98-100.

24. John Locke, *Concerning Civil Government, Second Essay: An Essay Concerning the True Original Extent and End of Civil Government,* sect. v, par. 43 (1690). The Project Gutenberg EBook of Second Treatise of Government, by John Locke: http://www.gutenberg.org/files/7370/7370-h/7370-h.htm. Retrieved May 21, 2013.

25. Mark Sagoff, "Can We Put a Price on Nature's Services?" *The Economy of the Earth: Philosophy, Law, and the Environment,* (Cambridge: Cambridge University Press, 2008), pp 87-92.

26. Richard C. Foltz, *Worldviews, Religion, and the Environment,* (Toronto: Wadsworth/Thomson Learning, 2003), p 456.

27. Alan Drengson and Bill Devall, *The Ecology of Wisdom: Writings by Arne Naess,* (Berkley, CA: Counterpoint, 2008), p 28.

28. David Landis Barnhill, Roger S. Gottlieb, eds., *Deep Ecology and World Religions: New Essays on Sacred Ground,* (New York: State University of New York Press, 2001), p 6.

29. Roger S. Gottlieb, ed., "Statement by Religious Leaders at the Summit on Environment," *This Sacred Earth: Religion, Nature, Environment* (2nd ed.), (New York: Routledge, 2004), p 731.

30. Ibid.

31. Ibid.

32. Ibid., p 734.

33. Roger S. Gottlieb, ed., "Declaration of the 'Mission' to Washington: Joint Appeal by Religion and Science for the Environment," *This Sacred Earth: Religion, Nature, Environment* (2nd ed.), pp 735-737.

34. Lydia Dotto, *Ethical Choices and Global Greenhouse Warming*, (Waterloo: Wilfrid Laurier University Press, 1993), p 31.

35. Ibid., p 32.

36. Rabbi Arthur Waskow is an American author and political activist. He is also a rabbi associated with the Jewish Renewal movement and is director of the Shalom Centre, a prophetic voice in Jewish, multireligious, and American life.

37. Arthur Waskow, "And the Earth Is Filled with the Breath of Life," *Worldviews, Religion, and the Environment*, p 309.

38. Lydia Dotto, *Ethical Choices and Global Greenhouse Warming*, p 33.

39. Ian Bradley, *God Is Green: Ecology for Christians*, (New York: Image Books, 1992), p 90.

40. Ibid., p 33.

41. Ibid., p 70.

42. Lydia Dotto, *Ethical Choices and Global Greenhouse Warming*, p 32.

43. Abul A'la Mawdudi, Towards Understanding Islam (USA: The Message Publications, 1988), p 154.

44. Lydia Dotto, *Ethical Choices and Global Greenhouse Warming*, p 34.

45. Christopher Chappel. "Hinduism and Deep Ecology," *Deep Ecology and World Religions*, (New York: State University of New York Press, 2001), pp 61, 53, 66, 70-71.

46. The Chipko movement: http://edugreen.teri.res.in/explore/forestry/chipko.htm. Retrieved May 23, 2012.

47. Vasudha Narayanan, "Water, Wood, and Wisdom: Ecological Perspectives from the Hindu Traditions" in Richard C. Foltz, *Worldviews, Religion, and the Environment*, pp 132-133.

48. Christopher Key Chappel, "Jainism and Ecology: Transformation of Tradition," *The Oxford Handbook of Religion and Ecology*, (Oxford: Oxford University Press, 2006), pp 149-153.

49. Ibid., pp 150-151.

50. Lydia Dotto, *Ethical Choices and Global Greenhouse Warming*, p 34.

51. Ian Harris, "Ecological Buddhism?" Richard C. Foltz, ed., *Worldviews, Religion, and the Environment*, p 179.

52. Stephanie Kaza, "To Save All Beings: Buddhist Environmental Activism," Richard C. Foltz, ed., *Worldviews, Religion, and the Environment*, p 194.

53. Mary Evelyn Tucker, "Ecological Themes in Taoism and Confucianism," Richard C. Foltz, ed., *Worldviews, Religion, and the Environment*, pp 218-219.

54. Ibid., p 220.

55. Ibid., p 221.

56. Ibid.

57. Ibid.

58. Ian Bocking, "Japanese Religions," Richard C. Foltz, ed., *Worldviews, Religion, and the Environment*, p 249.

59. Ibid.

60. Ibid., p 261.

61. David Kinsley, *Ecology and Religion: Ecological Spirituality in Cross-Cultural Perspective*, (Upper Saddle River, NJ: Prentice-Hall, Inc., 1995), p xv.

62. Jay McDaniel, "Ecotheology and World Religions," *EcoSpirit*, (New York: Fordham University Press, 2007), p 24.

63. Roger S. Gottlieb, *A Greener Faith: Religious Environmentalism and Our Planet's Future*, (Oxford: Oxford University Press, 2006), p 3.

64. Gary T. Gardner, *Inspiring Progress: Religions' Contributions to Sustainable Development*, (New York: W. W. Norton & Company, Inc., 2006), p 43.